Marine Aquarium

Handbook

SECOND EDITION
Robert J. Goldstein, Ph.D.

With 140 photographs
Illustrations by Michele Earle-Bridges

Dedication

This book resulted from the tireless instruction and encouragement of my mentor to the reef hobby, Jeff Voet of Raleigh, North Carolina. Blame him.

Photo Credits

Zig Leszczynski: 2, 7, 20, 27, 36, 42, 65, 84, 89 (bottom), 93 (top right, and bottom right), 115, 123, 127, 128, 129, 130, 131, 135 (top and bottom), 136 (top and bottom), 137 (top and bottom), 138 (bottom), 140 (bottom), 141, 143, 144, 145, 149 (bottom), 156, 158, 159, 160, 161 (top and bottom), 162, 163, 164 (top and bottom), 165 (top left), 166, 167, 168, 169 (top and bottom), 170, 171, 172 (top). All other photos by Robert J. Goldstein.

All inquiries should be addressed to:
Barron's Educational Series, Inc.
250 Wireless Boulevard
Hauppauge, New York 11788

ISBN-13: 978-0-7641-3674-0
ISBN-10: 0-7641-3674-7

Library of Congress Catalog Card No. 2007005497

Library of Congress Cataloging-in-Publication Data
Goldstein, Robert J. (Robert Jay), 1937– .
     Marine reef aquarium handbook / Robert J. Goldstein ; with
170 photographs ; Illustrations by Michele Earle-Bridges.
          p.   cm.
     Includes bibliographical references and index.
     ISBN-13: 978-0-7641-3674-0 (alk. paper)
     ISBN-10: 0-7641-3674-7 (alk. paper)
     1. Marine aquariums. 2. Coral reef animals.
3. Marine aquarium fishes. 4. Marine invertebrates as
pets. I. Earle-Bridges, Michele. II. Title.
SF457.1.G63   2007
597.177'073–dc22   2007005497

Printed in China

9 8 7 6 5 4 3 2 1

Cover Photos

All cover photos by Zig Leszczynski.

Acknowledgments

Many generous people reviewed chapters and good-naturedly offered constructive advice and information for the first edition. Chapter 1 on natural reefs was reviewed by Dana Riddle; Chapter 3 on water quality by John Farrell Kuhns of Aquascience Research Group; Chapter 5 on the nitrogen and carbon cycles by Stan Brown; Chapter 9 on UV sterilizers and ozonizers, and Chapter 11 on light and lighting by Stan Brown and Dana Riddle; Chapter 12 on plants Dr. Rick Searles of Duke University and Dr. Steven Miller of the National Undersea Research Center; Chapter 13 on corals by Stan Brown, Patrick MacMillan, and Dana Riddle; Chapter 14 on coral diseases by Dr. Ernest H. Williams, Jr. of the University of Puerto Rico and Dr. Esther C. Peters of Tetra Tech, Inc.; Chapter 16 on molluscs by Dr. Ron Shimek; Chapter 22 on fishes by John Tullock and J.R. Shute; and Chapter 23 on diseases of fishes by Dr. Ed Noga of North Carolina State University School of Veterinary Medicine.

Note

The marine aquarium hobby had its beginning in the 1950s when clownfishes and their host anemones, damsels, and butterfly- and angelfishes were first widely kept in captivity with the introduction of synthetic sea salt mixes. It was another twenty years before coral reef aquaria became popular, following the introduction of actinic light, trickle filtration, and finally the development of the Berlin system of light, live rock, and protein skimmer total water quality management. For the origins of successful reef aquaria, we must thank the pioneer Dietrich Steuber, mentor to today's leaders, Alf Jacob Nilson, Peter Wilkins, Charles Delbeek, and Julian Sprung. Other equally important and still active pioneers are Walter Adey, Bruce Carlson, Larry Jackson, Martin Moe, Mike Paletta, George Smit, Dana Riddle, Albert Theil, John Tullock, and J.E.N. Veron.

The marine hobby is rapidly evolving as technology is incorporated from environmental engineering, molecular genetics, and aquaculture. New methods of water quality regeneration and technical advances in larval nutrition and delivery have enabled laboratory and commercial production of myriad type of marine fishes from groupers to giant tuna. These exciting revelations have vastly increased commercial farming of corals and fishes. Twenty years from now, this book will be quaint and naïve, but when you are in exciting times, today is everything.

Contents

1. **Natural Reefs**   1
   Reef Classification   3
   Reef Habitats   4
   Nutrients   5

2. **Basic Equipment**   6
   Aquarium Tank   6
   Stand   6
   Power   8

3. **Water Quality**   9
   Makeup Water   10
   RO, DI, and Distilled Water   10
   Motion, Powerheads, and Wavemakers   12
   Nutrients   13
   Tap Water   13
   Nitrite and Nitrate   14
   Phosphate   14
   Salinity   16
   Salt Mixes   16
   Temperature   16
   pH   17
   Dissolved Oxygen   17
   Ozone   18
   Carbon   19
   BOD, COD, and TOC   20
   Carbon Dioxide   21
   Calcium   21
   Hardness and Alkalinity   22
   Strontium   24
   Iodine   25
   Copper   25
   Iron   25
   Trace Elements   25

4.	**Rock, Gravel, and Sand**	**26**
	Live Rock	26
	Bottom Media	29
	Aragonite	30
5.	**The Nitrogen and Carbon Cycles**	**33**
	Cycling the Aquarium	35
	Carbon	37
6.	**Powerheads and Water Pumps**	**38**
7.	**Filters**	**40**
	Hang-on Power Filters	40
	Canister Filters	40
	Trickling Filters	41
	Fluidized Bed Filtration	43
	Algal Mat Filtration	44
8.	**Protein Skimmers**	**46**
	Cocurrent Skimmers	46
	Downdraft Skimmers	47
	Venturi Skimmers	47
	Needle-Wheel Skimmers	48
	Spray Injection Skimmers	48
9.	**Sterilizers and Ozonizers**	**50**
	Ultraviolet Sterilizers	50
	Ozonizers	51
10.	**Temperature Control**	**53**
	Overheating	53
	Controlled Heating	54
	Cooling	54
	Chilling	54
	Monitoring	55
11.	**Light and Lighting**	**56**
	Wave Length	57
	Kelvin Degrees	57
	Color Rendering Index	57
	Ultraviolet Light	57
	Intensity, Lumens, and Lux	58
	Photosynthesis	59

	Metal Halide Incandescence	59
	Fluorescence	61
	Combination Fixtures	62
12.	**Algae and Plants**	**64**
	Detritus	64
	Algae	64
	Green Algae	65
	Brown Algae	69
	Red Algae	71
	Golden-brown Algae	72
	Dinoflagellates	73
	Blue-green "Algae"	74
	Nuisance Algae Control	75
13.	**Corals**	**76**
	Coral Metabolites	77
	Mixing and Matching Corals	77
	Life Cycle and Classification	77
	Classification	80
	Hydrocorals	81
	Anthozoa— Soft Corals	82
	Ceriantharia	82
	Antipatharia	84
	Alcyonaria	84
	Clavulariidae and Cornulariidae	84
	Tubiporidae	85
	Helioporidae	85
	Alcyonaceans	85
	Alcyoniidae	86
	Nephtheidae and Siphonogorgiidae.	87
	Xeniidae	88
	Gorgonacea and Pennatulacea	88
	Zoantharia	90
	Actinaria	90
	Corallimorpharia	94
	Zoanthinaria	95
	Scleractinia—Stony Corals	95
	Pocilloporidae	96
	Acroporidae	97
	Agariciidae	99
	Siderastreidae	99
	Fungiidae	100
	Poritidae	101

Faviidae 103
Oculinidae 106
Meandrinidae 107
Merulinidae 107
Pectinidae 108
Mussidae 109
Caryophyllidae 110
Dendrophylliidae 113
The Evolution of Corals 114

14. Diseases of Corals **116**
Coral Reef Bleaching 116
White-band Disease, White Plague, and
   Stress-related Necrosis 118
White Pox 118
Black-band and Red-band Disease 118
Skeletal-eroding and Brown-band Disease 119
Yellow Blotch and Yellow Band Disease 119
Other Bacteria 120
Aspergillosis 120
Rapid Wasting 120
Growths and Tumors 121
Pink Grub and Pink Spot 121
Algal Nodules 121

15. Sponges **122**
Demospongia 123
Calcarea 124
Sclerospongea 124
Hexactinellida (Hyalospongia) 124
Sponges for Reef Tanks 124

16. Molluscs **125**
Gastropoda 125
Bivalvia (Pelycepoda) 128
Tridacnid Clams 129

17. Crustaceans **132**
Barnacles 132
Copepods 133
Crabs 134
Shrimp 135
Lobsters 138

18.	**Echinoderms**	139
	Feather Stars	140
	Holothuroids	141
	Echinoids	142
	Ophiurioids	144
	Asteroidea	145
	What's In a Name?	146

| 19. | **Annelids** | 147 |

20.	**Chordata**	150
	Cephalochordata	150
	Urochordata	150

21.	**Fishes: Foods and Feeding**	153
	Brine Shrimp	153
	Brine Daphniae	154
	Live Fish	155
	Prepared Foods	155
	Macroalgae	156
	Vegetables	156

22.	**Fishes: Care and Breeding**	157
	Guidelines for Keeping Fishes in Reef Tanks	157
	Acanthuridae	158
	Zanclidae and Siganidae	159
	Pomacentridae	160
	Pomacanthidae	162
	Gobiidae and Eleotridae	163
	Grammatidae and Pseudochromidae	164
	Clinidae, Blenniidae, and Pholidichthyidae	165
	Tripterygiidae and Callionymidae	166
	Apogonidae	166
	Plesiopidae	167
	Antennariidae	167
	Serranidae	168
	Labridae	170
	Cirrhitidae	170
	Breeding Reef Fishes	171
	HUFAs	173
	Which Live Food?	175
	Rotifers	175
	Trochophores	176

Copepods 176
Ciliates and Mixed Infusoria 177
Handling Larval Fishes 178

23. Diseases of Fishes **179**
Environmental Stressors 179
Infectious Diseases 179
Bacterial Diseases 179
Antimicrobial Drugs 180
Fungal Diseases 181
Protozoal Diseases 181
Parasitic Worms 181
Parasitic Crustaceans 182
Noninfectious Diseases 182

Appendix **184**
Relationships 184
References 186

Glossary **192**

Index **195**

Chapter One
Natural Reefs

Coral reefs are marine islands and cities populated by beautiful and bizarre invertebrates and barely visible plants. Coral animals live everywhere, from the polar to the tropical oceans, and build reefs where the water is clear enough for light transmission, nutrient poor, and within a narrow range of salinity. Some corals get most of their nutrients from photosynthetic symbiotic algae; others by eating plankton. It's likely that corals yet to be found near undersea volcanic vents will be found capable of building reefs using chemical energy. Today most reef aquarists keep photosynthetic corals or specialized non-photosynthetic plankton eaters. One day aquarists will keep deep sea chemosynthetic corals yet to be discovered.

Corals are of two ecological types, those that build reefs as a waste product of their symbiotic algae (hermatypic corals) and those that have symbionts but do not build reefs (ahermatypic corals). Other "corals" and their relatives, the anemones, may or may not have symbiotic algae; those without feed on plankton. It is the reef builders (hermatypic corals) that most excite reef aquarists, although many soft corals (not reef builders) are also favorites in the hobby.

The hermatypic and many non-reef building corals rely on light mediated photosynthesis for most of their nutrition. Many ahermatypic corals and their relatives obtain nutrition by capturing and digesting zooplankton and phytoplankton from the water column. They are less reliant on light and can live inside caves, shipwrecks, and at depths where sunlight cannot reach. Not all corals are tropical. Polar and subtropical corals and those in the cold depths build slow growing reefs in the most unexpected habitats.

The familiar hermatypic corals are abundant in warm, shallow water (less than 300 feet deep), and never in darkened caves. The non-reef-building fire corals predominate in shallows and in caves and other dark areas. Hermatypic corals derive only a small proportion of their nutrition by capturing plankton. About 95 percent of their nutrition is supplied as the waste of the symbiotic microalgae living in their gut cells. Using light as an energy source and waste ammonia of the coral as a plant fertilizer or nutrient, these symbiotic dinoflagellates (genus *Symbiodinium*) manufacture and excrete excess amino acids and carbohydrates that are then absorbed into the flesh of the host coral polyp.

These intracellular dinoflagellates are called zooxanthellae. In corals with zooxanthellae (and that's most of them), the algae photosynthesize sugars and sugar alcohols and emit excess amino acids. Part of the two-step process of photosynthesis uses carbon dioxide from the water or the coral host. In reef building or hermatypic corals, the process is linked to removing dissolved

Amphiprion perideraion, *the pink skunk clown, has a close relative that is orange and with a different white mark. All the Amphiprion are popular for both reef and fish aquariums.*

calcium from the surrounding seawater and excreting it as solid calcite, a form of calcium carbonate and the principal component of coral reefs. Hermatypic corals, in concert with their internal zooxanthellae, are among the most important builders of coral reefs, but not the only ones.

Corals build just a part of the coral reef. Calcareous red, brown, and green macroalgae (among others) are also reef builders. The photosynthesis of these macroalgae generates more calcium carbonate, stiffening their tissues and enabling them to withstand surge and resist predation. In some cases the calcium carbonate outweighs the plant protoplasm. Red algae are the most important calcite contributors to structures on reef tops (called ridges) and to most of the cementing deposits between stony corals everywhere. While reef macroalgae may go unnoticed by snorkelers and divers, without them there would be no tangs, parrotfishes, or coral reefs as we know them.

Coral reefs as we know them evolved 65 million years ago, just after the Cretaceous extinction. Before then, "reefs" (fossilized mounds of marine calcareous algae, molluscs, and other invertebrates in a loose silty, calcite matrix) were composed mostly of ancient bivalve-like molluscs called rudists. The rudists, which arose over 160 million years ago in the ancient Tethys Sea of Europe (the Mediterranean is a fragment), spread westward mostly in the northern hemisphere and lasted 100 million years, these rudist reefs disappearing at the time of the Cretaceous extinction.

Symbioses arose early in the history of the planet, most notably between *Symbiodinium* (and perhaps other microalgae) and the protozoans called foraminifera. Foraminifera and *Symbiodinium* survived the extinction, and thrived, with *Symbiodinium* expanding into newly available niches. Early marine animals had several algal symbionts that enabled them to form calcite deposits. But after the Cretaceous extinction, *Symbiodinium* spread into reef-building and non-reef-building cnidarians, soft anemones and soft corals, giant clams, and many other invertebrates. The genus *Symbiodinium* today contains 2,000 species sorted by biologists into seven related lines of evolutionary descent called clades. All *Symbiodinium* have one set of chromosomes instead of pairs (they are haploid), which has eased the analysis of their evolution. Some host corals contain two species of *Symbiodinium* and others even two kinds of microalgae (*Symbiodinium* and a *Chlorella*).

Modern coral reefs are less than five million years old, coinciding with the first coral grinding parrotfishes. No living reef today is more than 5,000 years old, when sea levels rose as temperatures warmed after the last ice age, 26,000–18,000 years ago. The calcite remains of older reefs, uplifted on volcanic islands and tectonic plates around the world, are evidence of previous warm periods between ice ages. We have much older foraminiferan (protozoan) sediments, demonstrating that *Symbiodinium* zooxanthellae were important long before they invaded corals, so think about them next time you see a picture of the white cliffs of Dover. The zooxanthellae are far more ancient than the corals.

Coral reefs seem hard as rocks, but are as ephemeral as sand. Storms batter and destroy branching corals unprotected by barriers or depth, while massive boulder corals flourish. No matter their depth or location, the relentless erosion of corals by boring worms, snails, clams, and the peculiar fishes that live among them is more subtle and steady than dramatic, intermittent storms.

Reef Classification

For all their similarities, reefs are the product of the creatures that build them and the oceanic forces that mold and erode them. Shallow reefs associated with continents (e.g., the Florida-Belize-Honduras barrier reef and Australia's Great Barrier Reef) are called shelf reefs because they develop at the continental shelf edge and landward of the shelf in warm areas of all the continents.

Reefs that grow upon mid-oceanic islands, undersea mountains (sea mounts), and oceanic volcanoes (e.g., the Hawaiian islands) are called oceanic reefs. Atolls (e.g., Johnston, Etawetok) are circular reefs that grow along the rims or slopes of volcanoes or mountains that have since been submerged by a falling sea floor or a rising ocean. Atolls are abundant in the tropical

The Cretaceous Extinction

The Cretaceous extinction was triggered by a massive meteorite slamming into the Earth 65 million years ago with a force of 100,000 billion tons of TNT at what is now called the Chicxulub crater, just north of Mexico's Yucatan Peninsula. The signature debris of this collision has been found all over the planet in a thin layer dating exactly to this time. The debris filled the atmosphere and blacked out the sun, raising firestorms throughout the world, and sparing little. The early birds and mammals survived, but the Age of Dinosaurs, which had existed for 100 million years, ended. Some 65 percent of marine life was also lost, probably from boiling seas and lack of sunlight. It's extraordinary that not everything was killed, as it nearly was in the earlier Permian extinction that wiped out 95 percent of sea creatures.

Pacific, and uncommon in the younger tropical Atlantic.

A *barrier reef* is an outer reef that protects a large area from the battering of the open ocean. A barrier reef develops atop an old shoreline or old barrier island. We have barrier islands along the entire Atlantic and Gulf coasts. Imagine a coral reef developing upon a string of these islands, and you'll see how a barrier reef can arise. The Florida Keys are the remains of old coral reefs that developed on sand islands in the distant past. A barrier reef might be a hundred feet or a mile wide. The outer edge may slowly slope to a shallow plain or suddenly drop straight down into deep water. On the continental shelf, the drop can be as much as 150 feet. Barrier reefs on an oceanic island can drop 300 feet to the lowest depth at the edge is called a wall. Scuba divers flock to walls, which are often visited by oceanic sharks and other large predators. Some southern Caribbean volcanic islands such as Bonaire have oceanic barrier reefs an easy swim from shore, and whose outer walls drop off suddenly into deep water.

Reefs inshore of the barrier reef and in shallower water are called *fringing reefs*. An atoll surrounding a lagoon can be both a barrier reef and a fringing reef. Small and scattered isolated fringing reefs of an acre or so protected by a more seaward barrier or fringing reef are called *patch reefs*.

A *bank reef* is a shallow water reef that has grown upon an elevated plain or a shallow part of a shelf. Many islands and reefs in the northern Caribbean have developed upon the extensive limestone Bahamas Banks that extend northward along the continental edge as far north as the Carolinas. A deep hole, called a blue hole, in a bank occurs when the roof of a limestone cave collapses onto the floor below.

A blue hole is not merely a pit, but an entrance to an underwater cave that may extend for miles.

Reef Habitats

The outermost area of a reef faces the ocean. During storms, swells crash upon the reef, destroying fragile branching corals. This part of the reef is called the *reef front* (front referring to fronting the ocean) or *fore reef*. The top and highest part of the reef most often exposed to wind, tides, and intense heat and ultraviolet rays is the *reef crest*. The shallow, quiet area shoreward of the reef crest is the *back reef*. Closer inshore there may be continuous fringing reefs or isolated patch reefs.

Fossil coral reef on Bonaire dates to the Quaternary of the Pleistocene, long after the previous Cretaceous extinction that wiped out earlier rudist reefs. The massive height of the fossil coral reef is attributed to the low frequency of reef-blasting hurricanes well below the hurricane belt of the middle Caribbean.

which hermatypic corals survive, yet the slope of the mountain continues another 1,000 feet onto the abyssal sea floor. If the coral reef dropoff is vertical,

Because reef zones are exposed to the elements in different ways, they are colonized by different coral species, different growth forms of the same corals, non-coral invertebrates, and algae. The zones are also inhabited by different kinds of fishes and other invertebrates.

Corals living closest to the surface in the most equatorial areas have pigments that block ultraviolet radiation that could burn their tissues. Their zooxanthellae, like that of other plants, photosynthesize mostly, but not exclusively, in the red range of electromagnetic radiation.

Deep water coral zooxanthellae receive very little red light, which is almost completely absorbed by water at a depth of 30 feet. Some deepwater corals have energy-shifting pigments that convert higher energy blue light to lower energy green and yellow light, enabling the zooxanthellae to photosynthesize. Other deepwater corals are capable of harnessing the extremely weak red light that manages to reach these depths.

Reef areas exposed to moderate wave action and moderately bright light are colonized by fast-growing but delicate staghorn and elkhorn (*Acropora*) branching corals (now protected in the United States). During violent storms, the *Acropora* forests are battered into fragments that become hard surfaces that other corals colonize; the nubs of the original reef begin to grow new branches. On the fore reef, the pounding oceanic swells do not permit growth of delicate staghorn corals, so surge-tolerant boulder corals are abundant here. Boulder corals also thrive on windy shores where wave action keeps their surfaces clean of hitchhikers.

Calcareous macroalgae also adapt to different zones. Encrusting coralline red algae grow on exposed rock, while upright red, brown, and green algae grow where the surge is moderate.

Nutrients

Plant nutrients (fertilizers) are scarce in tropical ocean water far removed from river mouths and land runoff. Nutrients reach well-lighted surface waters (the photic zone) when deep currents are diverted upward by submarine mountains or rocky outcrops, or crash into an opposing current. These swirling eddies roil the sediments, releasing minerals that sweep upward into surface waters.

The calm waters of lagoons allow its inhabitants to retain and recycle nutrients. As a result, lagoons are richer in corals, algae, and other animals than the reefs, which are continually washed by open ocean waters. Fishes consume attached algae as fast as it grows and their wastes remain in the immediate reef vicinity to refertilize more algae. On an outside reef, those wastes are dispersed. Many herbivorous tangs are also coprophagous, consuming fecal droppings of other fishes falling through the water column, then passing them through their intestines for further biological degradation. For fishes that eat plants and plant fragments (detritus), tangs provide an additional round of digestion of the plant particles and the microbes that live upon them.

Coral rubble supports growths of microalgae, and this is consumed, ground up, and used as a food source by parrotfishes. Parrotfish droppings contribute to reef sand used by sediment burrowing microinvertebrates (infauna, meiofauna) and microbes. Few nutrients are exported from reefs, which grow more massive with time.

Chapter Two
Basic Equipment

The basic reef tank equipment consists of a tank, stand, and light.

Aquarium Tank

Reef tanks can be constructed of acrylic or glass. Modern acrylic systems combine the tank, cabinet stand, fanned lighting fixture, and filtration, and can be molded to any shape. However, the curved front or flat polygon shapes of some acrylic tanks distort or repeat images. The inner walls of acrylic tanks must be cleaned periodically with a blade, sponge, or filter floss to eliminate unsightly algae, and the acrylic is easily scratched by a sand particle caught by a wiper or a knocked over coral. Scratches create tracks where algae grow leaving an unsightly line that can only be removed by draining the tank and polishing the acrylic. Glass tanks are less expensive and scratchproof and for these reasons most aquarists prefer glass tanks.

A good reef tank will be braced for strength and constructed to work with a sump. Large tanks should have braces connecting the front and back panes at the top and bottom. Get your tank factory-drilled for a 1–1.5-inch PVC bulkhead fitting at an upper side panel for drainage to a sump. If you are converting an old tank to reef use, ask your dealer to drill the tank. Note that some tanks have tempered glass that will shatter, and glass becomes brittle with age. If you cannot make use of a drilled bulkhead fitting, consider a prefilter/surface skimmer that siphons water just under the upper frame to the sump, or ask your dealer for recommendations.

Stand

A reef tank can be a beautiful furnishing in your home. Carefully consider where you want to locate it by evaluating the support below and access to its plumbing and electrical systems. The underlying floor support—2″ × 4″ or 2″ × 6″ wood frame studs, concrete—limits tank size. A slab concrete floor in a den or basement is usually safe for a large tank, but cracks in a settling house can tilt the floor into separate planes. Although a wooden stud floor in a corner should support most tanks, even a slight sag risks stress on the bottom frame, resulting in glass panel separation or a cracked bottom. The strongest location on a wood floor in an upper storey room is in a corner.

The average reef tank is 70–135 gallons. It will probably have 1–2 pounds of rock (see Chapter 4) per gallon tank size, and perhaps 2–4 inches of sand or gravel. The remaining 75 percent of tank capacity will be filled with water. Let's calculate the weight of a fully set-up tank.

The weight of a tank and stand averages 1.5 pounds per gallon, more for larger tanks. A 55-gallon tank and stand weighs about 85 pounds, a 100-gallon set-up about 175 pounds, and a 135-gallon set-up about 250 pounds. About 75 percent of the tank is filled with water weighing 8.25 pounds per gallon. About 25 percent of the tank will be occupied by rock and sand or gravel at 17 pounds per gallon, or 17 pounds times 25 percent of the capacity of the tank.

Let's estimate the weight of a 135-gallon set-up. We're already estimated tank and stand at 250 pounds. Next, measure the base of the tank. A 135-gallon tank will generally be 18 inches back to front (wide), and 72 inches side to side (long), equal to 6 × 1.5 feet or 9 square feet. Using the square foot method to calculate the aragonite gravel needed, estimate 6.5 pounds per inch of gravel depth per square foot of tank bottom. For three inches of aragonite gravel you will need 6.5 × 3 × 9 or 175.5 pounds of gravel. Gravel comes in 44-pound sacks, so four sacks will be just right (4 × 44 = 176). The square inch method to calculate the weight of aragonite sand needed to fill a tank to a particular depth is to multiply L × W × D (where D is depth of sand desired) in inches, divide the product by 1728, and then multiply by 70.

A 135-gallon tank is 24 inches high. After adding 3 inches of gravel, another 3 inches will be displaced by 1–2 pounds per gallon of live rock. At a minimum, the rock will weigh 135 pounds. If the tank is filled 75 percent with water, the water alone will weigh 835 pounds. And so the total weight of a 135-gallon reef tank in pounds will be 250 (tank and stand) + 176 (gravel) + 135 (rock) + 835 (water) = 1,396 pounds or almost three quarters of a ton, with the weight distributed to the four or six legs of the stand.

The weight of a reef tank precludes using a table or furniture as a stand.

Echinaster sentis, *the Caribbean spiny sea star, is not safe in a reef tank, as it might feed on tridacnid clams or scallops.*

Commercially-built stands are strong and reliable. Homemade wood stands should be constructed of 4″ × 4″ or larger studs bolted to 4″ × 6″ pressure-treated frames, with numerous cross braces to protect against warping. You cannot overbuild a stand.

Purchase a package of Styrofoam insulation panels, and place panels on the frame to absorb slight unevenness where the tank meets the stand. The stand legs should be shimmed to eliminate the slightest unevenness.

Finally, leave some distance between the tank and walls (4–6 inches) for the dissipation of heat. Keeping a reef tank cool is difficult, and air space helps vent the tank heat.

Power

We need too much electricity to share with your home entertainment center. Lighting consumes most of the electricity to a reef tank, and is discussed in Chapter 11. Talk to your dealer about what kinds of reef tank (what kind of coral) you will keep, and ask that dealer to help you select or design the lighting. Corals generally need four watts per gallon. A 135-gallon reef tank may be illuminated by a combination of two 175-watt metal halide incandescent lamps, two 48-inch, 40-watt fluorescent lamps, and two 60-watt high output (HO) fluorescent lamps for a total of 550 watts. Metal halide lamps emit heat and, if enclosed in a hood, should be cooled with a built-in fan. The fans, light timers, and submersible water pumps for circulation and operating the protein skimmer or other filters may add another 100 watts. We've already reached 650 watts, but could easily go to 1,000 watts with bigger air-cooled pumps, stronger metal halide lamps, and optional ozone generator (see Chapter 9). Finally, your tank may run so hot from metal halide lamps and submersible water pumps that a chiller unit (see Chapter 10) is required to hold temperatures at healthy levels (72°–78°F) for corals. Chillers use 500 or more watts.

Salt is a terrific conductor of electricity. The combination of salt water with this much electrical power warrants a separate line for the reef tank with a ground fault interrupter (GFI) outlet. An electrician can run a 15- or 20-amp line from your circuit breaker box to the reef tank location. Have the electrician install a GFI outlet on the first box on the line, and then additional box outlets downcurrent, with all outlets at least a foot above the top of the tank for easy access and to protect from salt spray. Placing the outlets above and to either side of the tank lets you plug in from anywhere, and offers protection from splashes.

Back-up Power

Short-term power outages can be mitigated with battery driven aerators to maintain dissolved oxygen concentrations. Long-term outages can kill everything from fishes to microbes. A back-up generator can be a lifesaver. A small, portable generator will be sufficient to keep the animals alive during an outage if you have enough fuel on hand. But small generators solve only small problems. A better alternative is a 2,800–40,000-watt (40 kw) whole house or industrial generator that will not only take care of your reef tank, but everything else in your home. To determine generator size suitable for your home, you need to place an ammeter at the circuit box to determine amps pulled when all major appliances are running, and add 50 percent for starting surge. An electrical contractor will do this for you. You can run the average house on 10 kw, but should figure another 5 kw for the largest reef tank. I overbuilt with a 40 kw generator, so I have plenty to spare for neighbors. If your house has natural gas, have a plumbing contractor run a pipe directly to the generator and you'll never worry about running out of fuel. Whole house generators are quieter than portables. An optional automatic transfer switch will turn the unit on even if you're not home.

Chapter Three
Water Quality

Your reef tank should be maintained at tropical seawater salinity (35 ppt) and temperature (around 72°–76°F). A temperature below 65°F or above 90°F can be lethal to some fishes and corals. Stress at sublethal temperatures encourages attack by disease-causing microbes. Unlike estuary or near-shore animals with physiological mechanisms for adjusting to tidal water conditions, strictly oceanic animals like corals and many coral fishes do not easily adjust to values outside normal experience. That is why a reef aquarium should be maintained within strict parameters. Many aquarists have not had problems when pH values fell below 8.0, the water warmed to more than 82°F, the alkalinity dropped to a third its recommended range, and calcium was half again the concentration it should be. Occasional alterations are tolerated, and frequent deviations from norms may even facilitate adaptation, so few rules are set in stone. In fact, many authorities recommend reducing salinity below seawater values to reduce the likelihood of infectious disease. That's fallacious, as microbe populations adapt to changed conditions. Microbial infections can be treated with osmotic shock, but a lower than normal salinity is just an opportunity for adaptation.

Seawater contains major and minor chemicals and trace elements to support marine life; indeed, many marine algae and early larval fishes absorb nutrients and trace chemicals directly from the water. In the early days of the marine hobby, aquarists had to collect water for their aquariums by hauling it home from the ocean. When mixed with tap water, today's synthetic salt mixes will provide the necessary chemicals in the correct proportions to sustain and even breed marine animals.

Ocean water doesn't vary much around the world, giving rise to the notion that corals and other marine animals have little tolerance for values far removed from typical seawater. In reality some corals (and most fishes) are tougher than you might imagine. Many can tolerate, at least for a time, drastic changes in salinity, temperature, and alkalinity. On the other hand, some chemicals in even slight concentrations are deadly. Ordinary aquarium medications such as copper, used to treat fish diseases, are lethal to most invertebrates, while ammonia, lethal to most fishes, is a nutrient for corals.

More important is what variation from normal does to the ecosystem within the aquarium. Some macroalgae compete for nutrients with corals and can overgrow them. Other algae and microbes release toxins. Water quality maintenance is important to promote survival and growth of corals, while limiting the growth of noxious microbes.

Municipal tap water in which you dissolve the salt mix is not pure water. Some municipal waters contain chlorine or chloramines, nitrates, phosphates, and silicates. The first time you set up an aquarium, you'll add all the above to the tank. There may be a brown smear on the glass, sand, and rocks for a few weeks as diatoms bloom, feeding on the silicates; there may be a filamentous algal bloom, fed by phosphates and nitrates. Noxious algae will continue to bloom if these nutrients are not diluted by regular water changes or removed by the growth of desirable algae such as *Caulerpa*. In general, the one time use of tap water to mix the salts for the reef tank poses no risk. Risks arise when tap water is used repeatedly as make-up water to replace evaporative loss, and some contaminants build to significant adverse concentrations.

In many municipalities, surface water is treated so thoroughly to remove nutrients that it poses no threat of algal blooms. On the other hand, groundwater may be rich in iron, nitrates, or silicates, and should not be used to make up evaporative losses unless run through a reverse osmosis (RO) unit. Call your local water supplier (the phone number is on your water bill) and ask for a copy of the annual comprehensive laboratory analysis.

Makeup Water

After filling the aquarium, switch on the pumps and filters but leave the lights off for six weeks. Do not add any invertebrates. This period of low light and new (low nutrient) water will retard noxious algae while favoring low light-tolerant coralline red algae. It will also provide the nitrogen cycle bacterial populations time to develop. If the tank is near a window, pull the shades to limit the light.

During these weeks, you will be surprised by how fast the water (but not salt) evaporates from the aquarium and sump.

This water must be replaced to maintain salinity and the balance of chemicals. In some cities tap water contains calcium, but not silicates, nitrates, or phosphates. In others the concentrations of those chemicals is high enough to promote algae blooms. We need a substitute.

RO, DI, and Distilled Water

Evaporation losses should be replaced with distilled (pure), deionized (DI), or reverse osmosis (RO) water. Most aquarists opt for an RO unit. Pure water has no salts or nutrients, but distillation equipment (stills) are expensive. You can buy distilled water at supermarkets for about two dollars a gallon. Tap water is usually unsuitable for make-up water because its dissolved chemicals build up in the aquarium over time, its nutrients promote growth of noxious algae, and municipal disinfectants (chlorine, chloramine) may require adding more chemicals such as sodium thiosulfate for neutralization.

Differences between DI and RO

DI and RO units produce good water at a reasonable cost. Both require maintenance. RO membranes clog and must be replaced when flow rates drop. Deionizer units must be recharged or their cartridges replaced. RO water takes hours to produce in multigallon quantities, whereas running tap water through a DI unit will produce all the water you need in a short time. RO units waste 75 percent or more of the water coming through the unit, while deionizers waste none. RO units must be run for hours, and accidental flooding from failure to turn the unit off is common. Both RO and DI product water should be tested with a total dissolved solids meter or a hardness kit to monitor that the units are still working.

DI and RO units in series produce excellent water, provide backup in case one unit fails, and increase the lifetime of the resins and the membranes. It may be worth the cost in areas with hard water, or where house plumbing contains lead or copper pipes. Where lead in tap water is due to lead in the copper plumbing or brass fittings, let the tap run ten minutes before taking water for drinking or aquarium use. The effectiveness of an RO or DI unit can be increased by combining it with a mechanical prefilter and activated carbon adsorption filter. The best quality water combines all of the above in the treatment train, but best is seldom necessary. RO alone produces perfectly suitable water.

Deionized Water

Deionization removes non-ionic gases, and is even purer than distilled water, which absorbs atmospheric carbon dioxide (not a bad thing, since it is used by zooxanthellae). A deionizer canister contains charged resin beads or granules that attract ions of opposite charge. Newer units use resins with differing attractiveness for calcium and magnesium and for the anions nitrate and phosphate (NO_3^-, PO_4^-). Units in series remove a broad spectrum of charged chemicals. Deionizers require either replacement of the resins or recharge of the resins in a laboratory using strong acids or bases. As with distilled water, you can purchase DI water in supermarkets for about two dollars a gallon.

Reverse Osmosis

Reverse osmosis removes a high percentage of minerals, nitrates, and phosphates, but not silicates. Tap water from your faucet passes through a semipermeable membrane at enough pressure to squeeze the water through while

Recommended Water Quality Values for a Reef Tank

temperature	72–78°F
specific gravity	1.022–1.026
salinity	32–36 o/oo
	or ppt
pH	8.0–8.4
alkalinity	6–9 KH
carbon dioxide	2–5 ppm
calcium	400–450 mg/L
oxidation-reduction	
potential	+250–375 mV
dissolved oxygen	>5.5 ppm
Ammonia	<0.25 mg/L
Nitrite	<0.25 mg/L
Nitrate	<30 mg/L
phosphate	<0.03 mg/L
iron	0.1–0.2 mg/L
movement	>5×tank
	volume (gph)

Symbols

°F	degrees Fahrenheit
gph	gallons per hour
KH	German degrees of calcium alkalinity
>	greater than
<	less than
mg/L	milligrams per liter
mV	millivolts
ppm	parts per million
o/oo	parts per thousand
o/o	percent or parts per hundred

blocking the passage of minerals and salts. An RO unit requires several hours of breaking in, but afterward might produce up to 100 gallons per day (depending on the unit) of 25 percent by volume oxygen depleted, cation-poor and anion-poor water useful for replenishing evaporativo losses. The remaining 75 percent by volume is wastewater, and contains 85–95 percent of the original ions and other impurities.

A reverse osmosis unit consists of a membrane cartridge and one or more water filter cartridges. Tap water entering the unit is forced against the membrane. Relatively pure water passes through the membrane while wastewater, with concentrated minerals, is discarded.

RO efficiency depends on the concentrations of impurities of the incoming water, local water pressure, water temperature (room temperature is better than cold or hot water), and the type and age of the semipermeable membrane. Cellulose triacetate (CTA) membranes are degraded by bacteria, and must be used in chlorinated water or they break down. Thin film composite (TFC) membranes can be damaged by chlorine and work better on nitrates, yet in most areas nitrates are not a problem. Vendors will advise you on the type (CTA, TFC) and size unit (gallons/day) for your applications. All membranes have limited life expectancy, so product water should be tested every couple of months with a total dissolved solids (TDS) meter or a hardness test kit.

You can divert the RO product water to a storage barrel and the wastewater to your garden or other locations in your fish room using the icemaker tubing and connectors from an appliance store stocking parts for refrigerators.

Motion, Powerheads, and Wavemakers

Corals cannot survive without water motion to wash away waste products. Outside power filters can provide some surface current and pass the water through granular carbon for purification. Submersible powerhead pumps can move water through all levels and corners, leaving no dead spaces above the sand to become oxygen depleted. Water flow across the bottom sweeps detritus (decomposing plant fragments) from nooks and crannies. It provides respiratory exchange for the sand surface, which is the lung for the minute animals living within the gravel and sand (meiofauna). Rocks should be slightly elevated so that the sand layer is washed by no fewer than two opposing powerheads. Powerheads or water pumps should turn over at least five times the tank volume per hour. In nanoreefs or small (5–10 gallon) reef tanks where the heat emitted by powerheads is significant, aeration with large (non-splashing) bubbles can provide adequate current.

The water flows on coral reefs are not tidal or one-way, but relentless back-and-forth surges. Surges can be produced in reef tanks by pointing the discharge ports of powerheads or filter returns on intersecting paths, by placing opposing discharges on timers so they alternate between blocking and not blocking their opposite number, using wavemakers (buckets on spindles that fill and dump contents into the tank) or large clam-shell type bubble collectors, or with motor-mounted rotating spindles on which a powerhead or sump discharge is attached (e.g., AquaGate, Osci-Wave), providing up to a 90 degree arc of discharge at a slow pace to replicate natural surge.

Commercial wavemakers use 2–4 or more amps, but can handle several plug-in powerheads; some can be programmed to provide a surge when a light sensor detects dimming in the evening. Rotating motorized spindles are simple and flexible but cost about a hundred dollars or more. They mount in a corner top of the tank and slowly turn an attached powerhead (or discharge from the sump) back and forth in an arc. The basic mechanical wavemaker is a bucket that fills from a small powerhead and empties when the water level exceeds the bucket's center of gravity. Because water will leak from the hole carrying the spindle, the bucket must be mounted inside the aquarium just above the water level.

Nutrients

The water surrounding oceanic reefs is almost devoid of nutrients, yet reefs reach full development in these conditions and fail to develop where nutrients are plentiful. Nearshore reefs don't survive where flooded with silt and nutrients in freshwater runoff, which is why those on tourist islands eventually become silted over or overgrown by macroalgae. Quiet coastal lagoons with their bright light, high heat, and low surge can provide habitat for tolerant soft corals adaptable to aquaria. Shaded reef areas in deep water, caves, and underhangs provide habitat for plankton-feeding corals that do not depend on light and symbiotic algae. These sturdy corals can be maintained in captivity on live foods or bits of seafood fed with a kitchen baster.

Oceanic reefs recycle nutrients and thrive on light energy. The symbiotic algae in corals produce sugars, sugar alcohols, and the amino acid alanine from carbon dioxide, bright sunlight, and waste ammonia of the polyp, incorporat-ing it before it can dissipate into the ocean. Macroalgae grazed from the reef by tangs, parrotfishes, and angelfishes are returned to the reef as fecal matter, as are feces of other fishes, inverte-brates, and the surrounding zooplankton. Tangs supplement their diet by consuming droppings of other fishes, adding one more round of nutrient cycling on the highly efficient reef.

A reef tank differs from a real-world reef in that it cannot recycle wastes. Every aquarium is on the way to becoming a box of marine manure if not controlled. Foods are continually added, cycled by the inhabitants, and emitted back to the water as waste. A reef tank is a closed system. If a good portion of the old waste-laden water is not replaced with new, clean water, the increasing waste concentration will either cause a bloom of noxious algae that will kill the corals or otherwise stress the inhabitants beyond endurance. A rule of thumb is to replace at least 1 percent of synthetic seawater daily after providing make-up RO or distilled or deionized water to compensate for evaporative losses. A 125-gallon aquarium contains about 100 gallons of water, so removing at least a gallon a day and replacing it with newly mixed seawater accomplishes the minimum 1 percent water change. For a tank half this size, change a gallon every other day. You can use the discarded water to hatch *Artemia* (brine shrimp) cysts.

Tap Water

Ideally a new reef tank should be set up with water treated through a DI or RO unit, but quantities for a large tank are difficult to come by. Most aquarists simply mix marine salts with tap water for the initial filling. Tap water can also be used to mix limewater or other buffering additives, or to top off the aquarium or sump in an emergency. Tap water contains additives provided by your municipal water purveyor, but for small additions it's safe to use.

Chlorine

Tap water should be dechlorinated before use. Several tests can detect chlorine in water. In the diethylphenylenediamine (DPD) test, free chlorine causes the test reagent to turn red. A negative result indicates enough dechlorinator was used. Other tests rely on free chlorine to liberate iodine that can be detected with a coloring reagent. Don't use kits based on the reagent orthotoluidine; they are unreliable.

Ammonia

Ammonia is too dilute in tap water to worry about. The only important source of too much ammonia is decomposition. Early in the cycling of an aquarium, ammonia can build to levels toxic to fish. When ammonia cycling by microbes is under control (this takes a few weeks), ammonia test readings should remain low. An ammonia spike in an established tank indicates sudden decomposition from overfeeding (dry food is the usual suspect), or the death of an anemone, a coral, a large amount of algae, or a large fish.

Tests for ammonia do not distinguish between ordinary ammonia (NH_3) and ammonium ion (NH_4^+), which are always in equilibrium. As pH drops, the equilibrium shifts toward non-toxic ammonium ion. As pH rises, the equilibrium shifts toward toxic ammonia. That is why there is no single "ammonia" reading with a test kit that tells you what is toxic and what is safe.

The standard test for ammonia in fresh water relies on Nessler's reagent, which generates deepening shades of yellow with increasing ammonia concentration. In salt water, Nessler's reagent is precipitated by calcium and magnesium, preventing the yellowing reaction. This precipitation can be blocked by adding EDTA or Rochelle salts, either of which keep Nessler's reagent in solution. Ammonia test kits lacking EDTA or Rochelle salts are not suitable for salt-water tanks.

An alternative test is based on formation of a blue pigment (indophenol) when ammonia reacts with phenol and hypochlorite.

Nitrite and Nitrate

Fish and corals don't produce nitrate and nitrite. They produce ammonia and urea, which are metabolized by bacteria in the tank to form nitrite and nitrate. In general, nitrite is the toxic first step of ammonia conversion; nitrate is the nontoxic second step. The standard test for toxic nitrite in water yields a reddish purple (azo) dye. Hach Chemical has a sensitive version that can read nitrites down to 0.25 micrograms per liter (0.25 μgm/L). Nitrates (NO_3^-) in the water will not interfere with the results.

Phosphate

Organic phosphorus occurs in animal and plant tissues, in dry feeds, and in agricultural organophosphates. In the dissolved, inorganic (orthophosphate) state it is a plant nutrient that causes blooms of nuisance algae. Ecologists term this dissolved inorganic state soluble reactive phosphate (SRP).

Phosphate is an important zooxanthellae and macroalgae nutrient occurring in seawater at about 0.07 milligrams per liter (mg/L); in synthetic salt mixes it occurs at even lower concentrations. Its

Milligrams per Liter (mg/L) versus Parts per Million (ppm)

Concentrations of trace elements and unwanted wastes (ammonia, nitrite, phosphate) are reported in ppm (parts per million). If "parts" in ppm referred to 1 gram, then ppm would refer to grams per million grams (= million parts). As long as the "parts" are identical then using "ppm" is accurate.

The term "mg/L" is a measure of mixed kinds of parts, milligrams (weight) and liters (volume). It is incorrect to refer to 1 mg/L of salt in water as 1 ppm. Here's why. One liter (1 L) of natural seawater has a mass of approximately 1.025 kilograms or 1.025 Kg/L (depending on temperature). Pure (e.g., deionized) water at 4°C has a density of 1.0000 or 1 Kg/L. If you measure nitrite in seawater from a marine aquarium and the value on the test kit is "1.00" (either as nitrite ion or as nitrite-nitrogen), what the test actually reports is 1.00 mg/L. This means that each liter of water contains 1.00 mg of the substance.

This same value, 1.00 mg/L, if reported as "ppm," would actually be 0.9756 ppm. That is because 1.00 mg/L is equivalent to 1 mg per (1 liter x 1.025 kilograms per liter); or 1 mg per 1.025 Kg; or 1 mg per 1,025,000 mg; or 1 part per 1,025,000 parts; or 0.98 parts per million parts (ppm). (Whew!)

This difference is only 2.5 percent, but it is a real difference. Better quality test kits usually report results in mg/L, and not in ppm.

concentration in the reef tank should not exceed 0.02 mg/L, as excess phosphate causes noxious algal blooms. Most algae won't grow at SRP concentrations below 0.02 mg/L. Phosphate gets into the reef tank from animal feed and wastes, and with some municipal tap water. Phosphate-free distilled or deionized water from supermarkets is superior to tap water for make-up or for preparing limewater (calcium hydroxide solution). Commercial phosphate remover pads impregnated with aluminum oxide must be replaced after 24 hours and then the replacement pad after 48 hours, making them expensive. Ceramic hydroxides (available in granular and other forms) last longer. Limewater added to the sump reduces phosphate concentrations by flocculation and precipitation. Aquaria without gravel should be vacuumed with a siphon to remove fecal waste, detritus, and precipitated phosphates.

Tests for phosphate rely on yellow or blue complexes. The yellow test reads down to 1 mg/L, which is too high for aquarium use. The blue antimony-ascorbic acid test reads down to 0.1 mg/L; ten times better but still no cigar. The blue tin method is best, with a sensitivity of 0.007 mg/L.

Phosphates cannot be avoided, but they can be managed by adding limewater and changing tank water. The most practical way to decrease SRP levels is to feed less, siphon detritus and wastes frequently, and remove algae that tend to store phosphates. In some public wastewater treatment systems, duckweed is used to remove nitrates and phosphates; it is grown, harvested, and landfilled. In marine aquaria, fast-growing *Caulerpa* can provide the same benefits if encouraged to grow, vigorously harvested, and the excess discarded. It may look like a pretty plant, but think of it as a trash bag.

Salinity

The offshore reef environment is remarkably constant. The composition of seawater everywhere in the world is about 35 parts per thousand of dissolved salts (35 ppt or 35 o/oo), which is the same as 3.5 percent (3.5 o/o). Seawater is dilute in estuaries (to about 15 ppt), hypersaline from solar evaporation in some lagoons (40 ppt), but the components and proportions of the elements remain the same. The Red Sea, an enclosed gulf that evaporates faster than it receives inflow from the Indian Ocean, is more saline than the rest of the Indo-Pacific, but that's the only large exception. Most marine invertebrates and fishes are quite comfortable at salinities of 30–40 ppt, and tolerant of tank evaporation by as much as 15 percent. Strict adherence to a salinity of 35 ppt or specific gravity 1.025 (see below) is unnecessary. Many oceanic forms can penetrate far up estuarine rivers rich in calcium, and almost all marine fishes are tolerant of protracted freshwater dips to eliminate surface parasites. These tolerances also occur in some invertebrates, but in general invertebrates cannot manage osmotic adjustments as well as fishes.

Aquarists measure salinity of marine aquarium water by determining the water's ability to displace a floating object. That floating object might be a glass hydrometer or a floating arrow in a plastic box. The latter is easier to read. Many marine fish breeders use a refractometer for its increased accuracy, which matters more to easily shocked invertebrate culture organisms than to generally tolerant larval fishes.

Salt Mixes

Commercial marine mixes are 99.9 percent sodium chloride, potassium chloride, calcium chloride, magnesium chloride, magnesium sulfate, sodium bicarbonate, potassium bromide, strontium chloride, boric acid, and sodium fluoride, with several minor elements (more than 1 microgram per liter or μgm/L) and trace elements (less than 1 μgm/L).

Calcium and strontium are absorbed by growing corals and must be replaced by calcium hydroxide and strontium chloride or through the dissolution of aragonite sand. Iodine is a minor constituent, important for soft corals and fleshy macroalgae that may use it to detoxify excessive oxygen produced under intense light. Trace elements are provided by feeding brine shrimp nauplii, copepods, liquid supplements, or partial water changes.

If you are using an ozone generator with a protein skimmer, select a salt mix with the lowest bromine concentration. The effects of ozone on bromine are discussed in Chapter 9.

Temperature

Water temperatures at coral reefs vary from the surface to the depths, seasonally, and with exposure to sunlight and oceanic or nearshore tidal currents. The greatest diversity, abundance, and

Temperature, Salinity, and Specific Gravity

ppt	sp.gr. at 60°F	sp.gr. at 70°F	sp.gr. at 80°F
20	1.015	1.013	1.012
25	1.018	1.017	1.016
30	1.022	1.021	1.019
35	1.026	1.025	1.023
40	1.030	1.028	1.02

stability are where temperatures are within 70°F–78°F, there is little seasonal variation in light levels (closer to the equator), and the populations are either outside the hurricane belt along the trade wind routes or deep enough to survive storms. Where temperatures seasonally drop below 60°F or rise above 85°F, coral species diversity is low. The marine reef aquarium should be maintained close to 75°F and never allowed to exceed 80°F.

A reef tank maintained in the mid 70°s F will support estuarine invertebrates acclimated to summers along the Pacific coast or the northeastern United States. Many cold-water brilliant red or blue anemones, sea stars, and nudibranchs will thrive in a reef tank, but often must be hand fed.

pH

pH is best measured with electronic meters calibrated against standardized buffers. The meter is no more reliable than the buffers against which it is calibrated, so buffer quality is important, as is the age of the probe because the tips wear out. Electronic meters must be kept in good working order and calibrated before use.

In the field (or the fish room), pH can also be measured by titration, the addition of measured amounts of test water to a vial containing an indicator dye that changes color sharply at a specific point or points. The test kit color change should be proportional to concentration to be valid, which means it follows Beer's Law. The concentration (depending on the test) can be protons (H+, acid), phosphate, metals, or lots of other substances detectable with color tests and spectrometers. Beer's Law states that absorbance of monochromatic light by a solution is proportional to the concentration of the solute. Simply put, this relationship validates interpretations from dye tests and spectrographs.

The pH of oceanic water is 8.0–8.4 everywhere. At this pH, carbonate deposition is optimal and corals and calcareous algae grow fastest. At lower pH, hard corals won't survive, soft corals slowly decline, and non-calcareous nuisance algae and cyanobacteria overgrow hard coral surfaces. In aquaria, the main contributors to lowering pH are bacterial nitrification and photosynthesis. The pH should be maintained at or above 8.1 by regular partial water changes, minimal supplementary feedings, avoidance of liquified or suspension food supplements (despite commercial hyperbole), the regular addition of calcium hydroxide (Kalkwasser) solution, or (in an emergency) the addition of sodium bicarbonate (baking soda), sold as pH "upward" buffer.

Dissolved Oxygen

The most accurate way to measure oxygen concentration is with an electronic oxygen meter, an expensive instrument. Titration kits are time consuming and inaccurate. The simplest way to maintain (rather than measure) a high oxygen concentration is with low temperatures (not higher than 76°F) and strong turbulence. The appearance and health of the animals can be the most practical indicator of oxygen concentration.

Oxygen concentrations in the sea and in marine aquaria depend on temperature, salinity, and the oxidizable organic compounds in the water. Oxygen is saturated in tropical oceanic reef water at about 4–7 ppm at 75°F, but can be supersaturated in quiet, shallow, sunny lagoon waters rich in algae. Oxygen supersaturation is seldom stressful to corals, but can be stressful to fishes and gilled invertebrates. Oxygen concentrations drop in stagnant waters with decomposing organic materials, such as sewer outfalls and in polluted bays. Occasional slight depressions from saturation are not important, but sudden massive depletions or chronically low levels are stressful. The sudden drop of 2–3 ppm when decay microbes grow on dead animals, dead algae, or leftover food is often accompanied by a rapid build-up of ammonia/ammonium, a drop in pH, and an increase in dissolved carbon dioxide, all of which contribute to stress and, combined, can be lethal.

Oxidation-Reduction Potential

An oxidation-reduction potential (ORP) meter measures the drop in electrical potential, in millivolts (thousandths of a volt), across a probe. A sudden drop in voltage suggests a sudden drop in water quality. The absolute ORP reading is less important than any rapid decrease of 50 or more mV, suggesting that a water pump has failed or something in the tank has died and must be removed.

In the wild, the oxidation-reduction potential of seawater at reefs has been measured at +250 to +350 mV. Although that's the level recommended for reef aquarists, your tank's ORP is less important than whether the fishes and decapods are active and in good color, the corals are spread and their polyps open, and the animals look as healthy as if they were in the ocean. An ORP meter by itself is expensive and of limited usefulness. A drop in ORP can be set to trigger delivery of carbon dioxide or to start up an ozonizer, but it is not critical equipment.

If the animals look stressed, check the temperature, then the pumps. If neither of these are the problem, look for a decaying animal in the tank Once it has been removed, the quickest way to correct degraded water is with a massive water change. Filtration is merely an attractive short-cut and prolongs unacceptable conditions.

Ozone

Oxygen (O_2) energized with electricity or ultraviolet light forms ozone (O_3), is a highly reactive oxidizer. In aquaria, ozone oxidizes anything organic, including rubber gaskets, O-rings, and ordinary airline tubing. It can also damage fish and invertebrate tissues. Its major use is destroying bacteria, nuisance microalgae, parasitic protozoa, and clarifying yellow (organic-rich) water by oxidizing tannins, lignins, and phenols. Removing color and odor are the main reasons for using it in reef aquaria, but don't overdo the dose.

Ozonizer units have a stainless steel ground electrode separated from a ceramic or glass dielectric material, all enclosed in a case to protect from splash water or burning yourself. Filtered air from an air pump enters the influent port, passes across a desiccant to remove water vapor, and proceeds across the gap. High voltage AC current generates a charge across the gap that reacts with dry oxygen in the air, or with pure oxygen, if provided. The higher the electrical energy, the more ozone formed. A portion (about 1–10 percent in industrial units) of the oxygen is ionized, and immediately reacts with molecular oxygen to produce O_3 (ozone) that then reacts with anything organic. Ozone and air exiting the ozonizer is piped to a skimmer or sump, and released by an air diffuser constructed of sintered glass or sandstone, but not wood, which is destroyed by ozonization.

Locate the ozonizer above the tank to protect it from backflowing water in a power outage. Every six months, disassemble the unit and clean the generator tube and contacts of grit, and replace or regenerate the desiccant. The efficiency of the unit drops with humidity and the accumulation of dirt or dust. These wastes also block heat dissipation, which can damage the unit.

How much ozone is enough? You can rely on an ORP controller to manage output by turning off the ozonizer when ORP is high, but that's complex and expensive. Just 10 mg/hr per 50 gallons of aquarium water will deliver a substantial prophylactic dose with little danger of overdosing. Be aware that UV sterilization also produces some ozone.

Ozone reduces the output of a protein skimmer by breaking large, sticky molecules into units too small to capture on the water-air interface. Ozone also oxidizes effluent in the collection cup, producing a noxious odor that can be adsorbed with activated carbon.

Ozonizers are more often used on fish tanks to control microbial diseases than on reef tanks where they also destroy plankton. They are useful for reef tanks with algal mat filtration that produces yellow water from leaking macroalgal organics.

Burning of fishes by ozone can be avoided by cutting back ozonization, but this may solve the wrong problem. Your ozonizer output may not be too strong, but your marine mix may contain too much bromine. Excessive bromine in some salt mixes produces excessive, stable hypobromite (OBr^-), a powerful oxidant that irritates gills and skin. Selecting a salt mix with a low bromine level allows safer use of ozone. Alternatively, reduce the ozone generator output directly or through your ORP controller.

Carbon

Carbon is the backbone of all life, the defining element of organic compounds. It is the element of coal and diamonds, adsorptive, hard, and reactive. Charcoal is the carbon residue when organic substances (usually wood or coconut husks) are burned slowly. Coal is the carbonaceous remains of ancient plants and animals subjected to geologic heat and pressure. Diamond is carbon subjected to greater heat and pressure from the earth's interior, associated with volcanoes.

Activated carbon is carbon heated to burn off substances blocking the natural pores. It is more effective than charcoal or coal for adsorption of organics, colors, toxins, and medications. The two major forms are powdered (finely ground) and granular (coarsely ground). The finer the grind, the more surface area, higher the cost, and greater effectiveness. The commercial terms are granular activated carbon (GAC) and powdered activated carbon (PAC).

Many water treatment plants use inexpensive GAC to adsorb colors and odors in drinking water. It is also used in wastewater treatment plants for these properties, and because the pores later become colonized by anaerobic bacteria that feed on dissolved nitrates and release free nitrogen gas (denitrification).

PAC is finer and has greater adsorption capacity than GAC. Its capacity is measured in how much of its own weight (milligrams of substance per gram of carbon) it can adsorb of small molecules (iodine and methylene blue) and large molecules (molasses). A good grade of PAC with an iodine number of 1,000 (1,000 milligrams of iodine per gram of carbon) can adsorb its own weight in iodine.

Contact time (Tc) describes the time for optimal reactivity to occur. For sub-

Many hermit crabs are reef-safe detritivores, and safe with spawning fishes, but check them out species by species. Large hermits are especially good cleaners in clownfish brood tanks.

water. Replace no more than a third of the total at a time. Old GAC becomes colonized by nitrogen cycle bacteria and is useful forever in this capacity, but its capacity for adsorption is limited to a couple of months.

Activated carbon may remove some trace elements, but these are easily replaced by occasional feeding and normal water changes. Commercial trace element solutions always risk overdosing.

Cheap GACs may leach phosphates to the water, and should not be used in a reef aquarium until rinsed in freshwater. You can test for phosphate leaching of any GAC with a simple aquarium phosphate test. Poor quality carbon, when new (unrinsed) will read above 2 mg/L of orthophosphate; the preferred level is below 0.1 mg/L.

Biological Oxygen Demand, Chemical Oxygen Demand, and Total Organic Carbon (BOD, COD, and TOC)

Carbon-containing substances are excreted, leached, and emitted from living and dying animals and plants as nitrogenous wastes, sexual products, hormones, pheromones, pigments, and other metabolic products. The water and the surfaces of the rock will develop bacteria, protozoa, fungi, and algae. The broken cells of microbes also leach organic substances. These waste substances can cause yellowing of the water. The sum of this material from all sources is called total organic carbon (TOC). High quality water has low TOC, and low quality or nutrient enriched (or simply enriched) water has high TOC.

TOC can be removed by foam fractionation (protein skimming), ozonization,

stances requiring a short Tc to be effective, such as PAC, a small volume in the filter is sufficient. For GAC with its much longer Tc, effectiveness can be increased by using a larger volume of carbon or a small volume for a longer period.

PAC is useful with diatomaceous earth filtration for emergencies (yellow coloration of the water, noxious odors, accidental excessive doses of chemicals). GAC can be used permanently to remove noxious gases and colors before they become nuisances. GAC can be placed in nylon net bags in the sump, in the overflow chamber, or mixed with a surface layer of aragonite gravel. GAC should be replaced or more added at the first hint of yellowing of the aquarium and/or carbon adsorption. No simple test kits are available or necessary, since yellow water is a reliable indicator of high TOC. Protein skimmers remove large molecule TOC; small molecules are removed by activated carbon adsorption.

Another standard water quality test analyzes biological or chemical oxygen demand (BOD or COD). In different ways, these measure the organic constituents in water and provide an estimate of dissolved organic substances. The lower the BOD or COD value, the higher the water quality. Today, there is a simple test for COD based on permanganate demand. It's inexpensive but less accurate than measuring ORP.

Carbon Dioxide

All the corals, algae, fishes, macroinvertebrates, and many of the microorganisms in a reef tank require oxygen for aerobic respiration, and expel carbon dioxide as respiration's waste product. The small amount of dissolved carbon dioxide in the water is a nutrient for algae and some microbes, and a growth promoter for symbiotic zooxanthellae in corals and tridacnid clams, and for the macroalgae on live rock. Carbon dioxide also reacts with carbonates to form the bicarbonates that buffer seawater at about pH 8.3.

Ordinarily we don't measure dissolved carbon dioxide in the reef aquarium, but its effects on pH. By reading pH, we determine whether we need to generate more or less carbon dioxide, or correct the error another way. Commercial carbon dioxide pH controllers monitor aquarium pH and, upon detecting an elevation in pH above 8.3, slowly inject compressed gas from a refillable cylinder into the aquarium water to bring the pH back to 8.3. They are suitable for both freshwater and marine applications, as the desired pH can be programmed to the controller unit. However, controllers are expensive. Carbon dioxide injector systems are popular with freshwater plant enthusiasts, and in marine tanks can increase the growth rate of stony corals, but they are not necessary equipment for ordinary reef tanks.

There are no simple test kits to measure carbon dioxide in seawater. Even if there were, the results would vary with temperature, pH, alkalinity, and time. Laboratory methods to compute carbon dioxide concentrations are not adaptable to home aquaria.

Calcium

Calcium is essential to the growth of stony corals. Hard corals and coralline algae rapidly deplete dissolved calcium in water that must be replaced if growth is to continue. Because soft corals need less calcium, an aquarium containing only soft corals and having aragonite gravel will maintain adequate calcium levels with just periodic water changes.

Calcium in seawater competes with magnesium for carbonate ions and is depleted by algae, hard corals, and some invertebrates. Without high concentrations of magnesium (1,350 mg/L in natural seawater), calcium would combine with so many carbonates that it would precipitate out of solution. The average calcium concentration in seawater is 400 mg/L. Many synthetic marine salts, when dissolved in municipal tap water, meet this concentration because tap water usually contains some calcium. When marine salts are dissolved in reverse osmosis (RO), distilled, or deionized (DI) water, calcium should be added.

Calcium's constant removal by hard corals requires its replacement by a saturated solution of calcium hydroxide $Ca(OH)_2$, limewater or "Kalkwasser," calcium oxide (CaO), calcium chloride ($CaCl_2$), slow dissolution of aragonite gravel, or regular water changes. (Calcium chloride requires an additional step of buffering with bicarbonate.) You can make "Kalkwasser" by adding 2 tablespoons of granular calcium hydroxide per gallon of RO, DI, or distilled water in a 5 gallon bucket and mixing with a submerged powerhead. (Delbeek recommended 1.5 grams of calcium hydroxide per liter, which is about 6 grams per gallon.) Should you decide to make the Kalkwasser in phosphate-contaminated municipal tap water, mix it for not less than half a day to induce phosphate precipitation, then discard the surface scum and sediments before use.

Kalkwasser (about 800 mg/L Ca^{++}) should be added to the sump at night when reef tank pH is normally slightly depressed to 7.8–8.0. The pH 12–13 calcium hydroxide solution can elevate tank pH, but at night this remains within normal tolerances. Addition of the high pH solution during the day might push the reef tank above pH 8.3, which is not advised.

How much and how often calcium hydroxide should be added to replace calcium ions depends on your tank's stony coral and coralline algae community (soft corals do not need calcium additives), hours of bright light during which calcium ions are taken up, and the growth rates of the inhabitants. Measurements of calcium concentrations with a test kit are the only way to tell when and how often to add supplements. Aragonite gravel may eliminate the need for supplementary calcium in soft coral tanks, as the gravel (if deep) dissolves fast enough to maintain a 400 mg/L calcium concentration. Moderately higher concentrations (450–500 mg/L) are not harmful.

Calcium carbonate cannot maintain alkalinity in the absence of carbon dioxide. Automated calcium reactors mix calcium carbonate granules and inject carbon dioxide gas into the aquarium water. This eliminates the need for periodic hand mixing and delivery of Kalkwasser. Levels of calcium must still be monitored. Problems with reactors are their tendency to induce filamentous algal blooms (too much carbon dioxide) and elevated phosphate levels. Kalkwasser does not induce those side effects.

You can purchase (rather than make) Kalkwasser from your pet store. An inexpensive water treatment from Seachem that contains calcium, magnesium, and strontium in seawater ratios (100 to 5 to 0.1) is better than Kalkwasser or the expense and maintenance of calcium reactors.

Hardness and Alkalinity

Hardness is primarily the concentration of calcium (Ca^{++}) and magnesium (Mg^{++}), the two most important metal cations with more than a single positive charge, but in aquarium usage it sometimes also refers to alkalinity. Real alkalinity is the acid-neutralizing capacity of all the negatively charged ions, but mostly phosphate (PO_4^-), carbonate, bicarbonate, silicate, and borate. Aquarium "alkalinity" and "hardness" can also be expressed as mg $CaCO_3$/L or milliequivalents per liter (meq/L). Aquarium "hardness" is usually reported as mg/L of calcium carbonate, but in reality hardness should only refer to the calcium concentration. When we talk about milliequivalents, we are really referring to the amount of base or alkali (OH^-) it will take to neutralize the concentration of anything with a positive or acidic charge

Alkalinity, Hardness, and pH

Of all the concepts inherent in aquarium water chemistry, the two most confusing are hardness and alkalinity. One reason these concepts are confused is that German aquarists, who introduced the idea to the hobby, use the term "general hardness" to refer to hardness and "carbonate hardness" to refer to alkalinity. But the term "carbonate hardness" is an oxymoron. This is because anions (phosphates, silicates, borates, hydroxide, carbonate and bicarbonate) work together to produce cumulative alkalinity.

In the ocean, the constant influx of clay (anionic aluminosilicates) from coastal rivers provides the alkalinity that buffers nearshore oceanic pH. In aquariums, bicarbonate and carbonate provide the alkalinity to stabilize pH. Do not use clay to buffer your aquarium. Think of alkalinity as "acid-neutralizing capacity."

The hardness of water is its ability to form suds when mixed with soap, and depends on the concentration of polyvalent metals. Polyvalent metals mixed with soap form insoluble salts, so suds do not form. The major polyvalent metals that determine seawater hardness are calcium (Ca^{++}) and magnesium (Mg^{++}).

Hardness does not determine pH or alkalinity. However, in healthy seawater systems a high hardness is usually associated with a high alkalinity and a high pH. In the aquarium, these parameters need to be monitored with test kits and adjusted as necessary. It is not unusual to have a high calcium concentration but a low alkalinity that prevents coralline algae and hard corals from taking up the abundant calcium.

Strontium and Iron cations are numerically insignificant to hardness but physiologically they are important to red algae and corals.

(H^+) or more than one charge if it is a metal (Mg^{++}) rather than an acid.

One test for hardness is the EDTA titration method. A dye added to the sample water complexes with calcium and magnesium and turns the water wine red, after which EDTA is added until the red solution turns blue. The number of drops of EDTA needed for the change to blue is proportional to total hardness. We measure alkalinity in a somewhat similar manner, using a dropwise test with either of the common indicator dyes phenolphthalein or metacresol purple.

It is important to raise aquarium concentrations of calcium to that of seawater and alkalinity even higher for three reasons:

1. Calcium, depleted by stony corals and coralline algae, must be replaced.

2. Alkalinity helps maintain a high pH needed by corals.

3. Calcium saturation will precipitate phosphates, protecting the aquarium against nuisance algae blooms. (Calcium carbonate is less soluble than calcium phosphate.)

Should you use baking soda (sodium carbonate) to adjust alkalinity? Absolutely not. Commercial preparations for raising alkalinity are balanced mixtures of sodium carbonate and sodium borate. In the right ratios, they can adjust alkaline reserve without suddenly raising pH. Baking soda alone will rapidly raise the pH and stress the inhabitants.

Measuring and Relating Alkalinity and Hardness

In a nutshell, hardness refers to the concentration of calcium and magnesium cations, and alkalinity refers to the concentration of carbonate and bicarbonate anions.

Americans measure total hardness in meq/L or in grains of $CaCO_3$ per gallon. In all but soft water, alkalinity and cation hardness are expressed as calcium carbonate equivalent. The relationships are as follows:

$$1 \text{ meq/L} = 50 \text{ mg/L } CaCO_3$$
$$= 2.8 \text{ KH, GH, or dH}$$
$$= 2.92 \text{ grains } CaCO_3/gal$$
$$1 \text{ mg/L } CaCO_3 = 0.02 \text{ meq/L}$$
$$= 0.056 \text{ KH, GH, or dH}$$
$$= 0.058 \text{ grains } CaCO_3/gal$$
$$1 \text{ grain } CaCO_3/gal = 0.34 \text{ meq/L}$$
$$= 0.96 \text{ KH, GH, or dH}$$
$$= 17.9 \text{ mg/L or ppm } CaCO_3$$

mg/L Ca	mg/L $CaCO_3$	meq/L $CaCO_3$	dH, GH, or KH
40.00	100.00	**2.0**	5.6
100.00	250.00	5.0	14.0
200.00	500.00	10.0	28.0
300.00	750.00	15.0	42.0
400.00	1000.00	20.0	56.0
440.00	1100.00	22.0	61.6
460.00	1150.00	23.0	64.4
480.00	1200.00	24.0	67.2
500.00	1250.00	25.0	70.0

These relationships are for calcium or for calcium carbonate equivalent. Seawater has 400 mg/L of calcium and an alkalinity of just over 2.0 meq/L, one tenth the concentration predicted by the relationship in pure water.

In practice, we keep the calcium concentration and alkalinity of a reef tank higher than natural seawater to promote rapid growth of corals and coralline algae.

Strontium

Strontium's concentration in natural seawater is 8–9 mg/L, and varies from 0.2 to almost 14 mg/L in synthetic mixes. You can purchase commercial supple- ments of strontium chloride to add weekly to your aquarium, or you can make your own. Mix a 10 percent (w/v) solution by adding 100 grams of stron- tium chloride ($SrCl_2$) to a liter of water, and then add 1 ml (20 drops) of this solution to each 30 gallons of reef tank water volume (not total tank size) weekly. Strontium supplements improve growth of hard corals. Aragonite gravel should release enough strontium to eliminate the need for this supplement.

Strontium is difficult to detect because it is masked by calcium. There are no reliable and practical kits for measuring strontium in a reef tank.

Iodine

Iodine as the iodide ion, I^-, is a micronutrient for macroalgae, microalgae including symbiotic zooxanthellae, and many soft corals. It is used up rapidly and must be replaced for good growth. Commercial supplements typically consist of 1 percent potassium iodide, with instructions to add 1 ml per week per 20–25 gallons. Delbeek and Sprung recommended weekly dosing of 1 drop per 20 gallons with pharmaceutical over-the-counter tincture of iodine. Overdosing can cause blooms of noxious filamentous algae in the presence of high nitrate concentrations. Some synthetic salt mixes provide iodine; daily water changes of 1 percent may provide sufficient iodine and preclude the need for supplements. Poor red algal growth may improve with a combination of supplementary iodine and calcium, and a longer but not brighter photoperiod.

Copper

Copper is a micronutrient for algae. Even small amounts are toxic to invertebrates, and large concentrations kill algae. The principal source of copper in aquaria is fish medications, which should be avoided. A copper test good for marine tanks is the neocuproine method, which works at pH 3–9 to yield a yellow (not orange) product.

Iron

Iron is a nutrient for macroalgae and for some microalgae, including the zooxanthellae in corals, but we don't know how much to use. In one outstanding reef aquarium, the iron concentration was 0.15 mg/L, but there is no generally agreed optimal level. We don't have good tests for iron, so when using iron supplements, watch the aquarium. If you get an algal bloom, cut the dose.

Trace Elements

Molybdenum, manganese, zinc, and cobalt are important trace elements for plants, including the microalgae used to feed rotifers and copepods, the symbiotic zooxanthellae (dinoflagellates) of corals, attractive macroalgae like *Caulerpa*, and nuisance filamentous algae. These trace elements in salt mixes are used up quickly, and should be replaced by liquid supplements or water changes. Combinations are safer than single element preparations because they're mixed in the biologically correct ratios (10 Fe: 4 Mn: 5 Zn: 2 Co: 4 Mo). Daily 1 percent water replacement with new synthetic seawater will reduce or obviate the need for trace element supplements. Supplements sometimes produce lush growths of desirable macroalgae and improve the growth of soft corals, but can also stimulate outbreaks of hair algae in water high in nitrates and phosphates. Peter Wilkins reported changing only 1 percent of water per month to replace trace elements, noting that tap water in his city in Germany will replace manganese and iron as well as liquid supplements, yet not induce algal blooms. In the U.S. many groundwater supplies are rich in manganese and iron, but also, unfortunately, silicates that induce diatom blooms.

Chapter Four

Rock, Gravel, and Sand

The rocks, gravel, and sand of the reef aquarium have several functions. The more obvious are decorative and as platforms for corals. The less obvious are filtration and chemical water stabilization.

Live Rock

The term "live rock" refers to coral rubble colonized by marine organisms, and cleaned for reef tank use. Its most important characteristics are origin, porosity, cleanliness, and what grows upon it.

Live rock is one key to the reef aquarium (the other is intense lighting). Some corals are sensitive to the high levels of nitrate ordinarily found in marine aquaria with large carnivores. Live rock provides a vast surface area of deep pores where denitrifying bacteria take up and destroy the nitrate thereby keeping its concentration below that which might stress corals.

Natural live rock consists of storm-broken pieces of weakened coral that have tumbled to the reef base as rubble. It originated as healthy coral of years past. But coral is home to more than the animals that made it, and the older it gets, the more it is invaded, drilled, dissolved, and weakened. Unseen by man, boring clams, mussels, worms, protozoa, and sponges live within its structure or find protection for their soft parts. Other plants and animals grow on the outer surface of both dead and live stony coral, which provides secure footing in strong currents and surges or above a sandy bottom. Instead of producing an adhesive such as the barnacle's glue or the blue mussel's byssus threads, many marine creatures dissolve the coral's skeleton, forming a deep hole in which to live or a shallow hole to provide anchorage. Over time, the myriad holes created by invaders weaken the calcium carbonate reef structure. A storm arrives, enormous forces pound the exposed parts of the reef, and the most weakened corals break from their supports to tumble down and about, killing the polyps, and leaving only rubble.

In most parts of the world, it is the *Acropora* group of branching corals that grow fastest and suffer most during storms. Caribbean coral rubble consists mostly of elkhorn coral (*Acropora palmata*) and staghorn coral (*Acropora cervicornis*), for no reasons other than their abundance in the storm susceptibility zone. There are other corals making up rubble, and a walk on the beach will hint at the diversity of corals out from the shore.

As the rubble is rolled, ground, broken, and eroded, it is invaded by more boring organisms. Over time the rubble becomes pebbles, gravel, and finally sand. The base of the reef is covered in rubble in various stages of demolition, sorted by the surge into areas of rock, gravel, and sand. The rock and sand continue to support algae and microorganisms between the grains and pebbles and within the pores, and provide habitat for bottom dwelling invertebrates and small fishes. It's valuable habitat still, and that is why Florida and the South Atlantic and Gulf of Mexico Fishery Management Councils placed it under legal protection so that wild rubble can no longer be collected in south Florida. Several Indo-Pacific nations have followed suit.

In Florida and around the world, the legal limitations and continuing demand have supported a live rock aquaculture industry. Live rock can be made from mined limestone, from concrete and seashell aggregate, and other materials. Several aquaculturists in Florida place mined Caribbean limestone (ancient dead reef rock) on shallow bottoms leased from the state (inside the three-mile limit) or federal government (outside the three-mile limit). Native Florida limestone would work as well, but the law requires that the rock be from an identifiably remote site in order to prevent illegal trade in real, as opposed to cultured, wild rock.

Natural "live rock" is available from outside the United States. Wild and/or cultivated rock is available from the Caribbean, Singapore, the South Pacific, and the Philippines. Names such as Tonga rock, Fiji rock, and Marshall Island rock are often marketing ploys unrelated to origins.

The quality of live rock depends on its structure and how it was treated prior to sale. In nature, coral rubble is overgrown with algae and invertebrates, the complexity of the community varying by depth and increasing with time. The best pieces for the reef aquarist contain an encrusting layer of red coralline algae and little else. Nature, however, is not that cooperative.

Larger rocks are valuable for denitrifying microbial surface area, for coralline algae that encrust exposed portions not

A live rock reef display at the New Jersey state aquarium.

buried in sand, for the attractive invertebrates or plants that may live on them in quieter waters, and as decorative pieces for forming bridges and caves. The best pieces for microbial denitrification are large and flat, derived from outer branches of elkhorn coral. More massive pieces derived from boulder corals or elkhorn coral bases are heavier, and may support attractive live invertebrates and denser concentrations of coralline algae that develop on rubble not subject to tumbling.

Larval Recruitment or Supply Side Ecology?

How do mollusc and coral larvae decide where to settle? How are larvae of sessile invertebrates recruited to specific habitats? Studies of artificial reef materials have compared cement, steel, and old tires, but scientists were looking for love in all the wrong places. In fact, corals and other larvae recruit by sniffing out chemicals. Here's how. Some encrusting coralline algae leak an amino acid attractant plus a peptide containing a neurotransmitter (a chemical that triggers impulses between nerve cells). According to Daniel and Aileen Morse at the University of California at Santa Barbara, coralline red algae known in the food industry as *isoyake* produce the amino acid lysine and a peptide containing the tiny molecule gamma-amino butyric acid (GABA). Lysine attracts nearby larvae to home in on the red algae. The GABA-peptide then induces attach-ment and metamorphosis of at least 13 species of abalone and probably other molluscs. Another neurotransmitter, dihydroxyphenylalanine (DOPA) induces settlement and metamorpho-sis of other molluscs, including clam and oyster larvae. That's not all. The plant cell walls of some isoyake algae contain a sulfated polysaccharide (gly-cosaminoglycan) that induces settle-ment and metamorphosis of two species of *Agaricia* larvae (lettuce coral and leaf coral). Species of coralline algae differ in their chemical messengers and presumably induce different species of invertebrate larvae to settle and metamorphose. It's a con-tinuing story, with new relationships and chemicals found all the time. If you want your reef tank's coral larvae to settle and grow, try growing coralline algae from both Atlantic and Indo-Pacific live rock.

Wild rock must be cleaned and cured. Commercial collectors remove clumps and layers of green, red, and brown macroalgae, sponges, sea squirts, worms, predatory crabs, anemones, and other life. Most of it is too massive or risky to ship, or is unsuitable for a reef aquarium. After clearing away excessive growth, the coral is stored away from bright light for one to six weeks. During this period, most of the remaining life on the rock dies off and decomposes, but a few of the smallest invertebrates and algal holdfasts survive, as do encrusting coralline algae and many microbes. As surface area is made available by die-offs and decomposition of competitors, some of the coralline algae, which require little light, spread over the rock.

When the rock has only a slightly fishy odor or none at all, and all the mud and debris have been removed, it is ready for the reef aquarium. Adequately cured live rock will not develop a fuzzy, white, or gray film. If it does, it should be removed from the aquarium and placed in a barrel of seawater for further curing with strong aeration. Otherwise, the rock should remain in the newly set up reef tank for not less than two weeks for further curing with the lights off, and all the water pumps operating to provide good current, aeration, and circulation.

As the remaining marine life on the rock continues to die and the coralline algae and microbial population in the rocks increase, the fungi, bacteria, proto-zoans, and worms comprising the decomposer community digest the remaining organic material to carbon dioxide, water, and ammonia (NH_3). Ammonia at the high pH of seawater (about 8.3) may be toxic to fishes and invertebrates. Ammonia initiates the nitrogen cycle (Chapter 5) and is food for both algae and the bacteria known as the *Nitrosomonas* group. These bacteria consume and oxidize the ammonium, producing nitrite (NO_2^-) as a waste product. The rising nitrite concentration triggers a bloom of other bacteria (the *Nitrobacter* group), which consume the nitrite, excreting nitrate (NO_3^-) as a waste product. This process (conversion of ammonia to nitrite and then to nitrate) is called nitrification.

Both the *Nitrosomonas* and *Nitrobacter* groups are called nitrifying bacteria, and they live on all the surfaces of the aquarium, wherever there is enough oxygen and food, metabolizing ammonia to nitrate. (In fact, *Nitrosomonas* and *Nitrobacter* may not be the real workhorses of the nitrogen cycle in marine aquaria. Instead, other genera do the work, with these two playing barely any role.)

Now the value of live rock comes into play, for without it the nitrate would accumulate to unhealthy levels. The removal of nitrate (denitrification) is a separate and anaerobic process. The live rock's pores are deep enough to become anaerobic at the bottom. And here is where denitrifying bacteria now undergo a bloom, converting the abundant nitrate in the aquarium water to harmless nitrogen gas (N_2) and oxygen gas (O_2) that rapidly dissipate out of the pores and the aquarium. (Denitrification also occurs in deep gravel beds.)

If the protein skimmer is turned on when the rock is introduced to the tank, it will remove much of the dissolved organic material from the water before it

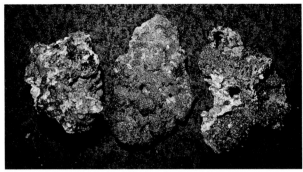

Live rock from the Gulf of Mexico (left) is rich in red sponges. Florida east coast rock (right) is lighter. Highly porous Fiji rock (center) often has purple coralline red algae.

can be broken down into ammonia by the decomposers. That slows development of the nitrite peak and the nitrifying bloom, leading to a delay in the fully functional biological filter that includes denitrification inside the rock pores.

Marine aquarists didn't invent this process. Today most wastewater (sewage) treatment plants process waste through "tertiary" treatment, the removal of nitrates and phosphates. The tertiary treatment plant process is called BNR (biological nutrient removal), and it can be achieved by the simple expedient of alternately turning the aeration equipment on and off in the same pit, something you would not want to do in an aquarium.

Bottom Media

Reef tanks can be set up with or without sand or gravel. A bare bottom aquarium is easy to clean, but provides fewer habitats, has lower species diversity (no meiofauna), and lacks the opportunity for localized denitrification. Tanks with gravel/sand bottoms risk developing deep anaerobic pockets that can generate hydrogen sulfide, lower pH, and release bacterial toxins into the water. The advantages of gravel or sand

Coralline red algae on rock becomes a base for attaching corals.

include increased reflection of light, another medium for both nitrification and denitrification, release of strontium, and as habitat to support more diversity.

Alternative bottom media are gravel or sand, shell hash, and crushed coral. These materials have different concentrations of different minerals. Most aquarium sand is finely eroded quartz rock (silica base). Some sands mix silica and limestone (calcium carbonate). The black sands of some Pacific beaches (Hawaii in places, Iwo Jima) are volcanic, rich in phosphates, and unsuitable for reef aquaria. Shell hash is rich in calcium and magnesium carbonates, but may have phosphate inclusions. Crushed coral consists of ground materials of recent age (aragonite type of calcite), or mined fossilized limestone of different calcite composition.

The best material for reef tanks is the gravel and sand that accumulates around the base of the reef itself, the product of reef erosion. It may be collected where it accumulates on beaches near shore or from beneath the sea. Aragonite gravel and sand is available in uniform grades of 1.75–3.00 mm (coarse), 1.25–1.75 mm (fine), less than

1.25 mm (sugar), and sold as dry reef sand. It is also collected from submerged localities and shipped out immediately for use in reef tanks (live sand). This wet material, because of its increased weight from water, is more expensive than dried product. Live sand introduces live meiofauna to your reef tank, but you never know what you're getting. A small amount of live sand, wild or from another reef tank, will seed the meiofauna for your new reef tank, so it's pointless as well as expensive to purchase large quantities.

Aragonite

Aragonite is recently deposited crushed coral, a marine limestone or oolite secreted by modern corals and coralline algae. (Ancient reefs were laid down mostly by rudite molluscs.) Aragonite is 97 percent calcium carbonate, less than 1.5 percent magnesium carbonate, with traces of aluminum oxide (<0.15 percent), sodium chloride (<0.25 percent), and strontium oxide (<0.125 percent). Strontium, similar in chemistry to calcium, is essential for the coralline algae and coral skeletons. Magnesium, also taken up by corals and algae, is adequately replaced by the gradual dissolution of aragonite, so supplements are not required.

The depth of the aragonite sand layer is proportional to its grain size. Coarse sand is filled to a depth of up to four inches, while "sugar" aragonite is effective at less than an inch deep. Too deep a layer risks creating anoxic conditions that promote black colonies of hydrogen sulfide-producing iron bacteria.

New aragonite gravel should be washed (one or two rinses) to remove black fragments of dried plants. Don't continue washing assuming that the murkiness is from dust. Aragonite sand dissolves during washing, so the rinse water always appears cloudy even when dust-free. Washed aragonite will initially cloud the tank water, but the water will clear in a few days.

Aragonite has several advantages over limestone and shell hash. Its composition and particle size promote a growth of sand-living microbes and minute invertebrates (infauna or meiofauna). These infauna protect the sand from blooms of noxious hydrogen sulfide-producing anaerobic iron bacteria (gray-black pockets and gas in the gravel). As high pH (8.1–8.4), highly oxygenated water diffuses into the sand, the oxygen is depleted by the infauna. The mostly aerobic infauna feeds on the wastes from the reef corals and fishes, stirring it into the sand as they consume oxygen diffusing downward from the water. Their metabolism releases carbon dioxide, water, and simple acids. The acids produced by decomposition immediately react with the carbonate of the aragonite sand, dissolving it and releasing calcium ions that diffuse back into the aquarium water. The reaction is fastest at lower pH and accelerates in the deeper sands. With time, the sand becomes filled with life and dissolves, dropping up to an inch in depth per year. This pH-mediated release of calcium ions into the water may replace the calcium ion uptake by coral growth. At the least, aragonite calcium release reduces the need to make up the calcium deficit with limewater.

In the deeper parts of the sand, the oxygen concentration is low enough to promote development of denitrifying bacteria. These bacteria complement those in the deep pores of the live rock, perhaps doubling the capacity of the aquarium to remove nitrates.

There are degrees of anaerobic (airless) conditions. If the sand goes from microaerophilic (very low level of oxygen) to anoxic (no oxygen at all), acids and hydrogen sulfide gas may be produced, threatening the corals and fishes. The sand should be deep enough to encourage denitrifying bacteria, but shallow enough that some oxygen can diffuse to all areas. With aragonite sand, the proper depth is 1–3 inches, replenished as necessary. Shell hash, although coarse, should be no more than an inch deep because its abundant stagnant pockets promote anaerobic decomposition. Media other than aragonite also promote development of denitrifiers, but without aragonite's continuous calcium (and strontium) release into the water.

Hydrogen Sulfide

Anaerobic bacteria produce hydrogen sulfide (H_2S), a gas with the odor of rotten eggs. Stripped from the water by an ordinary protein skimmer, it is then passed into the surrounding air. An experimental process for removing H_2S in an aquarium protein skimmer oxidizes the H_2S with ferric ions, keeping the ferric and ferrous ions in solution with a chelating agent. The final product is elemental sulfur that is removed by adsorptive plastic balls. The overall process is $H_2S + \frac{1}{2}O_2 \rightarrow S + H_2O$. Used for treating drinking water supplies, the process can probably be adapted to reef systems having deep sand layers. (See Nagl, 1996. References page 189.)

The Plenum System

Dr. Jean Jaubert at the Monaco Aquarium developed a way to rid aquariums of nitrate using a system of deep gravel beds separated horizontally by a screen, and containing a subterranean space (called the plenum) that is filled with water. The gravel above the screen developed a rich population of aerobic small invertebrates and nitrifying bacteria that promoted nitrification. The lower layer was screened from the small invertebrates in the upper gravel so it wasn't continually burrowed and mixed, and subsequently became oxygen-deficient, promoting denitrifying bacteria. The nitrogen and oxygen gasses of denitrification percolated upward out of the layers. Jaubert operated this aquarium as a completely self-sufficient, virtually closed system.

Some reef aquarists in the United States use plenum systems, but it is easier, in my opinion, to manage a reef aquarium with water changes, additives, and good husbandry than to create a working plenum that operates as a closed system. That said, here is a simple method for creating a plenum system.

Place an undergravel filter plate or plastic egg crate on the bottom of the aquarium to a depth of 0.75–1.0 inch, and cover it with plastic window screening. Place a 1- or 2-inch layer of calcareous sand on the screen and cover that with another layer of screening. Then add a final top layer of 1–3 inches of calcareous sand.

This results in two layers of sand above a layer of water. The top sand layer supports a diverse infauna of worms, other small invertebrates, and nitrifying microbes. Wrasses, gobies, and jawfishes also stir this layer, so it stays aerobic.

The lower sand layer is screened from invasion by the fishes and the infauna above. It doesn't become stirred, and develops a microaerophilic community of denitrifying bacteria.

The lowest layer is just stagnant water. It exchanges minute amounts of oxygen and carbon dioxide with the sand above, preventing complete anoxia. The water layer must be thick enough that temperature differences from top to bottom cause it to slowly circulate within its confined space. The water layer of the plenum is close enough to the very top surface of the sand layers (not more than a few inches deep) that gasses can diffuse from bottom to top. There should be just enough light to see the plenum water layer, but not enough to promote algae that can crash and cause a bloom of anaerobic bacteria.

An alternative to the plenum system and a simpler approach is to use up to 3 inches of aragonite gravel and up to 2 pounds of live rock per gallon of water. The rock and the deeper parts of the gravel provide sufficient denitrifying bacteria. Elimination of the plenum space and deeper gravel eliminate the risk of a large confined space that can become anoxic.

Sand collects detritus. Although unsightly, detritus is also a food source. Rather than siphon or vacuum it out of the aquarium, blow it about with a powerhead every few days to feed the corals. Any excess detritus blown into the water column will be captured by the sump or skimmer.

Chapter Five
The Nitrogen and Carbon Cycles

Fishes, corals, and other invertebrates feed on plants and animals, breaking down proteins into peptides, peptides into amino acids, and eventually to wastes. The principal wastes of protein metabolism are eliminated as urine in mammals, uric acid in birds, urea in sharks and rays, and ammonia and urea in bony fishes and most invertebrates.

Ammonia (NH_3) is toxic to many fishes at 0.2–0.5 mg/L, and can cause stress at less than 0.1 mg/L. The ionized form or ammonium ion (NH_4^+) is non-toxic. Both forms are in equilibrium in water, with their relative concentrations determined by total ammonia-ammonium, pH, and temperature.

Ammonia is an energy source for certain aerobic bacteria in soil and presumably in marine environments. Well-known bacteria (*Nitrosomonas, Nitrosococcus, Nitrosospira, Nitrosocystis*) oxidize ammonia to nitrite (NO_2) in soil. Nitrite is toxic at concentrations of 5 mg/L. Unlike ammonia, it cannot be converted to a non-toxic form by pH.

Still another group of aerobic bacteria use nitrite as an energy source. These genera (*Nitrobacter, Nitrocystis, Nitrospira, Nitrococcus*) oxidize nitrite (NO_2) to nitrate (NO_3), again in soil and presumably in some aquatic and marine environments, but we're not certain. Studies of the bacteria in aquarium trickling filters have identified an entirely different mix of nitrogen-metabolizing microbes.

Nitrate is relatively non-toxic to fishes. High concentrations can be useful to macroalgae and even to some soft corals, but stressful to some fishes and invertebrates, including shrimp, at levels exceeding 40 mg/L; most important, nitrates trigger nuisance algal blooms. There is no particularly dangerous level of nitrate for all organisms, although its removal cannot but benefit the reef aquarium. Nitrate is removed by macroalgae, by symbiotic microalgae in tridacnid clams and corals, and by denitrification in live rock pores and deeper, oxygen-poor layers of aragonite gravel. It is most quickly and efficiently removed by water changes.

The toxicity of nitrate to many aerobic animals is caused by competition of NO_3 with O_2 for attachment sites on the hemoglobin molecule. Because nitrate binds irreversibly, affected animals develop methemoglobinemia and suffer oxygen starvation that can cause death or chronic debilitation. Although nitrates have not been demonstrated to damage corals, prudent reef-keeping warrants keeping the level low in mini-reef aquaria.

Not all nitrates are taken up by macroalgae. Certain bacteria in the genera *Denitrobacillus, Micrococcus, Thiobacillus, Pseudomonas*, and *Sulfomonas* can live aerobically or anaerobi-

Ammonia and Ammonium Toxicity

At high pH and at increased temperatures, the ammonium-ammonia equilibrium shifts to a toxic form. Even slight amounts of ammonia in a marine tank can kill the inhabitants. (Many freshwater swamp-dwelling fishes can live in virtual organic soups at pH 5.0 because almost all ammonia is ionized to non-toxic ammonium.) For the marine aquarist, there is danger when adjusting pH upward to normal seawater levels of 8.3 required for fish and invertebrate health. At high pH, non-toxic ammonium is converted to ammonia and the animals are stressed or killed from toxicity in the form of methemoglobinemia or other abnormalities. Aquarium industry shippers do not put buffers into shipping water. As the pH in shipping water drops (from respiration and wastes), the shift from ammonia to ammonium ion protects the animals from the toxicity of their own wastes.

cally. Under anaerobic conditions, they reduce nitrate for energy. These bacteria often live deep in soil or in oxygen-deprived sediments in lakes and oceans. In the mini-reef aquarium, some grow deep inside thick sponge filters, down under the gravel, and most importantly at the bottoms of pores of live rock. At low pH (as deep within the gravel) reduction of nitrate (denitrification) breaks the NO_3 into nitrogen and oxygen gasses (N_2 and O_2) that are eliminated as bubbles or dissolve into the surrounding water.

Without these microbes, nitrate concentrations would rise beyond the capacity of macroalgae to utilize them until they stressed the sensitive invertebrates.

Solutions for reducing nitrate concentrations are water changes and anaerobic bacterial decomposition. Water changes dilute more than nitrates and are good husbandry in any aquarium. Anaerobic microbial decomposition is safe, easy, and efficient, promoted by moderately deep (1–4 inch) beds of gravel or by an abundance of live rock. A large block sponge filter in the sump of a trickling filter will also encourage nitrate decomposition.

Four additional mechanical methods are available. The first, using low-voltage electrical decomposition, is unsafe for marine aquaria, because salt drift can pass current from almost any electrical device to the water. The second is the coil denitrator. The principle of a denitrator is that water with organics enters a small diameter coil such as 15–50 feet of airline tubing, and moves through at the rate of about three liters or quarts an hour. As water passes slowly through the coiled narrow tube, aerobic bacteria on the walls near the entrance oxidize the organics. Eventually, somewhere along the tube, the oxygen is used up and only anaerobic bacteria grow on the wall and are available for organic decomposition. From here on, the anaerobes begin reducing nitrate in the tube to nitrogen gas and oxygen. If oxygen levels fall completely but too high an organic load continues through the tubing, there is danger of hydrogen sulfide generating bacteria blooming in the tube and producing noxious H_2S gas. If organics are low but nitrates are high, then the bacteria need supplementary food. The system depends on a long and slow passage through a coil with an extensive anaerobic component and low organics.

The third commercial unit is a modified calcium reactor that uses both calcareous and sulphur media. The advertisements proclaim that after you get the nitrates down to zero, you can buy some more parts and use the unit as a calcium reactor. But it ignores the problem that nitrates, once removed, will come back. It's also an expensive solution to a simple problem.

The fourth type of equipment is the ball nitrate reducer. This consists of a tall vessel filled with spheres of denitrifying bacteria in a protective medium. Water passing through these nitrator-balls is denitrified, and eventually the balls of bacteria must be replaced. It's simple to use, but costly to purchase and replenish.

Cutting to the chase, live rock does the job with less care and cost than coil denitrators or ball nitrate reducers. Coil denitrators require a food source (70 percent lactose, 30 percent sucrose dissolved in RO water to a final concentration of 15 percent or 15 grams per 100 ml of water). This sugar solution is delivered to the reaction vessel mounted above the sump at a rate of 5 percent of tank capacity four times a day (use a timer). Tank water enters the reaction tubing for denitrification at the rate of 3 ml/minute. It takes several weeks for the tubing in the reaction vessel to develop a stable anaerobic bacterial flora with denitrifiers predominating and hydrogen sulfide producers only a minor component. Finally, the effluent should pass through granular activated carbon to remove traces of hydrogen sulfide before dripping into the sump. The units require constant monitoring of the effluent, and can undergo sudden microbial population shifts resulting in failuro to denitrify, production of excess hydrogen sulfide, or the production of other noxious chemicals. The Nitrate Reducer is easy to set up and maintain, but refills

Hepatus epheliticus is a common inshore crab from South Carolina to Florida, but not reef safe, as it's a predator.

of reducer feed add up quickly and, unless you monitor water quality regularly, you won't know when or how far the nitrates are building up. I've said it before and I'll say it again. An aquarium is a pretty urinal. If you don't flush it to change the water, it gets worse and worse. And nobody has yet invented anything faster and cheaper than a bucket and siphon.

Cycling the Aquarium

Bacteria increase in numbers by cell division. One bacterium becomes two, two become four, four become eight, etc. Mathematically, the growth of the population is logarithmic to the base 2. This doubling of the population can occur every 20–60 minutes if the tem-

Some sponges can be propagated by macerating them in a blender and pouring the slurry into a new tank with aeration but no filtration.

conversion of ammonia to nitrite by the *Nitrosomonas* group or equivalents. Eventually, the nitrite level will be high enough to allow them also to undergo logarithmic growth, and the nitrite levels in the aquarium will suddenly plummet.

This 4–6-week period for growing large populations of ammonia- and nitrite-oxidizers is the break-in time for an aquarium, during which it should have only hardy animals (damselfishes, hermit crabs) tolerant of ammonia and nitrite and vigorous aeration to promote the process. Alternatively, one could start the cycle chemically by adding ammonium chloride or even urine to the water.

The end result of this bacterial metabolism is nitrate. Over time, the concentrations of nitrate can increase markedly. With ordinary marine aquaria, the easiest control of nitrate levels is through water changes and algal growth and harvest.

Until recently, we had no inexpensive way to eliminate nitrates sufficiently to keep corals in captivity. That changed with the recognition of live rock's surface and deep pore microbiology. In the mini-reef aquarium with live rock and/or deep gravel, nitrate levels will first peak and then plummet as anaerobic bacteria at the bottom of the rock pores and in the gravel attain logarithmic growth and maximum population size. At this point, chemical readings for ammonia, nitrite, and nitrate should all be near zero. The tank is now completely cycled.

Cycling of the mini-reef tank takes about 8–10 weeks. The cycle can be accelerated by using abundant live rock or a large dose (a five-gallon bucket) of live sand (soaked sand/gravel/shell hash from an underwater source rather than dry sand from the beach) to increase the initial numbers of bacteria. You can also accelerate the cycle by

perature is optimal, nutrients are freely available, wastes are rapidly eliminated, and nothing else interferes with reproduction. That's an ideal rate that seldom continues for long, but the better all conditions, the faster the population increases.

In a new aquarium, there are few ammonia-oxidizing and nitrite-oxidizing aerobic bacteria other than those introduced with rock, coral, contaminated hands, nets, etc. There is little ammonia and virtually no nitrite. Gradually, animal metabolism adds ammonia to the water. When the ammonia builds to optimal levels, *Nitrosomonas* and/or other ammonia oxidizers grow at a logarithmic rate, and suddenly are able to metabolize all the ammonia as fast as it is produced. In the meantime, *Nitrobacter* and/or other nitrite oxidizers await the adding *reef mud*, a microbial sludge containing a mixed population of recycling species of microbes. Once cycled, the tank will remain stable if you feed small amounts of food at a time. Large fluctuations in feeding and livestock populations can promote overgrowth by bacteria that displace nitrifiers, allowing a build-up of nitrites to harmful concentrations (>0.1 mg/L). As a practical matter, this is seldom a problem in a coral-only tank. It can be a severe problem in marine tanks containing large predators such as lionfish, groupers, toadfish, or anglerfish, all of which eat and regurgitate or defecate intermittently in large quantities.

Carbon

Carbon dioxide in the atmosphere freely dissolves in water. That's important, because dissolved CO_2 can be incorporated into living tissues. Carbon is the backbone of living tissues. Chemical structures containing carbon are called organic compounds. The study of carbon compounds in living systems is called biochemistry.

Water is not quite H_2O. Its reactivity will be better understood if we write it as $H^+{}^-OH \leftrightarrow HOH$. In other words, a certain percentage of the proton (H^+) and hydroxyl (^-OH) ions making up water is available to react with other molecules. One of those molecules is carbon dioxide (CO_2).

Carbon dioxide reacts with water to form carbonic acid ($H_2O + CO_2 \rightarrow H_2CO_3$). Carbonic acid in turn is in equilibrium with free protons (H^+) and bicarbonate ($CO_3{}^{2-}$).

The pH of water is affected by the relative concentrations of carbon dioxide, acidic carbonate, and alkaline bicarbonate. Ocean water is stable at pH 8.1 to 8.4 because the bicarbonate and carbon dioxide equilibrium absorbs and disposes of acidic protons (H^+). In aquaria, pH can vary dramatically and should be monitored.

Calcium Carbonate Deposits

Carbonate cations react with calcium anions to form calcium carbonate ($CaCO_3$) salt. Carbonate also reacts with strontium, magnesium, etc. to form strontium carbonate, magnesium carbonate, and other compounds found in clams, corals, fishes, algae, and other marine life. Most limestones and shells are mixes of calcium, magnesium, and strontium carbonate deposits. The most common mix occurs in ancient limestones laid down by foraminifera. Other ancient limestones laid down by rudist molluscs are not common anywhere. Dolomite is another type of calcium carbonate formed by more recent reefs. Aragonite is derived from modern corals and macroalgae. These materials are good pH buffers, because they are easily broken apart by the protons (the acid part) in water molecules. They are able to buffer the water as the calcium is split from the carbonate, feeding back into the carbonate/bicarbonate equilibrium. Most of these solids are slow to dissolve. Aragonite (oolite), deposited by corals and calcareous algae, is the least stable and most recent limestone. The pH of deep gravel beds is low, allowing aragonite to readily dissolve and release calcium cations and carbonate/bicarbonate anions. The released carbonates once more are taken up by growing corals and calcareous algae, while the bicarbonates buffer the seawater by neutralizing acids (protons) from water, waste, and decomposition.

Chapter Six
Powerheads and Water Pumps

All powerheads and water pumps are centrifugal pumps whose intake port must be below the surface of the water. They cannot pull water upwards, but they can push it with a force that depends on design (head pressure) rather than electric power consumption. You must select the right pump for the application, and that means gallons per minute pushed to a specific height. Powerheads with the same rated flows can differ in head pressure performance.

Head pressure is the pump output rating in pounds per square inch; for water pumps, it indicates how high water can be pushed upward, while for air pumps, it is an indicator of how deeply air can be pushed below water level or how far it can be pushed through narrow pipes. If you just want to stir water about, you don't need head pressure, and inexpensive submersible powerheads are sufficient. If you want to raise large amounts of water several feet from a floor sump back to the top of the tank, then you need a pump that offers several feet of head pressure. That can be either a large submersible powerhead (internal water pump) or an external water pump. With that in mind, let's look at pumps for reef tanks.

Submersible powerheads are used to drive water flow through undergravel filters. They are inexpensive and use little electricity. Because powerheads are submerged, water flows into the vane cavity to prime the pump, so power-

heads generally don't cavitate. Reef keepers use submersible powerheads (or larger water pumps) to create currents in reef tanks, to return water from sumps, or to drive some (not many) venturi protein skimmers. Few powerheads can push water six feet upwards.

Powerheads of different designs can push 20–200 gallons per hour at zero head. Most are inadequate for running large Venturi-driven protein skimmers or the return upward flows to high tanks. Powerheads typically run water through a half-inch port. Powerheads are bathed in water and shed waste heat to the tank (or sump) water, but burn out if allowed to run dry. Metal spindles (on which the vanes are mounted) can corrode. The better powerheads have corrosion-free ceramic spindles. Many powerheads have screens, but they clog quickly. Because there is no other filter between their intakes and the tank water with all its drifting debris, the spindles may become wrapped in algal or polyester fibers, causing the unit to slow, burn out, and fail.

Large air-cooled water pumps are not submersible. Mounted outside the aquarium and sump, they can move large volumes to a considerable head pressure, some pumps pushing 1000 or more gallons per hour at five feet of head. They are protected from damaging fibers by filter pads, and can be further protected by inserting a settling basin barrier to collect debris between the tank or sump and the

A nylon impeller spins rapidly within the electromagnetic field of its powerhead. Some powerheads have a venturi port for feeding air into the discharge stream. The intake is screened to keep debris away from the impeller.

pump's intake port. Some have air slits and fans to disperse heat, while others radiate heat through a thin metal skin. Some small air-cooled pumps produce little heat that can be carried away by the passage of water. Most pull 85–250 watts, the larger in the $\frac{1}{10}$th horsepower

range. Water pumps must be primed by flooding before being switched on or they cavitate (spin in a pocket of air) and fail to work. Most have thermally protected motors that shut off before they overheat.

A word of caution about external water pumps—get one larger than you need, and then plumb an adjustable flow restrictor into the PVC piping near the output port. The most common flow restrictors are ball and gate valves that can be finely tuned to control output. The valve must always be mounted on the discharge side of the pump. If mounted on the intake side, it will cause the pump to work hard and burn out. For the same reason, the intake side should be kept clean to prevent flow restriction into the pump. Pumps don't work hard to push water upward. They're built for it. They burn out, however, if they pull against resistance (from clogging). The principle of always putting the flow restrictor on the outlet side of a water pump applies equally to air pumps.

Large external water pumps provide volume and head pressure, and should be plumbed with PVC, putting the narrower pipe at the intake port and the larger PVC at the discharge end.

Chapter Seven
Filters

We filter reef aquaria to remove wastes through mechanical, chemical, and biological means. Years ago, marine tanks relied on undergravel filtration to break down nitrogenous wastes in the gravel. That gave way to trickling filters with far more efficient aerobic organic decomposition. Then Eng reported success without filters, using only sunlight and rock collected from the shore. Eng's "natural system tanks" had no measurable nitrate. Other aquarists recognized that the deep pores in the rock provided denitrification. Subsequently reef aquarists began adding wild (live) rock to tanks equipped with trickling filters and protein skimmers. Later, German aquarists reported that removal of the trickling filter in a tank with live rock lowered nitrates from little to almost none. Aquarists rushed to disconnect their trickling filters. The combination of brilliant lighting, live rock, and a protein skimmer without a trickling filter is known as the Berlin system, and is the most widely used reef tank technique today.

The Berlin system relies on skimming (foam fractionation) to remove organics and on porous rock and/or aragonite gravel to provide nitrification (mineralization) and denitrification of the nitrates to nitrogen and oxygen gases. It would seem that other types of filtration are superfluous, but that is not the case. Activated carbon is useful for removing toxic chemicals emitted by soft corals and yellow tints produced by macroalgae. Activated carbon must be placed somewhere accessible to replacement, cleaning, or regeneration, and there is no better place than in a box filter, power filter, or canister filter.

Hang-on Power Filters

Hang-on outside power filters provide a simple location for activated carbon. Avoid models professing trickling filter capability (in my view it's simply marketing hyperbole) and filters driven by open-vented electric motors should also be avoided, as they readily short circuit when exposed to accumulations of salt spray. Look for a motor with sealed magnetic drive, adequate finger space for removing the impeller for cleaning, replaceable parts, UL-listing, and replaceable filter cartridges combining floss for mechanical filtration and activated carbon for chemical filtration. Measure the width of your aquarium rim to be certain the reverse U-shaped lip with which the filter hangs onto your aquarium is sufficiently wide; many models are not built for large aquariums with thick frames.

Canister Filters

Canister filters force water through various layers of foam, granular carbon, and coral, shell hash, or aragonite. They provide mechanical and chemical filtration. Use one pound of GAC in the canister per 25 gallons of aquarium water, and change a third of the GAC when the water begins to yellow. More than any other aquarium equipment, canisters vary in quality of materials, so rely on dealer recommendations and warranties, and never forget the O-ring. Avoid units with pored discharge wands that tend to clog. Avoid top-heavy units (motor above rather than at the base), those with thin toggle on/off switches (they get wet and fail), and units with flimsy media baskets. Look for the capability to use diatomaceous earth filtration, multiple configurations, and interchangeable parts among models. Look for ease of assembly and disconnecting for service, and for readily visible discharges, because a clogged filter will restrict flow and burn out the motor.

Internal canister filters are awkward to service, may clog and not reveal the interrupted flow, and offer unwanted extras such as heater ports and bioballs for nitrification.

Trickling Filters

Trickling filters are no longer popular in coral tanks because they mineralize compounds to nitrate, rather than remove them entirely from the system, as do protein skimmers. The trickling filter is beneficial in tanks with a large biological load of fishes (especially those that are carnivorous) that excrete and eject large quantities of wastes. If you keep groupers, anglers, or lionfish, trickling filters are a good addition to the system. In any case, trickling filters for coral tanks may not be necessary, but are good back-ups should the protein skimmer fail. Their production of nitrates is of little concern; their increased evaporation is more important, but this is a maintenance rather than a water quality issue.

Trickling filters should be prefiltered with a layer of floss to first remove particulate debris. The debris-free water with its heavy organic load falls or trickles downward as a thin film over inert pebbles, small rocks or plastic "bioballs." Water running on any substance anywhere develops a film of microorganisms that use the organics in the water (carbon compounds, nitrogen compounds) for energy and food, leaving the water cleaner than when it entered the system. The difference in trickling filters versus submerged filters is that when a thin film of air is used over the wet medium, the colonizing organisms are more efficient because the air adjacent to the wet (as opposed to submerged) bacteria is 20 percent (200 ppt) oxygen, far higher than the oxygen in tank water. This is beneficial because the higher the oxygen concentration, the more efficient the aerobic bacteria. In a trickling filter, the microbes degrade virtually all organics coming into the system. In a completely submerged filter, a smaller portion is degraded, limited by the low concentration of dissolved oxygen in deep water.

In all filters, but especially trickling filters, when the bacteria, fungi, protozoa, rotifers, algae, nematodes, and others initially coat the inert surfaces, they form a thin film, and oxygen is available to all the "bugs." As the microbes remove nutrients and convert them into new bugs or biomass, the thickness of the living layer increases, becomes visible, and eventually is unsightly. Now the biological community is thick enough (and this varies with the system and flow rate) to cause the inside bugs to starve for oxygen, and they die off, lose their grip on the surface, and the colony sloughs away, falling to the bottom of the sump as *mulm*. Immersed under

Tridacnid clams need intense light but can be harmed by strontium supplements.

stilled water, the surviving biological mulm organisms also die from lack of oxygen. This mulm or gunk must be removed or it will become a source of anaerobic decomposition, producing hydrogen sulfide gas. That's why a trickling filter requires cleaning. You cannot just set it and forget it.

A trickling filter is a useful supplement that may be redundant in a Berlin system, but the Berlin system depends on intense light, strong currents, and abundant live rock. Any of these can fail. Some low levels of nitrate resulting from a trickling filter are not a problem for most corals; the much higher levels that might result should a skimmer fail are a danger for which a backup system should be provided.

You can build a trickling filter from a five-gallon plastic bucket filled with bioballs (or scrap plastics) and with a discharge port at the bottom. Locate a boating marina store, and purchase a through-hull fitting that consists of a discharge port and locking nut. At a hardware store, purchase a plastic cutting head for a power drill and a matching bit. Be certain your through-hull fitting and cutting head are the same size. Bring along a powerhead and six feet of plastic tubing that will fit over the powerhead discharge. Get a shorter length of wider tubing that will fit over the discharge port of the through-hull fitting. Your discharge port and tubing should always be far wider than the intake tubing to avoid flooding. Drill a hole an inch above the bottom of the bucket (to allow room for the locking nut) and insert the through-hull fitting from the inside, then tighten the locking nut on the outside until it barely deforms the bucket. A glob of silicon sealant will protect against leaks. A powerhead sitting on the undergravel filter stem outlet or lying among rocks sucks up tank water, and pushes it through the long plastic tube into a small hole cut into the lid of the bucket. Driving a stainless steel nail (twice as long as the hole in the lid) through the hose end inside the bucket keeps the hose from pulling out. The pumped water trickles down the bioballs and exits the bucket at the port below, falling by gravity back into the aquarium, a sump, or elsewhere for later pumping back into the system. In my basement fish room, I've placed bucket trickle filters on plate glass bases on the tops of freshwater and marine tanks. My wife never visits the fish room.

Commercially available trickling filters range from hang-on retrofit units to monsters that could drive the space

Ammonia Stripping—Fact or Fantasy

Bioballs come in various sizes and configurations of void spaces, and some advertisements for bioballs and trickling filters claim their products have optimal void space to strip ammonia. That may be true in industrial applications, but not in the home aquarium. In industrial facilities and public aquariums, ammonia stripping is made feasible by the large scale of the equipment. Great volumes of compressed air are driven at high speed from the bottom of the filter bed upward some eight feet through the medium to provide a counter current to the rapidly falling oxygen-rich water. With so much vertical space and a powerful opposite airflow, and with a pH temporarily adjusted to around 10 (and adjusted downward after treatment), void space (the ratio of air to water film) does indeed affect the efficiency of ammonia stripping. For home aquarium applications, ammonia stripping is a myth. Trickling filter height is too short, there is no massive volume of compressed air to rush over eight feet of packed bioballs, and there is no way to raise the pH to 10 and back down again to 8 before returning the water to the aquarium. In short, in home aquaria usage, void space becomes irrelevant. For the limits possible in home aquaria, any inert medium, including scrap plastic, hair curlers, and loose filter floss, work as well as high-priced plastic spheres, so long as the material remains loosely packed and air can reach all parts of the thin layer of microbes. Be alert to the danger of packing down from a heavy organic load over time, which reduces aerobic decomposition in favor of inefficient microaerophilic (low oxygen) oxidation, and even less efficient anaerobic (no oxygen) decomposition.

shuttle's wastewater treatment needs. In some units, you can add carbon and clinoptilolite canisters to the water path to remove other dissolved substances, or provide fittings for dripping in additives, in effect using the trickling filter sump and bioball box for adding all sorts of chemical and physical media out of sight and away from direct contact with the tank's inhabitants.

Trickling filters are less important in tanks with small biological inputs (foods), especially tanks with big skimmers and abundant live rock. A rock-laden system with two skimmers can replace the need for backup trickle filtration and achieve even greater reductions in nitrate and phosphate levels. Double skimmers are a variation on the Berlin system. It is fine for reef tanks with small organic loadings, but risky where meats are fed to large fishes or invertebrates.

The Berlin system has been tested by many aquarists. When you remove the trickling filter after months of use, the nitrate and phosphate levels should drop from 5 mg/L and 0.5 mg/L respectively to zero.

Fluidized Bed Filtration

The fluidized bed reactor is based on colonization of sand particles by microbes that feed on nutrients in highly oxygenated wastewater, which they clean by mineralization (nitrification). Here's how. Untreated raw tank water is

A fluidized bed reactor's sandstorm should rise about halfway in the reaction chamber, as in this hang-on model.

forced into the lower end of a sand/water column under enough pressure to keep the sand in suspension about halfway up the column. The water at the top of the column, now mineralized, exits through an overflow back to the tank or sump. In some units, the reactor has another tube to carry the treated water downward so that it exits at the bottom.

Fluidized bed filtration provides a high degree of mineralization (nitrification), continuous removal of sediment and particles in the overflow, uses only a small space (hang-on units are popular), and eliminates the need to change or clean the medium because tumbling and friction prevent formation of biological mats on the sand grains. After a time (perhaps twice a year), you will have to replenish sand that escaped to bring the operating level back to half way. You can build your own system from a clear PVC tube and silica sand, and operate it with a powerhead mounted above or outside the filter to keep it from clogging with sand when the electrical power is off. A hole drilled in the upper side (or a notch at the top) allows water to overflow back into the sump or the tank. The flow should be monitored so that the sandstorm always reaches just above halfway in the tube. Silica sand is inexpensive and preferred because aragonite dissolves, defeating the purpose of a self-cleaning aerobic bacterial bed.

Algal Mat Filtration

Growing plants on animal wastes is nothing new. Farmers used manure long before packaged fertilizers, and many still do. Third world farmers use human waste (night soil) to fertilize field crops. Excess field waste washes off the fields and into ponds containing edible aquatic plants and fish (usually tilapia and carp) that consume algae and nuisance plants. Municipal wastewater treatment plants grow duckweed in wastewater settling ponds to take up nitrates, phosphates, metals, and other materials. The duckweed is then used for hog, cattle, or poultry feed, a soil amendment for crops, or daily landfill cover. Pondkeepers keep koi and goldfish ponds cleansed with edible duckweed.

Algal mat filtration provides alternatives for eliminating wastes. Methods of algal mat filtration are in-tank algal growth, growth in a refugium, and growth in an algal turf compartment. In-tank algal growth is insufficient for removing nitrates, organics, phosphates, metals, and toxins because bright lighting is not turned on more than a few hours a day. In-tank excessive algal growth may occur during nuisance (hair) algal blooms that can kill valuable corals, so hair algae conditions (including bright light) are kept to a minimum. Nonetheless, blooms serve to remove nutrients and metals, although some can also produce noxious chemicals. Many reef keepers use natural algae to take up wastes, but do it in a separate well-lit compartment away from corals.

A well-illuminated refugium seeded with macroalgae removes waste using a separate box connected by plumbing to the mini-reef. Water is pumped between the two aquaria, and algae grown luxuriantly, free of grazers. The refugium requires round-the-clock light to keep the macroalgae net oxygen emitters. Should the lights go off, the vegetation will take up oxygen from both aquaria. Preferred refugium algae are fast-growers that absorb waste nutrients as fast as they are produced making them a nuisance in reef aquaria. (Recall that a weed is just a plant growing where you don't want it to grow.) Fast-growing, attractive *Caulerpa* species are excellent refugium waste absorbers. You can also use a refugium to grow animals that would not survive in the reef tank—amphipods (which can be harvested for fish food) or attractive (and tasty) decorative shrimp, for example. Because the refugium removes wastes, excess macroalgae should be discarded. A refugium can cause yellowing of the water; ozonation or carbon filtration will remove the color.

A turf compartment similarly provides a refugium for algal mat filtration. An opaque box is mounted above or beside the mini-reef, filled with a large area of plates used as growing surfaces (plastic window screening or 1–3 mm plastic grids), and provided flowing tank water and bright, close, 24-hour light. Over time, the grid surfaces become coated with algae. As this turf grows, it absorbs wastes, converting them to algal biomass. Unattended, the mass can grow so large that fragments break away and wash into the reef tank, or water flow becomes blocked. The mass must be cropped to provide an optimal balance that will maximally filter nutrients from the tank without clogging or fragmenting. An algal mat should grow at a rate enabling harvest and washing once or twice a month. Cleaning less often may result in overgrowth of noxious cyanobacteria; cleaning more often risks washing away good algal growth. For details of the system, see W.H. Adey and K. Loveland, *Dynamic Aquaria,* Academic Press, NY. The system is used by a few aquarists and several public aquaria, but the technique is not widespread in the hobby because of its need for a separate lighted system and yellowing of the water.

Chapter Eight
Protein Skimmers

Cocurrent Skimmers

Protein skimmers (foam fractionaters) have been in the marine hobby for 60 years. The first skimmers used a four-inch wide vertical piece of glass glued to a corner just up from the bottom of the tank, extending just above the water level. A wooden air diffuser was attached to stiff airline tubing inside the V-shaped chamber. Tank water slipping into the chamber from the open bottom rose with the fine bubbles from the diffuser, rolled around inside the chamber, and eventually exited from the bottom slit. The fine bubbles rising to the top collected gunk from the water (the foam fraction) and confined it to the elevated part of the chamber, so that the surface of the tank did not accumulate scum. The confined gunk could be wiped from the chamber with a finger. Because the bubbles and air/water mixture rose together in the column, this early type of skimming was called cocurrent skimming. Various stand-alone models were sold, consisting of a tubular unit that could be attached to an air line and inserted into an established tank.

How do skimmers work? You've seen skimming in nature in the form of foam on an ocean beach during a windy day. Skimming (foam fractionation) consists of two physical activities: the denaturation of proteins and peptides, and the adherence of particles to the denatured materials. Denaturation of proteins and peptides is caused by bubbles rushing through water or wind blowing over waves. When you boil egg white (albumin is pure protein), the heat breaks the hydrogen bonds that give albumin its unique clear and mucilaginous structure. The albumin collapses upon itself in a process called denaturation, in which the albumin comes out of solution, becomes visible, and can no longer function. All proteins and peptides can be denatured by heat or turbulence. Denaturation can also be caused by adding vinegar or lime juice (hydrogen ions) to egg white (changing the pH) or to raw fish or shrimp, which change from translucent to opaque. (That's the principal behind ceviche and other lime-marinated seafood.) The use of heat, acid, alkali, or chemical and physical injury to the weak hydrogen bonds of proteins causes bond breakage, visible as a change from clear or translucent to opaque. In protein skimming the precipitating insult is violent thrashing by tiny air bubbles, mimicking the action of wind on ocean waves.

Fine air bubbles in violent motion denature dissolved proteins. That first stage of foam fractionation generates particles of—and this is important—sticky precipitated protein that adheres to the bubbles. In the second stage of foam fractionation, other materials adhere to the denatured protein around the bubbles. Those other materials include algae, bacteria, protozoa, fungi, dissolved organic compounds, nutrients, heavy metals, and pigments. The longer bubbles remain in the water, the more they collect.

Today, the major types of skimmers are downdraft (countercurrent), venturi, and spray injection. All three types are made in configurations for use inside, outside, or hanging on the side of the tank or sump. Skimmers are rated for nano-reef tanks (10–15 gallons), medium reef tanks (50–75 gallons), and large tanks (90–150 gallons). Many large aquariums have custom-made or multiple skimmers. What are the important considerations when choosing a skimmer?

Contact time (Tc) between bubble and water is important, as are bubble size and number. The more and finer bubbles you can crowd for the longest time into the contact chamber, the greater the removal efficiency of the skimmer. (It's analogous to using finely ground carbon rather than large granular or pebble carbon.) Bubble size is a function of the equipment generating the bubbles, and of the salinity and pH of the water; high salinity and pH are conducive to forming fine bubbles, which is why skimming is not practical for freshwater tanks.

Downdraft Skimmers

In the downdraft (countercurrent) skimmer, air under pressure enters the reaction vessel from a diffuser at the bottom, and water is forced into the same chamber from the opposite direction. The mixture is circulated in the reaction chamber, often through two or more passes. Because the rising bubbles are pushed back by the onrushing water, bubble contact time (Tc) is extended, delaying the rise of the bubbles and giving them more time to dena-

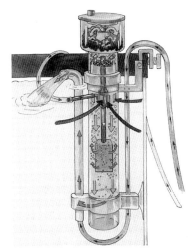

A hang-on countercurrent protein skimmer takes little space and requires no water level adjustment. If the air supply is from a pump passing water to a limewood air diffuser, that diffuser must be replaced when the bubble output is reduced or the bubbles seem larger. Both indicate the diffuser is becoming clogged and ineffective, and putting backpressure on the air pump.

ture proteins and grab onto particles in the water. Downdraft skimmers are inexpensive and cost-effective for small aquariums. Their air diffusers are usually ceramic and must be periodically cleaned or replaced because the pores clog, reducing air flow. Downdraft skimmers (and the other types discussed below) typically have a removable collection cup, where the foam collapses and concentrates into a blackish green waste product resembling motor oil. I recommend choosing a model with a cup that has an outlet port, which allows you to run tubing from the cup to a larger wastebucket.

Venturi Skimmers

Today, venturi skimmers have mostly replaced the air diffused downdraft variety. The venturi skimmer relies on water rushing past the tip of a conical pore, creating drag or friction that draws air from the outside (the base of the cone) through the pore and into the water stream. When water is siphoned from a tank through a clear hose a whirlpool of air will form from the water surface toward the base of the siphon tube. That's known as a *venturi effect;* the same phenomenon occurs in wind during violent cyclonic storms and in water at whirlpools.

Over time, the pore of the skimmer will clog with debris. To clear it, keep the skimmer running and fill a jar with hot water. Insert a length of airline tubing into the jar and place the free end of the tubing against the pore. This will draw the hot water from the jar into the skimmer, cleaning the pore. When the reaction chamber becomes overgrown with algae or slime, take the skimmer apart for cleaning. Allow room for an overflow bucket and access to the venturi pore when installing the skimmer and remember, you cannot have too large a venturi skimmer on a marine tank—especially one with large fish and therefore a larger waste load.

Needle-Wheel Skimmers

The needle-wheel skimmer replaces the typical impeller of the water pump with a multiple-armed impeller. All impellers break bubbles, but the needle-wheeled impeller does the job better, breaking already-small air bubbles as they form, multiplying bubble number, and reducing mean bubble size. The translucent homogenization of the air and water is as close to an air-water mix as you can get, so a smaller reaction vessel does the job normally associated with larger skimmers. On some water pumps, it's possible to replace the factory impeller with a needle wheel impeller, increasing the efficiency of the unit. If you do this, realize that running the pump harder than the workload for which it was designed risks overheating and shortening the life of the pump.

Spray Injection Skimmers

We've discussed pushing pressurized air into the water and pulling air into the water with a venturi pore. A simple, new type of skimmer is the spray injection skimmer, which uses a process similar to shooting water and air into the tank from a garden hose. A water pump pushes water to the top of the chamber (in this case a box rather than a cylinder) where it exits through multiple fine holes in a spray bar above the water line. As the pressurized water shoots down into the reaction area of raw tank water, the spray traps air and pushes the mixture down close to the bottom of the shallow reac-

---

Further Fractionater Facts

A vexing problem with many skimmers lies in determining the correct elevation in relation to the tank or sump water level. Often a minor adjustment in skimmer elevation obviates the need for a larger pump. Manufacturers recommend the correct level in relation to sump or tank. One of the best innovations is the hang-on skimmer. When draped over the tank rim, minor adjustments in water level or powerhead output result in optimal skimmer efficiency. There is no relationship of cubic inches of skimmer reaction chamber per gallon of tank. It is the organic loading of the tank that matters, and you cannot overdo it. Get the largest skimmer you can afford.

tion box. If you've seen the old Eheim canister filter return spray bars, you'll have a good idea of the principle. Spray injection skimmers take up less space and have fewer moving parts than venturi skimmers. The spray bars must be cleaned periodically, but splashing is confined to the reaction box. The cleaned (skimmed) water exits out the bottom, and the surface scum exits near the top.

Optional calcium reactors or ozone injection, oversized or portable collection vessels, and adjustable discharge and leveling ports operated by gate valves are just a few of the bell-and-whistle attachments available for your skimmer. Before you buy, consider that the more parts that make up your skimmer, the more opportunities there are for failure and the more places to clean. Simple venturi skimmers plumbed to discharge rather than merely store the waste are all that is needed, and those that disassemble easily are preferred. An exception is the use of mini-skimmers for nano-reefs. Skimmers are least effective when scaled down. Small skimmers store little waste, must be cleaned more often, and are not much cheaper.

Get as large a skimmer as possible. Many experts advise eliminating trickling filters to lower the nitrates to zero, but moderate levels of nitrate (5–10 mg/L) are generally harmless to corals. At the very least, the trickling filter is a redundant life support system providing additional mechanical and chemical filtration, aeration and degassing for a complex marine community whose existence is always precarious. Redundancy may not be necessary, but neither is insurance. Two skimmers may skim better than one, but we don't know if doubling up on skimmers will replace the benefits of trickling filters. Trickling filters also capture and kill disease

1. water inlet from sump
2. venturi fitting
3. venturi air injector
4. water returns to sump
5. carbon chamber
6. debris removal chamber

Larger floor or sump mounted venturi countercurrent protein skimmers are usually driven by an external air-cooled water pump. The venturi port draws in atmospheric air to fill the low pressure space where the pump-driven water suddenly flows into a larger chamber. The airline entering the venturi port should be placed into a glass of hot water once a week to clean the venturi and keep it from clogging.

organisms passing over the hungry biofilm, and probably remove chemicals not trapped by bubbles. Trickling filters are clunkers, not as sexy as skimmers and not their equal in reducing nitrogenous compounds. But there are pollutants other than nitrogenous compounds, and pollutants will induce populations of microbes that use them. No skimmer can make that claim.

Chapter Nine
Sterilizers and Ozonizers

Ozonizers and UV sterilizers are disinfectants used in public aquariums, aquaculture facilities, indoor fish farms, water treatment plants, and wastewater treatment plants. UV and ozone are safer than chlorine, with fewer problems from disinfection by-products. However, ozone in salt water containing bromine can produce disinfection byproducts just as noxious as those from chlorination in fresh water. Most public water and wastewater facilities are abandoning chlorination in favor of UV irradiation, which has no by-products.

Ultraviolet Sterilizers

Ultraviolet light is invisible energy in the range of 1900–4000 angstroms (Å), which are equal to 190–400 nanometers (nm). Energies higher than 200 nm fall into the realm of X-rays; even more energetic are the gamma rays produced by stars. All these high-energy waves of radiation are capable of oxidizing atoms and molecules into unstable, reactive ions, and all can destroy enzymes and nucleic acids.

Ultraviolet, the weakest ionizing radiation, breaks the DNA and RNA of microbes, which is most sensitive at 240 nm. Some microbes have enzymes that repair minor DNA damage shortly after it occurs, but excessive and prolonged UV exposure causes irreparable damage by destroying not only the DNA and RNA, but also the chromosomes, which are not repairable.

The optimal UV wavelength for water sterilization is 265 nm. The cheapest equipment is a standard mercury vapor lamp that emits at 253.7 nm, and this is what is used in the hobby. Because UV rays are absorbed by glass, water, and dissolved salts, the best germicidal effects require the 253.7 nm bulb be enclosed in quartz, through which the radiation can pass. To be most effective, UV sterilizers should operate above 100°F and pass the water to be sterilized (meaning the entrained microbes to be killed) within millimeters of the UV-emitting source for protracted contact time. Just as in photography, the effect of the radiation depends on intensity, distance from the light source, and exposure time.

A UV sterilizer consists of an opaque plastic tube to contain the water, a quartz sleeve around the mercury vapor bulb, a ballast, and O-rings to prevent leakage. UV sterilizers are designed to slow the movement of water as it passes the bulb so the period in proximity to the radiation is optimized to kill the most resistant organisms and cysts (50,000–100,000 microwatts per second per square centimeter of UV bulb surface). Martin Moe recommended a flow rate of no more than 30 gallons per hour, per watt. A slower rate per watt (less gallonage per hour) increases dwell time and thus effectiveness. Because effectiveness falls off with age and biofilm on the quartz tube, the bulbs should be cleaned monthly and replaced according to the manufacturer's directions. Many UV sterilizers have straight line sleeves that carry water past the length of the UV lamp. Other sterilizers, such as the Turbo-Twist, Gamma, and AquaStep, pass the water through a helical quartz coil that surrounds the lamp, increasing dwell time. Ask your dealer to recommend particular units and wattage for your marine tank, or check manufacturers' Web sites. UV units vary in construction materials, number of UV bulbs per unit (doubles and quads are available), rating by tank size and flow rate, and lamp tube length. The effectiveness of a UV lamp falls off with time, and different tubes may need to be replaced biannually or annually. UV lamps are manufactured in standard wattages (8, 15, 25, 40, 57, 80, 120, 160, and 240 W) of increasing cost. Because UV treatment is confined to the sterilizer and the unit is shielded, there is no danger of excess or escaping UV. Never turn on the lamp outside its containment or look at a lit lamp, as UV causes sunburn-like skin and eye damage. UV irradiation of oxygen molecules generates ozone, but so little that it is not a practical means of ozonization. Some of the UV unit manufacturers are Aqua Ultraviolet, Pentair Aquatics (Rainbow Lifegard), Coralife, AquaMedic, Aquastep, and Twist.

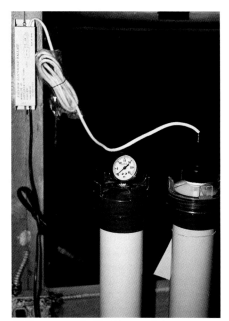

UV lamp mounted inside a canister.

Ozonizers

Ozone is another effective microbe killer. It destroys the microbial cell wall, DNA and RNA, and depolymerizes (denatures) proteins. It burns exposed tissues and should be used in a reaction chamber such as a protein skimmer. Ozone is produced by electrostatic generators (corona discharge) or in a few cases by UV lights. The corona dis-

charge is the basis of all home aquarium equipment. Public aquariums and fish farms might feed pure oxygen to the ozonizer. Air (19+ percent oxygen) is almost as good, but must be dried of all water vapor. Humid air wastes a lot of energy, so air is first passed over a desiccant to absorb water molecules. Then the oxygen or air under pressure enters the ozonizer and passes over the corona discharge unit, producing a small percentage of ozone or ozonized air. The ozonized air is discharged into the protein skimmer (preferably), but occasional small doses can be discharged directly to the sump or aquarium. The desiccant eventually can hold no more moisture and must be recharged by heating in the oven.

Ozone is more powerful, but more risky, than UV. It destroys rubber and many plastics, including ordinary airline tubing. Protein skimmers to be hooked up to ozonizers should be constructed of ozone-resistant plastics such as Kynar or neoprene. Ozone escaping into the atmosphere can irritate your mucus membranes and can harm pet birds. Ozone discharged to the skimmer increases efficiency. However, excessively oxidized gunk in the collection cup has a noxious odor.

Several skimmer manufacturers provide a deodorizing and ozone absorbing granulated activated carbon (GAC) container atop the collection cup through which wastewater and gunk odors and excess ozone must pass before entering the room. The GAC should be replaced whenever any sweet or foul odor is detected near the skimmer cup. Both odors can indicate that either too much ozone is being produced or the GAC's capacity for odor adsorption has been exceeded.

Avoid salt mixes containing a lot of bromide, which reacts with ozone to form hypobromite ion (OBr^-) that then oxidizes to bromate ion (BrO_3^-) at seawater pH (but not at pH 6.5). Bromate ion is a powerful oxidizer not unlike commercial bleach, and stable in seawater for several hours. It can quickly accumulate to toxic levels. The hypobromate ion can be converted to harmless bromide by granular activated carbon (GAC). Ozonization can form carcinogenic brominated hydrocarbons, so generate only the ozone necessary to decolorize, disinfect, or otherwise clean the water. Include GAC in the system, perhaps within an in-line container or within the return from the sump. In freshwater applications, lower pH and higher ammonia shift the equilibrium to somewhat less harmful hypobromite ion. Keep in mind that bromine salts not only form long-lasting toxic ionic compounds in seawater, but they prevent you from accurately monitoring the results of ozonization. Reef keepers and marine fish breeders use ozone or UV (but not both) for sterilization and decolorization of tank water yellowed from dissolved organic carbon (DOC) and pigments from algal (often refugia) secretions. Ionization by UV irradiation or by corona discharge-induced ozone will destroy the chemical bonds of DOC and microbial DNA and RNA and clarify the water.

Because ozone must be used at low doses in marine systems, the smallest commercial unit will be more than enough for a large reef tank. About 10 mg/hr/50 gallons of aquarium water is usually a safe and effective antimicrobial dose, but you may use more if you have a high DOC problem. Many aquarists combine intermittent ozonization with a redox controller that switches on the ozonizer when the oxidation-reduction (redox) potential drops below a particular setting for that individual aquarium. Ozonizers require maintenance. Every six months (or more often), the ozonizer should be disassembled and the electrostatic generator removed and cleaned. Even if you think it looks clean, scrub it with a dry cloth, but avoid scratching the unit. Ozonizers for aquarium use are offered by Red Sea and Aqua Medic. Industrial and commercial ozonizers are made by Ozotech for the water industry and other applications.

Chapter Ten
Temperature Control

Overheating

Corals do best at 70°–76°F, but can tolerate temperatures in the 60°s for hours or days. Overheating is more dangerous than occasional chilling. Common sources of unwanted heat are metal halide lights, powerheads, overheated pumps with clogged intake ports, and too little space between the aquarium and adjacent wall.

Hooded metal halide lights close to the water should be cooled by fans; pendant lights should have eight inches or more of space between water and the lamp. Powerheads and larger water pumps can overheat water several ways. First, there can be too many small pumps doing the work of a few large ones; if this is the case, consider using fewer and larger pumps. Second, a restricted flow causes overheating from back pressure. Clean the intake strainers, but do not remove them—an unscreened intake can trap fish and invertebrates exploring dark recesses. Do not use foam covers over intake strainers as the fine pores quickly clog, producing back pressure on the pump resulting in overheating, warping, and failure. When setting up the aquarium, use the largest diameter piping compatible with your skimmer and pumps; narrow pipes restrict the flow of water, resulting in unwanted heat. Try to match piping diameters with intake and (larger) discharge port diameters, although it is often safe to step up to a wider pipe. If all else fails, consider moving the aquarium 4–6 inches from adjacent walls to allow tank heat to dissipate.

In nature, excessive heat can kill almost all the symbiotic zooxanthellae in the local corals, causing bleaching as the corals expel dead microalgae. However, a minute number of symbiotic microalgae may be heat tolerant, perhaps one in a billion. Some of them will remain in their host corals and not be expelled. If enough are retained, the coral will survive. But in most cases, almost all the corals will expel all their microalgae (heat resistant or not), in the same way that your body will regurgitate everything in your stomach after ingesting a lot of good food but one bite of spoiled food. When good algae are expelled, they become available to other corals that have no symbiotic algae remaining, and are able to take up new ones from the water. Every bleaching event is different, and that's why some bleached reefs recover quickly, some take years to recover, and others may never recover if, in the meantime, the corals die and are overgrown by macroalgae. Early in a bleaching event, bleached (algal-deficient or algae-absent) corals may survive for days, weeks, or longer, but if starved of nutrients too long, they eventually die. Eventually the temperature-tolerant (heat-resistant) zooxanthellae, normally a minor part of the local population, repopulate the surviving corals (if any) to become the dominant microalgal type, and the local corals recover.

Heat-tolerant *Symbiodinium* species have a different mix of lipids (oils) in the membranes of their chloroplasts, which is thought to account for their heat resistance, although it could be coincidental. In your aquarium, the microalgal numbers are simply not large enough to provide the heat-resistant seeding option that occurs in the wild. That's why heat death of aquarium corals is permanent.

Controlled Heating

The two biggest killers of aquatic animals are chlorinated water and faulty heaters. Most tanks don't need a heater. The other equipment produces heat, and if the room is comfortable for you, it's comfortable for your fishes and corals. In colder regions, reef tanks may need to be heated with a submersible (waterproof) aquarium heater set at 72°–74°F. Many animals are killed when the old-style thermostat, consisting of two metal strips, welds itself shut from corrosion or age, and the heating element fails to shut down. If an older type heater is used, it should be sized at 2 watts per gallon so that if the thermostat welds and fails, the constant heat output will be insufficient to overheat the tank. Old-style heaters should also be replaced yearly—the cost of a replacement heater is insignificant compared with the cost of one coral.

Modern heaters offer silicon chip, solid-state technology with no moving parts and no metal strips to weld shut. They reliably deliver the dialed temperature, but you should keep independent thermometers in the tanks as a check on how well they are operating. (Trust but verify!) The better heaters have two separate solid state sensors: one to sense water temperature using the glass wall as a probe, and the other to detect differences in separate regions of the glass, signaling that the water level has dropped or the heater has been removed from the aquarium, either circumstance triggering a shut-off. The best heaters use titanium heating tubes and remotely dialed thermostatic controls with indicator lights. The heating unit can be placed in the sump (where it cannot contact any creature), and the thermostat in the tank.

Cooling

Reef tanks in hot climates can be cooled by setting the aquarium beneath an air-conditioning vent. Where direct sunlight, lack of air circulation, or metal halide illumination is the cause of excessive heat, supplementary cooling may be necessary. Aquaria that use trickle filtration benefit from evaporative cooling, but it may not be enough.

Chilling

The larger the aquarium, the lower the surface-to-volume ratio, and the less efficiently the tank surface dissipates heat. Large tanks (over 100 gallons) usually have multiple metal halide lamps that aggravate heat buildup, making the installation of a chiller necessary. Chillers are fan-cooled, industrial refrigeration units with a grid of titanium coils, a compressor, and a motor. Unlike your home refrigerator, which absorbs heat from the internal box and dissipates it to the outside air, the aquarium chiller is sealed with inlet and outlet ports for water delivered by a water pump (not included). Heat is absorbed from the water and dissipated to the air.

The two types of chiller are the stand-alone and the drop-in. A stand-alone chiller requires a water pump or a powerhead to drive water into the chiller and push it back out to the tank (varying with the design). Submersible powerheads are cheap, but add their own heat to the water, requiring you to compensate by going to the next larger model. External water pumps are more expensive than submersible powerheads, so it's a trade-off and either system will work. Because the pump is required to push water through the chiller, it should never be turned off while the chiller compressor motor is switched on.

A stand-alone chiller can be placed away from the tank for aesthetic purposes. The water lines between chiller and tank should be insulated. All chillers must be vented for heat dissipation efficiency, and must not be placed in confined spaces like closets. Chiller output is preset by the manufacturer or dealer to the individual aquarist's specifications. The options are generally 65°–80°F, 50°–65°F, and below 50°F. The compressor will probably (and should) be filled with R22 or MP39 refrigerant rather than R12 freon. The coldest chillers used for North Pacific marine animals (below 50°F) cost about $125–$200 more than those used for most mini-reef tanks which cost $400–$1000 for a ⅙ to ½ hp unit.

A cheaper alternative is the pumpless chiller with drop-in titanium coil heat absorber. The coil works like the hot-water heating coils used for warming a cup of coffee, except it absorbs rather than dissipates heat. The water around the coil must be in constant motion. The unit is intended to be dropped into the current of a sump with a running pump.

The type and size chiller for your reef tank is based on water volume and degrees of chilling. Thus you'll need a larger chiller for a 30-gallon tank of Icelandic lobsters than for a 100-gallon tank in which you're attempting to reduce heat by 10 degrees for corals.

The equipment cost is proportional to horsepower. Operational costs are proportional to size and where you live. Most chillers run on household (115 volt) current, and larger units (1 hp and up) on 230 volt current. You can estimate the base cost of a chiller in dollars at about its wattage. Some typical relationships are as follows, give or take about 25 percent.

hp	watts	cost
⅙	400	$ 450
⅕	500	550
¼	670	650
⅓	850	750
½	1,140	1,150
1	1,820	1,750

These prices do not include an electronic thermostatic controller (another $100–$200 depending on whether it operates only a chiller or both a chiller and a heater) or the power bill from your local utility. Costs per kilowatt hour also vary by region of the country.

Monitoring

No heater or chiller is safe to use without a separate digital thermometer to monitor water temperature. There is no substitute for an electronic digital thermometer, backed up by a scientific quality thermometer. Get an expanded scale alcohol or mercury thermometer from a photography dealer or scientific supply house, mount it where you can easily read the temperature, and scrub off scale and algae regularly. Discard any thermometer with a space within the registering liquid. All thermometers should be calibrated against each other, and checked regularly.

Chapter Eleven
Light and Lighting

We don't have reef aquariums. We have glass boxes with the animals arranged on rocks to simulate coral reefs. We need to know what a coral needs to live in a glass box. As we'll see later, some corals feed on plankton and are indifferent to light; others depend largely on symbiotic algae. Many but not all corals are symbiont-dependent, and not all symbiont-dependent corals are reef builders. Reef builders are those corals that produce abundant limestone as a waste product.

The reef builders are the familiar corals of shallow tropical seas. Their symbiotic microalgae are myriad strains in about seven clades (phylogenetic lines) of the dinoflagellate genus *Symbiodinium*. These microalgae live in the cells lining the blind sac or "gut" (or what was once a gut) in the coral polyp. Near the surface of the sea, these microalgae thrive on bright sunlight, and down a hundred feet, two hundred and sometimes more, they rely on either transformed blue light or are able to photomultiply the small amount of red light that reaches these depths, or some combination of these traits.

But wait. Corals and their microalgae can't see colors. They don't have eyes or brains. "Colors" refer to human perceptions of electromagnetic energy. The cones in our eyes respond to limited ranges of radiation that trigger a chemical reaction that produces an electrical impulse transmitted to our brains, which categorize these impulses into groups we call colors. If humans had evolved like some fish or bats, we might perceive electromagnetic radiation as sound or pressure or something else. This electromagnetic radiation stimulates *Symbiodinium* to initiate photosynthesis, triggering the microalgae to take up dissolved carbon dioxide from the water and the host polyp, and to manufacture sugars, sugar alcohols, and an amino acid, and in the process emitting waste oxygen and calcium carbonate. There is more physical chemistry involved, but certain wavelengths and intensities of electromagnetic energy (not "red light" or "blue light") are the triggers. Different strains of *Symbiodinium* have evolved to need little energy, a particular portion of the spectrum, to photomultiply incoming energy, or to filter the energy and harvest a portion of what is available. One day we will probably discover deepwater corals from mid-oceanic ridges or volcanic vents adapted to sulfur, iron, or other surrounding chemicals in a lifestyle based on chemosynthesis.

The symbiotic relationship of the reef-building corals is mutually obligatory. If the microalgae die, the corals cannot long survive, and the algae cannot long exist outside the coral host. To keep the algae and corals alive, we provide both with carbon dioxide, and the algae with the right type and intensity of electromagnetic energy for photosynthesis. The home reef keeper must evaluate and select artificial lighting that supports symbiosis. Reef aquarium equipment has characteristics of wattage, wavelength or energy (color), and intensity that are described in lux, nanometers, CRI, and technical terms. To understand the needs of the corals and their algae, and the capabilities of equipment to meet those needs, we need to understand these terms.

Wave Length

All electromagnetic waves travel at the speed of light (186,000 miles per second). The sun puts out its own distinctive mix of wavelengths of energy (based on its composition and age), as do other stars. Many wavelengths from the sun are absorbed by the atmosphere before they get to earth or by water before they penetrate very deeply. We are concerned only with those wavelengths that influence plant life. The wavelength of any kind of light is the distance between wave peaks or troughs, as measured in meters (m), nanometers (nm), or angstroms (Å). A nanometer is a billionth of a meter (10^{-9} meter), and an angstrom a ten billionth of a meter (10^{-10} meter). Several wavelengths energize photosynthesis in plants, green algae, red algae, brown algae, several kinds of bacteria, and even in cyanobacteria (blue-green microbes).

Kelvin Degrees

People are not too different from algae. Various kinds of electromagnetic radiation trigger photosynthesis in algae; in humans these types of radiation trigger the cones in our eyes to tell our brains the differences among wavelengths between violet (4,000 Å) and red (7,000 Å). Both processes are initiated by electromagnetic waves and both result in chemical reactions that have cascading effects. For us, when the waves to which we are sensitive (the colors) are combined, we "see" an intermediate color we describe as a specific quality of light. People interested in such things use a scale called Kelvin degrees of color temperature (K). There is a degree of Kelvin color temperature (an average color) resembling the total visible light of the sun at noon, another that resembles morning light, one that resembles daylight at noon at 40 feet beneath the ocean, and so on. Physicists and photographers are good at this.

Color Rendering Index

The Color Rendering Index (CRI) is a measure of an artificial light's similarity to the Kelvin value of the sun at noon at mean sea level at the equator. A color rendering index (CRI) of 100 would be equivalent to noon sunlight at mid-tide on the equator. High-quality stroboscopic lights for photographic film approach a CRI of 100 because they are designed to mimic sunlight at this time and in this place. Expensive aquarium lamps list their CRI next to the wattage. The higher the CRI, the closer the spectrum (mix of wavelengths) is to equatorial sunlight at noon. A standard incandescent bulb typically has a CRI of about 82, irrespective of watts.

Ultraviolet Light

The waves (photons, vibrations) of all light are forms of energy. Many forms of radiating energy can be harmful In excess, such as heat from infrared rays, ionizing radiation from UV rays, X-radiation and gamma rays from the stars, radiation from the radium series of elements, and the long wave radiation from your microwave oven. For aquarists, the energy of ultraviolet light is particularly important.

We distinguish three areas of the continuous ultraviolet (UV) portion of the spectrum, UV-A (least energetic), UV-B, and UV-C. The first two cause sunburn in nature, and in a reef tank they simulate high-energy sunlight in shallow water. UV-C, the most energetic, is an industrial product that is generated by sterilization equipment (see Chapter 9), but is too energetic to be used directly on clams, corals, other invertebrates, fishes, or algae.

Very High Output (VHO) fluorescent lamps and low-intensity (175 W) metal halide lamps emitting in the UV-A and UV-B ranges also benefit tridacnid clams and stony corals if placed about eight inches from the light source. At closer distances, UV energy may burn the corals.

Colorful pigments of the acroporid stony corals were once thought to filter harmful UV, but we now know UV-protective chemicals are colorless, and the enhanced colors of hard corals under brilliant lighting are a response to intensity rather than wavelength.

In the absence of intense light, the colorful pigments of shallow water corals may disappear and the coral turn tan or white. Corals from deep water, where UV doesn't reach, may burn when placed close to a metal halide lamp whether or not they are pigmented, so it's doubtful their (and perhaps most) pigments have protective value against UV.

Intensity, Lumens, and Lux

Intensity is not the same as energy, as we older guys are only too aware. In light, intensity is the volume of radiation emitted all at once. Compare, for example, the output of a 25-watt versus a 500-watt lamp. Although the wavelengths (colors) of the two lamps are the same, they differ in radiation intensity. So what is intensity? Intensity is the instantaneous volume of light emitted or lumens emitted at the source. But that isn't useful, because the effectiveness of light depends on how far away it is from the object upon which it shines. A 500-watt light 500 feet away will not do much for a reef aquarium, so intensity or lumens at the source is only half the story. The light that gets to the corals is what counts, and that light is measured in illuminance, or lumens per square meter of surface (lux). Lux matters most, because lux is the light received.

To summarize so far, our eyes and our brains "see" what we call visible light, that part of the electromagnetic wave energy (light quality) put out by the sun to which we ascribe colors, our skin "feels" another part (infrared or heat energy), and our tissues can be damaged by still other parts we don't "see" (X-rays, gamma rays, UV radiation). We use the word "light" to mean visible light: the part we see and, it seems, the part that plants "feel" since it triggers them to photosynthesize. Visible light quantity is measured in lumens or output at the source, and measured at the target in lux or lumens received per square meter. Which brings us to the photosynthetic algae inside the corals inside the aquarium.

Photosynthesis

The electromagnetic waves that induce the grass to grow on your lawn are not the same as the waves that keep deepwater corals healthy. The red and yellow parts of the spectrum used by grass are rapidly absorbed by water in the first 30–40 feet. The visible light that penetrates more deeply is blue light in the 4,000 Å or 400 nm range, and the most important part of the spectrum for symbiotic zooxanthellae photosynthesis. Not all photosynthesis is alike. The many kinds of algae, green, red, brown, yellow, etc., all photosynthesize through chloroplasts or other types of plastids. The ancestors of higher plants are the green algae, with similar chloroplasts and means of photosynthesizing mostly under red and yellow light rays. But the symbiotic zooxanthellae in corals are dinoflagellates, completely different from green algae, and photoeynthesis here is different. For one thing, symbiotic dinoflagellates use a lot of blue light and the

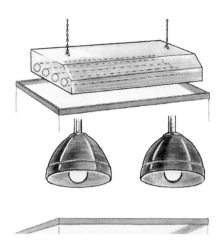

Heat is the enemy of reef tanks. Canopy or pendant lighting must provide either air space or fans for ventilation. The tank should also be far enough from the wall so that air can circulate all around and help cool the tank.

yellow and red parts of the spectrum are not as important. That enables corals to live in ocean depths where red rays cannot reach. It also explains why dinoflagellates, and not green algae, are the most widely distributed symbiotic algae in the ocean, occurring in corals, foraminifera, clams, and many other marine creatures. Green algae (*Chlorella*) also occur in some corals, but not exclusively and are never dominant in the ocean, as they can be in freshwater habitats.

Metal Halide Incandescense

Ordinary household tungsten lamps at high wattage offer excellent intensity in the yellow and red range, but miss the blue part of the spectrum needed by marine symbiotic algae.

High-intensity incandescent lights are usually oversized lamps on oversized mirrored reflectors, and they're filled with

Which Metal Halide is Best?

Your metal halide lamp(s) should be at least 175 W each. Two lamps are better than one for a 4–6 foot-wide aquarium. The lamps should be positioned at least 8 inches above the water to protect from heating and splashing, and fan-cooled if possible. Avoid metal halide lamps less than 5,000 K color temperature, selecting the best-priced unit in the 5,000 K to 6,000 K (for a replacement lamp) range, fine for large polyp stony corals (LPS) of shallow reefs. For small polyp stony corals (SPS corals) of deep water, 10,000 K and 20,000 K color temperature metal halides are better, providing greater intensity in the blue-shifted range that brings out pigment formation at the tips. Although CRI is not critical, look for CRI values above 85 to provide a natural look to the aquarium. Metal halide lights do all they need to do (get the symbiotic algae to photosynthesize) turned on for 4–6 hours a day. You can minimize heat and keep the aesthetics by using supplemental VHO or HO fluorescent fixtures when the metal halide lamps are switched off.

gas under partial vacuum (which can implode) or under 50 pounds per square inch of pressure (and can explode). Mercury vapor and sodium vapor lamps are of no use to reef keepers because they are short on the blue end of the spectrum. Halogen quartz metal halides are not expensive, but their spectra are also the wrong colors for photosynthesis by symbiotic coral algae.

Tungsten quartz metal halide lamps emit a broad spectrum of rays that often include blue light, making them suitable for growing the symbiotic algae of corals. The metal halide lamps offered in the aquarium trade are compact, brighter, and better color-balanced for blues than those stocked in hardware stores for space lighting.

Broad-spectrum metal halide lamps that produce blue light will also produce UV light. Some lamps have outer glass layers to block UV emissions. In lamps without glass protection, the UV emitted can damage your eyes and burn the corals. The heat and pressure of all metal halide lamps make them prone to explosive breakage if splashed while hot.

Most of the metal halide lamps in the hobby mimic sunlight at sea level with an average output of 5,500–6,500 Kelvin degrees color temperature, but the variety is great, with many having color temperatures of 4,300 K ranging to 20,000 K. Each requires a remote ballast specific to the wattage and type of lamp; one size does not fit all. Lamps with 150 W, 175 W, 250 W, and 400 W, at a color temperature of 6,500 K, all have enough blue radiant energy to support symbiotic algae in corals inside deep aquaria. For reef aquariums up to 20 inches deep, one or two 175 W lamps eight inches above the water will suffice; 250 W and 400 W lamps may be needed for deeper aquaria. The lamps can be mounted in wall fixtures next to the aquarium, in pendant fixtures over the aquarium, in canopies, or in combination hoods that hold one or two metal halide lamps and one to six fluorescent lamps. Hoods containing metal halide lamps should be fan-vented to dissipate heat, and far enough above the water to avoid splashes that can shatter the lamp's glass. Compact combination units include fittings (and bulbs) for metal halide and compact fluorescent lamps, and today you can find miniaturized combination units for nano-reef tanks.

When new, the metal halide lamp contains a small, clear chamber at about the middle of the bulb. When old, and failing, the metal halide bulb flickers erratically. Those familiar only with fluorescent lamps would assume the ballast has gone bad, but the bulb has probably worn out. Look for cloudiness in the center of the interior chamber and a black spray of carbon deposits near the base of the bulb to confirm the bulb has failed.

Fluorescense

Fluorescent tubes are filled with mercury vapor that emits ultraviolet light when energized by electricity. UV irradiation hits the coating on the inner walls of the lamp, and that coating fluoresces under this irradiation. There are all kinds of coatings for specialized purposes. Coatings developed for the printing industry emit strongly in the 4,200 Å blue range. These printer's bulbs are useful for deep-water corals. They are called O3 Actinic lamps and emit a dark blue light. While they support symbiotic microalgae of deep-water corals, they do not provide enough light for you to enjoy the colors of the fish and other animals. On the other hand, they cause many corals to fluoresce, a beautiful sight in a reef aquarium.

Some lamps sacrifice some blue in the 420 nm range and provide minor peaks in the red and green range by including rare earth phosphors in the coating. The loss of 420 nm blue output can be made up if needed with a second lamp or by increasing the lumens reaching the aquarium with a reflector. The combined (mostly) blue and (much less) red and green is a bright lavender lamp that enhances colors, makes corals fluoresce, and keeps the symbiotic algae happy. The so-called 50–50

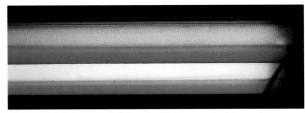

A four-unit fluorescent fixture holds two cool white and two actinic bulbs.

lamps consist of approximately 50 percent 6,500 K daylight and 50 percent 7,100 K actinic light, and are available with mirrored reflectors.

A reef aquarium can be illuminated by four to six of these lamps or any combination of actinic 03 and color enhancers and even cool white. Some reef units are combination actinic fluorescent and mirrored metal halide fixtures that direct all light output downward into the aquarium.

These inexpensive commercial units can be attached to customized overhead plywood platforms with metal foil reflective sheets positioned between the wood and bulbs. Fluorescent receptacles are susceptible to short circuiting from salt drift deposits. Sealed end caps and remote ballasts will protect against this.

Position the end-capped lamps next to each other with plastic clips, and keep them close to the water surface because intensity reaching the tank (lux) drops off as the square of the distance. It's not unusual to have 6 or 8 adjacent bulbs.

High Output and Very High Output Fluorescent Lamps

Ordinary straight tube household fluorescent lamps are low intensity units available in 15 W, 20 W, and 40 W or energy-saving 37 W. Higher intensity fluorescent lamps are not widely available, but better for reef aquariums. The High Output (HO) and Very High Output (VHO) lamps are available in 65 W and 110 W, 48-inch lengths, in both actinic and full spectrum outputs, and always require a remote electronic ballast. HO and VHO are alternatives to metal halide lamps for deep reef aquariums, but the cost of the electronic ballast is about the same as the cost of a complete metal halide fixture. Electronic ballasts are non-flickering and instant-starting, with little heat output. Locate them away from the aquarium to protect them from saltwater spray and salt creep. The electronic ballast for a VHO unit cannot be used for HO lamps, and vice-versa; the ballast must be matched to the lamp output type.

Compact Fluorescents

Compact fluorescent lamps are manufactured by Phillips, Panasonic, Osram Sylvania, General Electric, and others, and come in many shapes and sizes, including bulb-like, U-tube and helix designs. The compact fluorescent is powered at just one end. The ballast may be built-in (an integral unit) or remote, and can be magnetic (flickering and buzzing when you start up) or electronic (starting silently and instantly). The light output of an 18 W compact fluorescent puts out about the same lumens as 75 W of incandescent light. The CRI is not constant and varies from 60 to more than 85.

Small compact fluorescents for reef aquariums come in daylight (5,000 K), actinic (7,100 K), and 50–50 combinations of 5,000 K and 7,100 K. The ballast is remote, and the pins require a special fixture. These units are available in fan-cooled combination hoods holding one or two compact actinic and daylight fluorescent lamps plus a metal halide lamp.

Compact fluorescents are not made in high wattages. Their low intensity limits their usefulness to tanks less than 16 inches deep or in the 10- to 15-gallon range (nano-reef size) and to fire corals and anemones that don't require intense illumination.

Combination Fixtures

A good rule for minimum lighting is to use ordinary fluorescent lamps for a tank one foot deep containing soft corals, HO or VHO lamps for soft coral tanks 18 inches deep, and metal halide lamps for tanks containing hard corals irrespective of depth. Whenever you exceed the minimum, you expand the types of corals potentially suitable for the tank.

Although soft corals lacking zooxanthellae don't require blue light, it's a good idea to illuminate your tank with a blue source so that hard coral fragments may be added at any time. A 20-gallon tank can be adequately illuminated with four fluorescent lamps (two actinic and two full-spectrum daylight). A 29–55 gallon reef aquarium is deeper and requires at least two VHO and two ordinary fluorescent lamps. Tanks primarily for hard corals should, in addition to VHO, have one or two metal halide lamps. Compact fluorescents should not be used on a large tank.

You can easily find standard fixtures suitable for one or two 175 W–250 W metal halide lamps and one or two actinic (4,000 Å) blue fluorescent lamps in the 7,100 K range. For deep aquariums (150 gallons and up), increase the metal halide wattage (400 W and up) and look for a fan and a VHO actinic fluorescent fitting all in the same fixture.

Timers

Each lamp type should have a dedicated 24-hour timer. Ordinary fluorescents should be switched on for 10–14 hours.

Keeping Symbiotic Algae Happy: When You're Hot, You're Not

Photosynthesis in corals takes place in the chloroplasts of the symbiotic dinoflagellates and it is a rapid two-step process, with a brief period (merely an instant) between steps. If the interval is interrupted or delayed a fraction of a second by heat, for example, the oily chemicals produced in the first step are oxidized, fail, prevent the second step, and kill the algae, causing the polyp to expel them. This is the basis of heat-mediated coral bleaching.

In nature, the coral reef community consists of many kinds of corals containing only a few types of *Symbiodinium*, each association adapted for various temperatures, light levels, and spectral ranges (color temperatures). In cases of coral bleaching resulting from heat, damaged corals often recover after being reinvaded by heat-tolerant strains of *Symbiodinium*. The heat tolerant strains have higher concentrations of highly unsaturated fatty acids (HUFAs) in the lipid thylakoid membrane of the chloroplasts than do the typical strains. Because the thylakoid membrane lipids are more highly unsaturated, algae with more of these lipids are resistant to oxidation during interrupted photosynthesis. In nature, there is a mix of *Symbiodinium* types, with the dominant strains not heat resistant. When hot period bleaching kills the common *Symbiodinium* types, the corals may recover if there are enough heat-resistant *Symbiodinium* around with their higher amounts of HUFAs in their chloroplasts' thylakoid membranes, and it is these algae that come to spread through and dominate the recovering *Symbiodinium* populations. When the crisis has passed, the heat-resistant types may once more be displaced by the normal type.

Because they emit weak light, they should be the first to switch on in the morning and the last to switch off in the evening, simulating dawn and dusk, and not panicking the fishes. VHO lamps should be used 6–8 hours a day. Metal halide lamps use a great deal of power, and should be plugged into a heavy-duty, air conditioning type timer for a 2–4 hour photoperiod in the middle of the lighting cycle.

Some aquarists have induced corals to spawn in reef tanks by controlling light and temperature to mimic the annual cycle on the reef. This requires long-term timers to gradually decrease the photoperiod, and programming the chillers to mimic the approach of winter (longer use per day), then reversing the cycle to mimic spring (shorter use per day).

Replacement

All fluorescent and metal halide lamps lose intensity and shift color spectra over time. Fluorescent lamps should be replaced according to the manufacturer's directions or at six-month intervals, but gradually. Replace one bulb per week during the replacement period to avoid sudden color or intensity changes that might stress or shock the zooxanthellae. Metal halide lamps should be replaced when they begin to flicker.

Not only pretty colors are at stake, but the survival of the corals. Trying to squeeze another month out of a 25-dollar lamp may risk thousands of dollars in live coral and is a mistake rarely made more than once.

Chapter Twelve
Algae and Plants

In both fresh- and saltwater, the bottom of the food chain consists of equally important phytoplankton and detritus. Phytoplankton are drifting, floating, or swimming mostly unicellular algae. Many filter-feeding corals, sponges, and molluscs depend on phytoplankton.

Detritus consists of plant fragments and debris important for the microbes coating and feeding upon them. Bacteria and fungi break down the tissues, and protozoans, rotifers, worms, and other animal life eat the bacteria and each other. Many kinds of fish and shellfish larvae depend on detritus, and other types depend on phytoplankton.

On the reef itself, the most important plants are the symbiotic dinoflagellate algae (zooxanthellea) of corals and other invertebrates, the red algae that cement coral reefs together, and the calcareous green algae that also contribute to limestone beach sands. The symbionts absorb nitrogen mostly from the hosts and phosphates from seawater. Marine macroalgae get some nitrogen from nitrogen-fixing cyanobacteria on the reef, but most is from animal ammonia, recycling of detritus through the guts of tangs and parrotfishes and invertebrates. In general, nutrients are sparse on the reef. Distant mangroves, grasses, and kelps must be fragmented, pulverized, and in some cases dissolved to provide detritus and dissolved nutrients and finally reach a reef that can afford neither to waste nor interrupt its supply. Coral reefs take everything, reuse everything, and leave nothing but sand and rubble.

Detritus

A few species of higher plants have adapted to the marine environment at its edges. Primary productivity depends on these estuarine and nearshore mangrove and maritime forests, emergent estuarine marsh and coastal submerged sea grasses, and gardens of macroalgae. As mangroves and grasses undergo seasonal die-off or leaf-drop, their protozoan and microbial coatings feed small shrimp, crabs, worms, and fish larvae. The debris is churned through the intestinal tracts of a series of herbivorous, filter- and silt-feeding fishes, shrimp, crabs, worms, fungi, protozoa, and bacteria. The plant particles are called detritus, the fuel that maintains near-shore fish and shellfish production. It is also important to coral reefs. Out in the open sea, phytoplankton plays the same role throughout the water column, but detritus plays an important role on both shallow bottoms, and on the deepest bottoms of the abyss.

Algae

Algae are important in primary productivity, shoreline stabilization, and reef formation. The most important algae of the reef are the symbionts that keep reef-building corals alive and secreting calcium carbonate, and the green and red algae that glue the reef together. Algal types include the microalgae (phytoplankton, single cells or small groups), usually invisible unless there is a bloom that tints the water or kills the fish, and the highly visible macroalgae that coat rocks and sand with sheets and upright structures everywhere in the near shore zone.

Green Algae

Green algae (Chlorophyta) occur as single cells, sheets, filaments, or masses. Many are microscopic (microalgae), and others are large enough to be noticed and called macroalgae.

Green algae are food or habitat for many reef inhabitants. Some form mats or turfs, protected as private food sources by damselfishes until stripped by schools of tangs. Many green macroalgae accumulate calcium carbonate that stiffens them enabling upward growth while making them unpalatable to herbivores. They contribute to reef structure by cementing adjacent coral skeletons, and their ground remains become new sand.

Attractive Calcareous Green Algae: Nearshore warm habitats contain some beautiful green macroalgae suitable for an aquarium. Most require brilliant (metal halide) illumination, but others do well under household incandescent light.

Segmented Algae

Halimeda. The particulate limestone remains of *Halimeda* and other calcareous algae grazed by parrotfishes are a major part of beach sand. *Halimeda* plants are supported upright by a fibrous holdfast that grips rocks, coral, and sand. The uprights are calcified except at the joints, and bend in cur-

Banded coral shrimp meet atop a mass of Caulerpa.

rents. Some occur in bright shallows, others at dim depths and in caves. *Halimeda lacrimosa* has tear- or bead-shaped segments; *H. monile* segments resemble small cylinders; and *H. incrassata* segments are thickly bi- or tri-lobed. Flattened, plate-like segments and a central rib are characteristics of *H. copiosa, H. tuna, H. discoidea, H. opuntia,* and *H. goreaui,* distinguishable by segment size and shape, branching, and depth. In nutrient-rich aquaria, *Halimeda* might require thinning.

Feathers and Grapes

Caulerpa. Over a hundred species of feather and grape algae grow in rock and rubble zones in coastal shallows, the open ocean, in estuaries, and in tropical and temperate waters around the world. They spread mostly by asexual growth and fragmentation, and some grow rapidly under the brilliant lighting of nutrient-rich reef tanks, requiring thinning. *Caulerpa* are not prominent on reefs, but common inshore on mangrove roots, on sand, rock, or rubble beaches. These syncytial or acellular algae (their nuclei

Grape form of Caulerpa *extending over the bottom.*

side like bristles on a feather. Some forms develop only under certain lighting. *Caulerpa racemosa* resemble clusters of grapes, but the spheres are larger, fewer and flattened on top in the variety *peltata*; *C. nummularia* is similar, but its flattened tops look like unribbed umbrella algae; *C. prolifera* uprights look like smooth-edged seagrass, while *C. serrulata* resembles rough-edged *Sargassum* weed. *C. cupressoides* looks like spears of asparagus; *C. lanuginosa* looks the same, but has fine hairs along the rhizome providing additional purchase in the sand. In three popular aquarium species, the uprights are fronds; *C. sertularioides* is flat-bladed with fine branchlets or has three-dimensional uprights with thickened branchlets and a thick rhizome, and *C. mexicana* has straight-edged, tightly packed flat branchlets while *C. taxifolia* has loosely packed, tapering flat branchlets.

Caulerpa sometimes grows too rapidly in a reef tank, and must be thinned by hand. Tangs and pygmy angelfishes help keep it cropped. Several inshore species of *Caulerpa* do well in refugia, or in mini- or nano-reefs, and some do well in nutrient rich water with ordinary household incandescent lighting. Because no two locales are illuminated the same way, the *Caulerpa* form you buy, trade, or collect will likely differ from the form that develops in your aquarium.

are dispersed in a continuous cytoplasm not divided by cell walls) grow upright from a horizontal rhizome or runner that grips rock, sand, or mud with penetrating rhizoids. The upright may have a mid-rib from which small branches extend to the

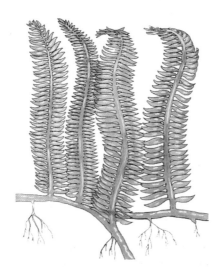

Caulerpa *species are identified by the form of the upright fronds, but all species grow over the surface by extending a runner or rhizome that attaches to the bottom by rootlike rhizoids.*

Cups and Brushes

Acetabularia. The finely ribbed umbrella, thin stalk, and cryptic holdfast of the mermaid's wine glass is a single, giant cell with a cup or dish up to three-fourths of an inch across. The stalk is attached to hard objects on shallow sand flats. Calcium carbonate protects against algae-grazing damselfishes. *Acetabularia* reproduces asexually by division at the base of the stalk. Sexual reproduction is by cysts released from rays of the cups, producing flagellated gametes. Two species available from Florida are the pale white *A. crenulata* with tiny teeth around the margins of the disk and *A. calyculus,* which is green and has smooth edges.

Polyphysa polyphysoides is similar, bright white with lime deposits, and smaller than the mermaid's wine glass.

Penicillus. The mermaid's shaving brush is a large, bristly, upright alga of shallow sand flats. It is hardened by calcium carbonate tissue, and its holdfast is a web of rhizoids anchoring it in deep sand. Three common Florida species are *P. capitatus,* 2–4 inches tall with a slender stalk; *P. pyriformis* at almost 4 inches, but with a stubby stalk and flat top; and *P. dumetosus,* 6 inches tall with a stubby base and rounded top. Brilliant light is required for all.

Rhipocephalus. The false shaving brush or ripweed is a calcified alga with plates instead of bristles. The single Florida species, *R. phoenix,* grows to 6 inches tall and ranges from shallow grass and mangrove flats to 120 feet deep on reefs, rock, or sand.

In reef tanks, cups and brushes require deep sand, intense light (they do best in shallow tanks), iodine and calcium supplements, and protection from tangs, pygmy angels, and snails. Their high nutrient requirements make them incompatible with hard corals.

Fans and Fingers

Udotea. Ranging from shallow flats to 50 or more feet deep, these hard fan algae have smooth, calcareous green plates on a stalk anchored by a holdfast in sand or muddy silt. The plates often have concentric lines of calcium carbonate deposits. The four common Florida

Penicillus dumetosus *attains up to 6 inches in height.*

species are *U. cyathiformis* with a cupshaped plate; *U. wilsonii* with a cluster of plates around the central stalk; *U. flabellum* with a cluster of dark green, leathery plates; and *U. occidentalis* with a cluster of light green, stiff plates. *Udotea* species are grazed by parrotfishes and important contributors to beach sand. *Cymopolia* has bristles at the tips.

Avrainvillea. The soft fans are blackish-green acellular (syncytial) algae covered with fine filaments giving them a suede-like texture. The holdfast is a massive ball of filaments rooted in silty sand. The finger-shaped *A. rawsonii* occurs in grass flats. The others are fanshaped and range from mangrove and grass flats to deep water. The 8-inch-high *A. longicaulis* has a regular outline while an irregular outline marks *A. nigricans.* The shorter *A. elliottii* has straight lower edges on the fan; the dinner plateshaped *A. asarifolia* has a 12-inch-high fan on a minute stalk.

67

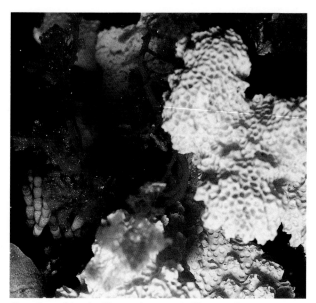

Fan-shaped Avrainvillea *and segmented* Cymopolia.

Anadyomene. The veined fans are beautiful but infrequent survivors on live rock. Under the microscope, *A. stellata* has regularly arranged cells among the veins, and *A. saldanhae* has irregularly spaced cells. Both require good current.

Neomeris. These short, stubby, green finger-shaped algae have calcified concentric white lines. They grow slowly forming an attractive upright turf.

Codium. These thick, rubbery, dark green algae have simple or complex branching, grow low to the rock or long and flowing in the wild. What look like thick fingers are actually bundles of fine acellular strands. These algae are usually removed or decay during curing of live rock. Surviving fragments do not get enough light in tanks to become pests.

Bubbles

Valonia and Ventricaria. Smooth bubble algae are among the largest single-celled plants. Each bubble is a single cell with tiny nucleic acid fragments scattered through the cytoplasm. *Valonia macrophysa* has large spherical bubbles; *Valonia aegagropila* forms bubbles three times as long as wide; *Valonia utricularis* has sausage-shaped bubbles. *Ventricaria ventricosa* occurs as individual green bubbles an inch or more in diameter. All species can grow fast in aquaria, even in dark spaces, and must be thinned. They reproduce sexually and asexually. There is a bubble stage of the nuisance alga *Derbesia* (called the *Halicystis*) resembling *V. ventricosa,* but it drifts when detached (*Valonia* sinks).

Dictyospheria. Rough bubble algae (*D. cavernosa* and *D. ocellata* sometimes called *Valonia ocellata, D. versluyii*) form mats of tiny bubbles that encrust rock. Their fast asexual growth compounded by sexual reproduction can make them a nuisance. Rough bubble algae form layers of 1 mm cells that cover rocks, prevent attachment by corals, and even overgrow corals. Limiting dissolved nutrients will not control them as they can get their nutrients from the activity of worms, crustaceans, and other small fauna beneath them. The only control is thinning by hand.

Nuisance Green Algae

Macro- and microalgae are usually controlled with herbivorous snails, sea urchins, tangs, and pygmy angelfishes. Supplemental iodine and iron accelerate growth, as do nitrates and nitrites. Nuisance algae overgrow coralline red algae on rock, preventing the rock from being used by corals. They require removal by hand, darkness, or immersion of the infested rocks in a killing bath containing erythromycin. Other controls are granular activated carbon (GAC) filtration, eliminating iodine supplements, keeping phosphate levels below 0.02 mg/L, frequent water changes, and constant, strong skimming. Connecting the reef tank to a refugium or an algal mat box can lead to initial and repeated infestations.

Ulva. Sea lettuce forms gelatinous sheets and blades attached to hard bottoms. *Ulva* grows so fast that it is harvested for food in the Pacific. *Ulvaria* is thinner and paler. Sea lettuce thrives under intense light in nutrient enriched water, and can be readily killed by a few days of light deprivation.

Enteromorpha. Tubular green filaments of this alga occur on rock or shell collected near shore. Related to *Ulva,* it is eaten by herbivorous fishes, but the best control is cleaning rocks and shells before putting them in a reef tank. *Enteromorpha* seldom spreads because of its strong light and high nutrient requirements.

Bryopsis. The sea ferns form clumps of tuft-like, soft, feathery algae. A type of turf alga, it arrives on live rock and may be adopted and cultivated by damselfishes.

Derbesia. A nuisance filamentous or hair alga forming dense yellowish green mats of delicate branched filaments. It sometimes appears in a marble-like bubble stage (sea bottle) resembling *Valonia,* but that stage subsequently gives rise to the filamentous form.

Chaetomorpha. Fine, light green, unbranched filaments form small algal turfs managed by damselfishes, or develop into vast masses of "mossy" nuisance algae. The variably sized cells have multiple nuclei, indicating incomplete wall formation following nuclear division. The nuisance alga *Chaetomorpha linum* is overgrowing Jamaican reefs and grass beds. This pollution indicator responds to phosphorus by

Fan-shaped Avrainvillea *and segmented* Cymopolia.

overgrowing everything in its vicinity, its 15-foot long strands wrapping around corals, grasses, sponges, and other algae, cutting off their light and circulation.

Cladophora and **Cladophoropsis.** Dark green, branched thin or thickened filaments forming tangles or tufts with a greasy texture resembling Cyanobacteria, these coiled hair algae are attached or floating, round clumps on or under the sand, or rolling in the current. Remove it by hand.

Brown Algae

Brown algae (Phaeophyta) are everywhere, and the most common algae in colder water. You have probably seen *Macrocystis* (giant kelps) on rocky Pacific shores or rockweed (*Fucus*) on the northeastern Atlantic coast. Drifting mats of just two species of *Sargassum* can cover acres of the

Fucus *in a Maine salt marsh.*

subtropical ocean surface, yet far more species are attached to hard bottoms. The few calcareous species are attractive but difficult to keep. Brown algae require strong current and supplemental iodine, grow slowly, and are readily smothered by epiphytic cyanobacteria. Brown pigment (fucoxanthin) masks the green chlorophylls. In the wild, the fast-growing tips have chemicals that resist attachment by epiphytes, but in captivity the plants don't grow fast enough to have this protection.

Attractive Brown Algae

Stypopodium. Individual fronds of this non-calcareous, tan-to-olive alga with white banding are attached to hard surfaces. Noxious chemicals in the fronds discourage herbivorous fishes.

Padina. Semicircular brown fronds of this calcareous alga pack hard bottoms. White bands or lines are colorless hairs

and deposits of calcium carbonate that discourage herbivores.

Unsuitable Brown Algae

Lobophora. Leafy orange, brown, or green fronds resemble curved snack chips or tightly packed lettuce leaves. It is fast-growing and attaches by holdfasts. *Lobophora variegata* can be a nuisance on nearshore reefs washed by runoff with excess nutrients. Its noxious-tasting chemicals protect it from herbivorous tangs, but it is eaten by *Diadema antillarum* sea urchins and often ripped away during storms.

Dictyota. This large genus of branched, attached, rubbery algae with flattened fronds sometimes has attractive surface beading, and the frond edges may be smooth or toothed. *Dictyota cervicornis* and *D. jamaicensis* are fast-growing pollution indicators that rapidly overgrow even deep coral reefs on densely populated islands. The delicately-thin *D. bartayresii* is a translucent, iridescent blue. Species of the similar *Dictyopteris* are distinguished by fronds with mid-ribs. Often attached to wild rock, no member of this group is suitable for mini-reefs.

Colpomenia. These brown bubble algae grow as gas-filled, rubbery spheres, irregular sinuses, or eruptions on hard surfaces in nutrient-rich aquaria. Portions that break away float. They would be pests were they fast growers.

Turbinaria. A foot tall, and with exquisite trumpet- or mushroom-shaped branches, this shallow water alga requires surge and brilliant lighting. It is used for food and fertilizer, and does not survive in marine tanks. (Note that *Turbinaria* is a generic name for both an alga and a coral.)

Sargassum. Two drifting species (*S. natans, S. fluitans*) dominate the floating weed pooling in the oceanic circulation known as the Sargasso Sea. Storms and the Gulf Stream carry masses northward along the Atlantic coast, where it blows onto shore (Florida to North Carolina) or is trapped by downwellings and sinks into the depths to provide food to the deep ocean. The floating mat contains over 200 species of fishes and invertebrates including endemics found nowhere else—such as the sargassum frogfish (*Histrio histrio*), the sargassum nudibranch (*Scyllaea pelagica*), and several species of sargassum shrimp. The marine community of the sargassum weed has its closest relatives on hard bottom habitats, prompting ecologists to call it a floating benthic habitat. Fishes of the sargassum weed community are the major foods for marlin, dolphin, some marine birds, and the floating weed is a critical habitat for baby sea turtles. Sargassum—and the sargassum frogfish—occur in all the tropical seas of the world.

The majority of *Sargassum* species grow attached (*S. hystrix, S. platycarpum, S. polyceratium, S. filipendula, S. bermudense, S. pteropleuron*), but broken segments float into the masses of drifting weed. The species can be identified by the shape of the frond and whether it has smooth or toothed edges and a mid-rib; the formation, color, and location of gas-filled flotation bladders (berries); and whether the berries have spiny tips. *Sargassum hystrix* responds to nutrient pollution by overgrowing deep coral reefs, along with *Dictyota* and *Lobophora*.

Red Algae

With more than 4,000 species, the red algae (Rhodophyta) are the most successful marine algae, growing from the intertidal zone to over 800 feet deep.

Many live below the depth to which red light penetrates. The pigments of red algae are chlorophyll *a*, phycoerythrin, and phycocyanin. Phycoerythrin and phycocyanin absorb high-energy blue light, and emit lower-energy red light. This extraction and conversion of electromagnetic radiation allows red algae to energize their chlorophylls at depths beyond the reach of the red energy of sunlight.

Some red algae contain chemicals that discourage herbivores and may have application to medicine. Red algae may be rubbery fronds with thick holdfasts or delicate membranes or dense masses of finely branched filaments. They include calcareous encrusting species critical for the reef and the successful reef tank. The encrusting calcareous coralline algae cement hard corals to rock or the reef base, holding the reef together, and their growth builds the reef crest, which is more algal than coral in origin.

Encrusting Coralline Red Algae

Goniolithon, Amphiroa, Jania, Corallina, Neogoniolithon, Lithothamnion, Mesophyllum, Titanoderma, Peyssonelia, Porolithon, Spongites, Sporolithon, Hydrolithon: These are pink-to-dark red, calcareous algae growing as a single crust or overlapping crustal layers. They range from the intertidal zone to great depths, and may resemble sponges, bryozoans, or red protozoans that form similar patches.

The most important reef-building red algae are *Porolithon pachydermum* in the Atlantic and *P. onkodes* in the Pacific, which make much of the calcium carbonate (calcite) that cements reef structure and absorbs the shock of waves, protecting the reef from destruction. The earliest reefs were mounds dominated by rudist bivalve molluscs and red calcareous algae, and existed eons before coral reefs appeared.

Both wild (collected) and cultured live rock should have large areas of encrusting coralline algae after weeks of darkness. The pink or red patches spread if provided supplementary calcium (>450 mg/L) in dim light. In the established reef tank, encrusting coralline algae cover the glass, filters, and other hard parts, providing a base for attachment of corals. Absent a liquid calcium supplement or aragonite gravel, coralline algae may be overgrown by undesirable green hair algae and cyanobacteria.

Non-Encrusting Red Algae

Erectile and massive red algae are discarded during live rock preparation, but fragments may survive and grow. Many red algae are too large and of little interest, while others are quite pretty.

Gracilaria. Cultivated throughout Asia for industrial use (cosmetics, anti-inflammatory drugs, microbial agar medium, food and food additives), and ubiquitous in reef tanks, *Gracilaria* may grow fast but is easily hand-cropped. It's commonly served with sushi dishes.

Botryocladia. Small, dull red bubble algae or sea grapes usually grow as two or more bubbles on a short stalk from crevices. The bladders contain a mucilaginous fluid.

Porphyra, Halymenia, and *Flahaultia.* Spreading sheet-like fronds of these algae appear similar to translucent, yellow to dark red versions of sea lettuce *(Ulva).* In aquaria, each frond may contain a large gas bubble within its fold.

Anotrichum, Antithamnionella, Bostrychia, Callithamnion, Ceramium, Griffithsia, and *Wrangelia.* Microscopic to fine filaments of these algae form tufts of turf algae on rocks in the wild and often in developing in algal mat scrub-

CLOD Pathogen

A mucilaginous rod-shaped bacterial agent causes coralline algae lethal orange disease (CLOD). The condition resembles black-band disease of corals in its rapid growth rate and demarcation by a distinct line and total necrosis leaving only bare coral skeleton behind. CLOD probably originated in the eastern Pacific and is on reefs worldwide. The stages of CLOD are marked by orange dots, then circles, and finally fingers of infection throughout the surface. In later stages, the mucilaginous colonies of gliding rods protrude as eruptive globules called propagules that are carried by waves to other coral heads and reefs. In laboratory tests, all species of encrusting red algae were susceptible. This emerging disease should be watched for in rock and reef tanks.

bers. *Ceramium* is an indicator of nutrient pollution, as the masses of this red "mossy" alga overgrow corals in shallows near sewage discharges.

Golden-brown Algae

The diatoms are the golden-brown or glass algae (Chrysophyta), characterized by a complex external skeleton or capsule (the frustule) of interlocking silica (glass) valves. With forms as diverse as snowflakes, entire books are devoted to diagrams of diatoms. Diatom species occur as single cells or filaments, clumps, attached or drifting. In aquaria, they form a light brown film over the glass, gravel, and rocks when there's abundant silica in make-up water and nitrates are high (silica alone will not cause a bloom). Attached diatoms are controlled by grazing herbivorous *Astraea* snails, *Ctenochaetus* bristle-tooth tangs, and *Centropyge* pygmy angelfishes. Drifting diatoms are removed by protein skimming. Some diatoms are nutritious algae able to manufacture essential highly unsaturated fatty acids, and are important food for rotifer and copepod cultures.

Dinoflagellates

Dinoflagellates (Pyrrhophyta) are extraordinarily diverse and important single-celled algae. Free-living forms have a body wall of two cellulose plates divided by a transverse groove and a longitudinal groove across them. One groove has a short flagellum and the other a longer one for motility. Most species are members of the phytoplankton community. Many planktonic dinoflagellates have high concentrations of HUFA oils in the membranes of their chloroplasts, and are important sources of HUFAs for zooplankton and the larval fishes that eat them. These and other important HUFAs are concentrated up the food chain, and important even to human neurologic development.

Zooxanthellae

Different kinds of dinoflagellates are free-living, parasitic, or symbiotic with corals, molluscs, foraminifera, echinoderms, and other marine animals. The common name for these symbionts is zooxanthellae, and for many years all the species in corals were believed to be *Symbiodinium microadriaticum.* Today we know that the *Symbiodinium* populations of corals, forams, molluscs, etc., are different groups of species, but don't know where to draw the evolutionary lines (so to speak). At this time we can do no more than place them in closely-related clusters of species called clades. DNA analysis shows that *Symbiodinium* were important dinoflagellates that formed symbiotic relationships with the foraminifera protozoans long before they were symbionts with cnidara. The foraminiferans, like corals today, excreted calcium carbonate skeletons. They were mostly drifting pelagic protozoans and, when they died, their calcium carbonate shells fell to the bottom where, over time, they formed limestone beds hundreds of feet thick.

Then came the meteoric impact with the earth that triggered the end of the Cretaceous period and wiped out 65 percent of marine animals, including many, but not all, the foraminifera. *Symbiodinium* survived and the extinction became an opportunity. Fossils of 5–10 million years later contain today's seven clades of *Symbiodinium* in all the invertebrate groups in which they now occur. Before then, coral reefs could not have existed because *Symbiodinium* had not yet become symbiotic with reef-forming cnidaria. The oldest fossil "reefs" going back some 450 million years are large mounds of calcareous algae, sands, silts, and mixed invertebrates dominated by rudist molluscs. They are not coral reefs, which are much younger.

The zooxanthellae of reef-building corals live inside cells lining the mostly nascent gut (hardly used since most nutrition is provided by the algae) where they photosynthesize using electromagnetic energy and the wastes of the coral polyp (phosphate, ammonia) as nutrients, and leak their own excess production of glucose, sugar alcohol, and alanine to the host. *Symbiodinium* zooxanthellae in tridacnid clams occur between rather than within cells, and are cultivated by the clam as a complete food to be periodically swept inside and digested.

Red Tide

A number of dinoflagellates (*Gonyaulax, Gyrodinium, Alexandrium,* etc.) produce noxious waste products. Under nutrient-rich conditions, they bloom and their wastes reach concentrations toxic to fish, crabs, and mammals, including humans sensitive to eye and lung irritation. Concentrated in shellfish, these toxins can be lethal to people. Red tides are natural phenomena but may be increasing from coastal eutrophication. They have not yet been documented in aquaria. Noga at North Carolina State University has determined that at least one freshwater "velvet" agent previously thought to be *Piscinoodinium* may in fact be a dinoflagellate related to red tide, which suggests that some marine skin infections may be more closely related to marine red tide dinoflagellates than to freshwater dinoflagellates.

Blue-green "Algae"

The blue-greens or Cyanobacteria are not algae, bacteria, nor fungi, but a group (or more than one group) apart from all others. Their cell walls are chemically different from all bacteria and algae, they produce unique chemicals, and they live where nothing else can survive. Today's Cyanobacteria are descendents of early 3-billion-year-old cells that could use carbon dioxide and nitrogen from the atmosphere and photosynthesize carbohydrates, and whose wastes became the oxygen in our atmosphere. Modern cyanobacteria often appear as greenish black and glistening films on rocks and glass. Many species produce malodorous and toxic wastes. Their chemicals make them distasteful to most fishes and invertebrates. They overgrow macroalgae under low light when phosphates are high, and form thick, slimy, acrid sheets. Their cyanotoxins stress or kill other aquatic life.

Blue-greens are divided into three Orders:

The Chroococcales occur as single cells or colonies. The Stigonematales form filaments with branches and divide in two planes; *Microcystis* is in this group, important for producing toxic microcystins that kill waterfowl and cause human illness. The Nostocales divide in one plane to form unbranched filaments; *Oscillatoria* often grows as a mat or turf; *Schizothrix* forms gelatinous sheets and *Lyngbya* slimy turfs in nutrient enriched habitats and important in artificial algal turf scrubbers; *Phormidium* is parasitic, causing black-band disease of corals. Other blue-greens that cause coral and perhaps other invertebrate and red alga diseases are also in this Order.

For most algae, nitrogen is a limiting nutrient and, when it is used up, the plants stop growing. Blue-greens are not nitrogen limited because they can fix atmospheric nitrogen into all the nitrate they need. They are, however, limited by the availability of phosphorus. You can limit their growth by employing phosphate removal pads and equipment, and by using deionized or reverse osmosis water to make up evaporation rather than tap water.

Other methods to control or kill blue-greens are copper sulfate, erythromycin (Maracyn) (~20 mg/L), chloromycetin (~10 mg/L), or neomycin (~4 mg/L). Maracyn is easiest to use, but it may also kill beneficial algae and Gram-positive bacteria.

The most effective phosphate adsorbers for reef tanks are ceramics (metal hydroxides). The important ceramic ferric oxide hydroxide is impregnated into textiles sold as replaceable adsorbant disks.

The disks quickly saturate and must be replaced when phosphate levels again rise. Among the ceramic liquids, granules, and impregnated pad brands are Phosphate Sponge, Chemi-Mat, PhosGuard, Phosphate and Silicate Magnet, Phos-Ban, Phos-Pure, and Phosphate Filter Pads. Canisters for impregnated granules of ferric oxide hydroxide include the PhosBan Reactor, Nautilus Phos Reactor, and the Kent Nautilus Phos-Reactor. All of them work on simple adsorption; the term "reactor" is hyperbole.

Nuisance Algae Control

Fast-growing algae (red, green, brown, golden-brown) and cyanobacteria are controlled in the wild by constant cropping (there is something to eat everything) and limited nutrients. We can simulate both methods in our artificial reef environments.

Limiting Nutrients

The principal nutrients to be limited are nitrogen as nitrate, phosphate as the inorganic form also called orthophosphate, and silica as silicic acid, a nutrient for diatoms that incorporate it into their skeletal tests. Nitrates, phosphates, and silicates may be minor contaminants of tap water, but only nitrates have adverse health effects in high concentrations. Groundwaters in coastal communities and in the Great Basin of the western states are often high in orthophosphates.

Nutrients in normal (N to P ratio) concentrations may increase green hair algae. Nutrients in abnormal concentrations may increase blue-greens (cyanobacteria). Control orthophosphate to keep it below 0.02 mg/L.

Reverse osmosis (RO) can greatly reduce nitrates and phosphates, but not silicates. Distilled or deionized (DI) water will reduce all three nutrients.

Protein Skimming

Macroalgae, bacteria, and cyanobacteria all form biofilms that become mats through succession. These biofilms and mats secrete dissolved organic chemicals (DOC) that provide nutrients for cyanobacterial growth. Foam fractionation (protein skimming) reduces DOCs in water, starving the cyanobacteria and shifting the growth advantage to red and green macroalgae. This shift occurs within two weeks of an aquarium being provided with protein skimming.

Housekeeping: The bare glass bottom of a reef tank without aragonite should be siphoned to remove animal wastes and the fungi, cyanobacteria, and other microbes living in the waste. Nuisance algae on rocks and glass should be scraped, clipped, power-washed with tap water, or the rocks removed to a darkened barrel of seawater with erythromycin (Maracyn) to kill the algae. Afterward, rinse the rock and quarantine it in clean seawater for a week when it should be suitable for return to the reef tank.

Herbivores

Herbivorous snails, fishes, sea urchins, and other animals graze and crop non-calcareous algae. Keep at least two herbivorous snails (*Turbo, Astraea*) per gallon of tank capacity, or fewer if you can get large snails. Some hermit crabs (*Clibanarius*) and Sally Lightfoot mangrove crabs (*Grapsus*) will consume cyanobacteria. Yellow, yelloweye, and sailfin tangs, Moorish idols, foxfaces (*Lo*), and pygmy angelfishes (*Centropyge*) are often voracious grazers, but powder blue tangs and lyretailed angels are planktivores, attractive but useless for algae control.

Chapter Thirteen
Corals

The Phylum Cnidaria (previously Coelenterata) includes jellyfishes, anemones, soft corals, stony corals, fire corals, sea fans, sea pens, and other hydroids familiar to visitors to tropical islands. (The related Phylum Ctenophora includes comb jellies, a few of which have been kept recently in public aquaria, but not in reef tanks.)

Most stony corals are important reef builders because the outer calcium carbonate skeletons adhere to adjacent and earlier or previous skeletons of any species, but some large individual corals live freely on sand and make no contribution to the growth of the reef. Soft corals, with rare exceptions, do not contribute to reef structure but are common reef inhabitants. Many soft corals emit terpenoids and other chemicals, natural fat-soluble polymers similar to lemon oil and terpentine, and toxic to other corals (allelopathic). Terpenoids may be concentrated by nudibranchs immune to the toxins. These nudibranchs digest the coral tissue and store the terpenoids for their own defense from predatory fish. Many terpenoids are pharmacologically active, and have important medical applications. Other nudibranchs concentrate stinging cells of corals for their own defense; they are discussed in Chapter 16.

Where corals occur on the reef makes for intellectually stimulating, but irrelevant, discussions. More relevant is the experience of aquarists successful with those corals or not. The surge and sunlight on the ridge top of a reef cannot be duplicated in an aquarium. You can pretend it does, but don't expect your corals to have the same imagination. Corals should be positioned according to lighting and current regimes that other aquarists have learned provide the best survival and growth, irrespective of where they occur in nature. Corals such as *Tubastrea* do not have zooxanthellae and do well in shade (but do not require it) when you provide them currents and zooplankton. *Tubastrea* in the wild live in caves and shade, not because they require it, but because corals needing light cannot compete with them in the shade. Delicate mushroom anemones need light for their zooxanthellae but cannot withstand strong currents at the outflow of a powerhead discharge. Mushrooms often occur in quiet, surge-free lagoons where other corals cannot survive the lower oxygen concentration and higher temperature. Free-living stony corals are often slowly mobile on sand in the wild and should be placed on sand in your tank rather than on a stack of rocks, as they tend to walk off cliffs. Reef-building corals should be sandwiched between pieces of live rock, tied to the rock with rubber bands or plastic twist ties, or cemented to the rock with non-toxic adhesives in order to withstand powerful currents. Soft corals may be attached to live rock with rubber bands, plastic ties, or toothpicks through the base and into the rock. If already attached to a shell or rock, they may be emplaced as for reef-builders.

Coral Metabolites

Many beginners keep hard and soft corals in a single long tank, with the soft corals downcurrent from the hard, and the aquarium provided with carbon filtration. It's a bad idea because soft corals often emit noxious chemicals (and some can move around), while hard corals often send out aggressive fighting and feeding tentacles. Mixing these types in one small confined space may look natural but it can be stressful to the animals.

Many soft corals emit chemicals that can poison hard corals (that's how they get living space in the wild), discourage predators, prevent nearby settling of larvae of other corals, act as sexual attractants or dissuaders, or have functions we do not understand. Many of the chemicals produced by anemones and soft corals can kill hard or unrelated soft corals.

The principal chemicals produced by soft corals are terpenes and terpenoids, prostaglandins and other prostanoids, and hormone-like polyhydroxysterols. Some are defensive, others prevent algal overgrowth, and still others fend off microbial diseases. Mostly, we know what the chemicals can do, but we don't know what they do in the wild. In the laboratory some specific terpenoids have anti-leukemia, anti-AIDS, anti-algae (preventing overgrowth), anti-bacterial, cytotoxic, and lethal effects, while other chemicals simply seem to be pigments. But pigments are in the eye (and brain) of the beholder and may have uses other than recognition or have chemical functions we do not recognize. Many recently discovered chemicals are being tested for medical applications. We also now know that some of these sub- stances are made by the corals even when bleached of their symbiotic algae.

Mixing and Matching Corals

Soft corals may sting, burn, or digest competitors, and should be far from immovable, vulnerable hard corals. Soft corals secrete copious mucus that can smother and kill a hard coral, so keep the hard corals close to the powerhead discharge, and soft corals downstream and distant (a separate tank is better). Fire corals (hydrocorals) are not true hard corals (scleractinians), but their calcareous skeleton makes them seem hard. Their powerful stingers and rapid growth are reasons to keep them away from all other species. The easiest tank to keep is one that contains photosynthesizing hard corals, soft corals, *or* fire corals, but not a mixture. It's easy to observe the interactions of incompatible fishes, but corals suffer silently.

Life Cycle and Classification

What makes a Cnidarian? All cnidarians have a unique structure called the cnidocyte (stinger cell), found in no other animals, and just two layers in the embryo called the ectoderm and endoderm (higher animals have a third layer between them). The ectoderm will generate the adult outer layer containing cnidocytes and tentacles; in some it also secretes a crystalline calcium carbonate or calcite called aragonite. The embryonic endoderm becomes the layer lining the gastrovascular cavity or gut, where the polyp feeds, excretes, and respires. If the cnidarian is to have symbiotic zooxanthellae, they will be located in the cells lining the gastrovascular cavity.

Classification Within the Phylum Cnidaria

Subphylum Medusozoa
  Class Hydrozoa
    Order Athecata (= Hydrocorallinae, = Anthomedusae)
      Suborder Capitata
        Families Moerisiidae, Sphaerocorynidae, Tricylusidae, Candelabridae, Acaulidae, Euphysidae, Corymorphidae, Paracorynidae, Tubulariidae, Margelopsidae, Halocordylidae, Dicylocorynidae, Corynidae, Velellidae, Cladonemidae, Eleutheriidae, Halocorynidae, Hydrocorynidae, Solanderiidae, Cladocorynidae, Zancleidae, Teissieridae, Milleporidae
      Suborder Filifera
        Families Eudendriidae, Calycopsidae, Protiaridae, Pandeidae, Niobiidae, Cytaeidae, Bougainvilliidae, Russelliidae Rathkeidae, Rhysiidae, Stylasteridae, Hydractiniidae, Ptilocodiidae, Clavidae, Polyorchidae
    Order Thecata
        Families Campanulariidae, Campanulidae, Lafoeidae, Bonneviellidae, Haleciidae, Syntheciidae, Sertulariidae, Plumulariidae, Mitrocomidae, Laodiceidae, Melicertidae, Dipleurosomatidae, Eutimidae, Aequoridae, Phialellidae, Calycellidae, Lovenellidae, Eirenidae, Timoididae, Phialucidae
    Order Limnomedusae
      Family Olindiidae
    Order Siphonophora
      Suborder Physophorida
        Families Physaliidae (=Chondrophoridae), Rhizophysidae, Apolemiidae, Agalmidae, Pyrostephidae, Physophoridae, Athorybiidae, Rhodaliidae, Forskaliidae
      Suborder Calycophora
        Families Prayidae, Hippopodiidae, Diphyidae, Clausophyidae, Sphaeronectidae, Abylidae
    Order Trachymedusae
        Families Geryonidae, Ptycogastridae, Petasidae, Halicreatidae, Rhopalonematidae
    Order Narcomedusae
        Families Cuninidae, Aeginidae, Solmarisidae
    Order Actinulida
        Families Halammohydridae, Otohydridae
    Order Pteromedusae
      Family Tetraplatidae
  Class Scyphozoa
    Order Stauromedusae
        Families Eleutherocarpidae, Cleistocarpidae
    Order Coronatae
        Families Nausithoidae, Atollidae, Atorellidae, Linuchidae, Paraphyllinidae, Periphyllidae, Semaeostomeae, Pelagiidae, Cyaneidae, Ulmaridae
    Order Rhizostomae
        Families Rhizostomatidae, Stomolophidae, Cassiopeidae, Cepheidae, Mastigiidae, Versurigidae, Thysanostomidae, Lynchnorhizidae, Catostylidae, Lobonematidae
  Class Cubozoa
    Order Cubomedusae
        Families Carybdeidae, Chirodropidae

Classification Within the Phylum Cnidaria (continued)

Subphylum Anthozoa
  Class Ceriantipatharia
  Class Antipatharia
    Order Antipatharia
      Families Antippathidae, Leiopathidae, Dendrobrachiidae
    Order Cerianthria
      Families Cerianthidae, Botrucnidiferidae, Arachnactidae
  Class Alcyonaria (= Octocorallia)
    Order Stolonifira
      Families Cornulariidae, Clavulariidae, Tubiporidae
    Order Testacea
      Families Telestidae, Pseudocladochonidae
    Order Alcyonacea
      Families Alcyoniidae, Astrospiculariidae, Nephtheidae, Siphonogorgiidae,
      Viguieriotidae, Xeniidae
    Order Coenothecalia
      Family Helioporidae
    Order Gorgonacea
      Families Briereidae, Subergorgiidae, Coralliidae, Melithaeidae,
      Paramuriceidae, Anthothelidae, Paragorgiidae, Parisididae, Keroeididae,
      Acanthogorgiidae, Plexauridae, Gorgoniidae
    Order Pennatulacea
      Families Veretillidae, Echinoptilidae, Renillidae, Kophobelemnidae,
      Anthoptilidae, Funiculinidae, Protoptilidae, Stachyptilidae, Scleroptilidae,
      Chunellidae, Umbellulidae, Virgulariidae, Pennatulidae, Pteroeididae
  Class Zoantharia (= Hexacorallia)
    Order Actinaria
      Families Gonactiniidae, Boloceroididae, Edwardsiidae, Halcampidae,
      Ilyanthidae, Andresiidae, Actiniidae, Alciidae, Phyllactidae, Bunodidae,
      Stoichactidae, Minyadidae, Aurelianidae, Phymanthidae, Actinodendridae,
      Thalassianthidae, Discosomidae, Actinostolidae, Isophelliidae, Paractidae,
      Metriidae, Diadumenidae, Aiptasiidae, Sagartiidae, Hormathiidae,
      Stichodactylidae
    Order Corallimorpharia
      Families Corallimorphiidae, Actinodiscidae
    Order Zoanthiniaria (= Zoanthidea)
      Families Epizoanthidae, Zoanthidae
    Order Scleractinia
      Suborder Astrocoeniina
        Families Thamnasteriidae, Astrocoeniidae, Pocilloporidae, Acroporidae
      Suborder Fungiina
        Families Agariciidae, Siderastreidae, Fungiidae, Poritidae
      Suborder Faviina
        Families Faviidae, Rhizangiidae, Oculinidae, Meandrinidae, Merulinidae,
        Pectiniidae, Mussidae
      Suborder Caryophylliina
        Families Caryophylliidae, Flebellidae
      Suborder Dendrophylliina
        Family Dendrophylliidae

Cnidaria occur in two life forms, the (sedentary) polyp form and the (drifting) medusa form. Generally the parts are the same, but one form attaches by its base and the other is unattached and drifts upside down. Many cnidarians have alternating stages in the life cycle, while others have abridged cycles in which one stage is reduced or absent.

The polyp is flat at the attachment end. The gastrovascular (gut and respiratory) cavity at the other end is surrounded by tentacles. Hard coral polyps secrete an aragonite cup called the corallite from the outer layer's base and lower sides. Some free-living corals consist of a single large polyp. Colonial polyps bud at the edges to produce more polyps, each then producing its own corallite. Growth is accompanied by the accumulation of many daughter corallites budding laterally and vertically. With time, the colony becomes massive and rock-like, and is called a corallum. A single polyp, free-living stony coral may have a corallite the size of a man's hand, and is both corallite and corallum. Other typical corallums are the massive brain corals, extensively-branching staghorns, and some large encrustations.

The unattached medusa stage drifts with the gastrovascular opening and tentacles pointing downward. It's plump, with a jelly-like matrix between the inner and outer body layers. That's why the common name for most medusas is jellyfish. The medusa develops sex organs that emit eggs and sperm. The fertilized egg (zygote) develops into an embryo that differentiates into a ciliated larval stage called a planula. The planula drifts, swims, and finally settles down to metamorphose into a polyp. The polyp grows larger and may simply grow into one large polyp, or it may divide into hundreds or thousands of small polyps attached to each other. Reef-building colonial polyps secrete an aragonite corallite that eventually separates from the base and produces a new layer on top, with a cavity between. The corallum thus becomes ever more layered and massive.

The epidermis contains the cnidocytes. The most common cnidocyte is the nematocyst, a pressurized capsule with a coiled, barbed filament ejected when the cell is stimulated. Some nematocysts are warheads within warheads, the tip piercing the prey, and the barbs along the filament injecting a paralyzing neurotoxin. Nematocysts sting zooplankton, phytoplankton, and ichthyoplankton to be used as food brought into the gastrovascular cavity by the tentacles. Another type of cnidocyte, the spirocyst, has a sticky filament that adheres to hard-shelled crustaceans that cannot be penetrated by stinging filaments. Many sea anemones feel sticky to the touch (spirocyst), but being brushed by the tentacles of a Portuguese Man O' War will cause searing agony (nematocyst).

Classification

The Phylum Cnidaria was traditionally divided into jellyfishes and their allies (subphylum Medusozoa), and the soft and stony corals (subphylum Anthozoa). Today, molecular genetics allows tracking relationships of corals through chromosomal and mitochondrial DNA, and even by their RNA or their proteins (proteinomics). Genes and parts of genes can be identified and mapped, correlated with genes or gene parts in other animals, the relationships statistically evaluated for most likely common ancestry, and relationships sorted, assisted by programs developed, tested, and proven time and again, making traditional taxonomy subject to rigorous checking. This has produced surprises and will continue to alter our perceptions of who is related to whom. Everything will be written anew and differently, as mutations (alterations, replications, deletions, translocations) of specific genes replace our intuitively derived taxonomy.

In this book I use a traditional classification scheme for sorting and putting things in comfortable order. How we perceive related groups (clades) will certainly change in coming years, so the scientific names should be used as labels or tags for identification, but not relied on for relationships. Most of the world's species of Cnidaria are not available because of protected status, depth or distance inaccessibility, difficulty in keeping them alive, rarity, or lack of interest. Local laws everywhere make it increasingly difficult to collect live corals from the wild, which is rewarding efforts at propagation. The hobby is expanding more because of new methods and equipment than new species. The availability of corals is getting better more from commercial propagation of fragments than from importations. New kinds of corals continue to be introduced by public aquariums in controlled releases. Some new corals may be identified only to the family level. Relationships provide starting points for considering the care of corals not in this book.

Hydrocorals

The Hydrocorals contain fire and lace corals, jellyfishes, and box jellyfishes.

The Milleporidae or fire corals are hard corals that are unique in develop-

Upright fronds of fire coral, Millepora alcicornis, *cover the nearshore bottom at Bonaire, while orange* Tubastrea *corals grow in their shadow.*

ing a tiny medusa-like reproductive stage in cups on the corallum. These medusa-like growths produce eggs and sperm that combine to form a zygote that develops into a drifting football-shaped, ciliated planula larva.

Fire corals have central gastropores (holes for the feeding polyps) surrounded by smaller dactylopores (holes for nonfeeding and powerful stinging defensive polyps). Both the hair-like tentacles of the polyps and the smooth surface of the corallum are armed with stinging cells. Contact causes a burning sting; snorkelers thrown by surge onto the smooth plates while trying to catch baby jewelfish learn not to get close again.

Fire corals are eaten by filefish and damaged by storms and hot water, but are rarely overgrown by algae and are

Sweeper Tentacles

Many anemones, soft corals, black corals, and stony corals have long, searching epidermal tentacles called acrorhagi used to sweep the surrounding areas for enemies or competitors. Acrorhagi can sweep areas far beyond the feeding tentacles, their nematocysts stinging other anemones or corals that come too close.

Other Cnidarians have elongated gastrodermal filaments called acontia that extend far outside the gastrovascular cavity to sweep the surrounding area for food. These nutritive filaments are extensions of the digestive tract that, alien-like, find and digest other cnidarians. Gastrodermal filaments or acontia defend against enemies resistant to stinging cells. In anemones, they're also called fighting tentacles.

Epidermal stinging tentacles and gastrodermal nutritive filaments are most active at night, and can be seen using a flashlight after dark.

less vulnerable to pollution than reef-building corals. Their zooxanthellae-bearing polyps are hidden beneath a stony yellow-brown crust. The Caribbean *Millepora alcicornis, M. complanata,* and *M. squarrosa* are differentiated by their growth forms. Pacific *Millepora* include the upright, leaf-like *M. platyphylla* and *M. dichotoma,* staghorn-like *M. tenella,* and the lumpy crusted *M. exaesa.* Fire corals also occur in arctic waters and at great depths, feeding everywhere on zooplankton. Fire corals grow rapidly but should not be housed with other corals, which they will sting and damage. They've reproduced sexually in captivity, turning the aquarium milky white and as odoriferous as a swamp.

The Stylasteridae or lace corals occur in caves and shade in fan-shaped or bush-like colonies. The name derives from the star-shaped gastropores, which, as in *Millepora,* are surrounded by dactylopores. *Stylaster* occurs in the Atlantic and Pacific, *Distichopora* only in the Pacific. All are suitable for reef aquaria, but delicate.

Jellyfishes are too difficult to feed, too large, or otherwise not suitable for aquaria. Box jellies are specialized small jellyfishes with extraordinarily toxic stinging cells. Box jellyfish kill swimmers every year, causing many tropical Pacific resorts to regularly close their beaches when they appear. Every reef aquarist wants to dive or snorkel a reef, and should be aware of this menace. Box jellies are a good reason to wear wet suits and swim lifeguard-protected beaches or travel with a professional dive company. If you see one in the water with you, there will be many more between you and the beach or the boat.

Anthozoa—Soft Corals

The Anthozoa contain the anemones and soft corals, 6,500 species of cnidarians that lack a medusa stage. Reproduction is mostly by budding or division. The occasional sexual reproduction results in a swimming larva that eventually settles and grows into a miniature polyp. Anthozoans in plankton-poor waters rely on symbiotic zooxanthellae for nutrition, while those in caves and plankton-rich waters use cnidocytes to feed on zooplankton.

Ceriantharia

Tube-dwelling anemones are inexpensive and pretty, but some of them eat fishes. The stinging tube-dwelling

Symbiotic Zooxanthellae

Many Cnidaria contain *Symbiodinium* zooxanthellae in their tissues. Reef-building hard corals with zooxanthellae are called hermatypic, and those not reef-builders are called ahermatypic. Many non-reef builders, soft corals, and anemones also contain symbiotic algae, as do clams, some echinoderms, some protozoans, and other animals. The corals do not digest the zooxanthellae for two reasons. First, the algae are within the cnidarian's gut cells, rather than on the outside (inside the gut) where they could be washed with secreted digestive enzymes (as they are in giant clams). Second, coral polyps, like most animals, lack the enzyme cellulase, required for dissolving plant cell walls. In some algae, the cell walls are porous or leaky, allowing digestive enzymes to get through. Some soft corals and acroporid hard corals that digest phytoplankton may feed by this method.

Zooxanthellae leak half their production of the sugar alcohol glycerol, the sugar glucose, and the amino acid alanine to the host polyp. In return, the polyp provides a place to live, protection from predation by zooplankton, and plant nutrients (phosphates, ammonia, other substances) acquired from the capture of prey by their tentacles and excreted as metabolic waste.

During extreme cold or heat, symbiotic algae may be expelled (coral "bleaching"). If the algae remain expelled very long, the corals may die of starvation; if temporary, the corals recover. So important are symbiotic algae to corals that they are passed on inside the fertilized egg during sexual reproduction. In the wild, many corals recover from bleaching as the polyps are reinvaded by local heat-tolerant strains of *Symbiodinium*. These zooxanthellae multiply and expand into the rest of the coral community. The replacement heat-resistance *Symbiodinium* have different proportions of unsaturated oils in their cells, and this difference may account for their heat resistance or simply be a coincidence.

With few exceptions, symbiotic zooxanthellae are limited by light to depths of little more than 200 feet and temperatures that do not fall much below 68°F. Corals that live deeper or colder rely on zooplankton and phytoplankton for nutrition and their own excretory functions for disposal of waste ammonia.

The zooxanthellae of the Cnidaria and other invertebrates are members of the single dinoflagellate group *Symbiodinium*, a large genus of mostly unnamed species clustered into seven groups or clades. The explosive speciation of *Symbiodinium* dates back about 50 million years, not long in evolutionary time, but their ancestors have been around far longer. Part of the problem in interpreting the evolution of *Symbiodinium* is that they're all haploid species with but a single set of chromosomes, making it difficult to determine how in the world they evolved into so many genetically distinct but separate types.

anemones (*Cerianthus, Isarachnanthus, Pachycerianthus*) have outer and inner rings of tentacles. There is no foot, nor calcareous skeleton. When disturbed, tube-dwellers withdraw into an extensive mucus tube up to three feet long

Cerianthus *tube anemones are carnivorous and need hand-feeding.*

Alcyonaria

The Alcyonaria, or octocorals, comprise 1,000 species of colonial soft corals with each polyp divided into eight segments, from the tentacles to the partitions down the gullet. The groups of aquarium interest are gorgonians, sea pens, mushrooms, and star polyps.

If a skeleton occurs, it is internal and can be calcareous or horny. The spicules are taxonomically diagnostic for many species, and are ornate in gorgonians and smooth in sea pens.

Generally, soft corals can do fine under full-spectrum daylight plus actinic VHO lamps, not less than 5 watts per gallon for 12 hours a day. They require strong but indirect currents to sweep away extrusions of slime and waste tissue, which may contain terpenoids. Some capture zooplankton, others do not. To determine feeding behavior, squirt newly hatched brine shrimp directly onto the tentacles with a food baster. The soft corals will either ignore the food or wrap their tentacles around it and deliver it to the mouth. Gorgonians also capture and eat meiofauna (tiny sand-dwelling invertebrates) and detritus stirred into the water column (hand stirring, powerhead blasting). Mushroom anemones are piscivorous, and appreciate an occasional dead guppy.

whose walls are strengthened by particles of shell and sand. Tube anemones sting other corals and will capture and eat small fishes.

Antipatharia

The Antipatharia or black and thorny corals are anemones that secrete a proteinaceous skeleton. Many tropical island nations protect the deepwater black corals *Antipathes, Cirrhipathes,* and *Stichopathes,* mostly branching, bushlike or whiplike colonial forms with a dark, horny support similar to skeletons of sea fans. Black corals have been overharvested for jewelry; the remaining colonies are jealously guarded by dive operators. Black corals are no longer kept in reef tanks and their protected status should keep them from further collecting for jewelry or the hobby.

Clavulariidae and Cornulariidae

The Cornulariiae and Clavulariidae (star and daisy polyps) are ideal corals for beginners, easy to keep and attractive, some fluorescing under UV light. They have a weak internal skeleton of calcareous spicules. *Clavularia* resembles a cluster of white palm trees with green centers. *Pachyclavularia* has green polyps with white centers and lives inside tiny purple tubes resembling organ pipe corals. *Cornularia*, *Clavularia,* and *Pachyclavularia* should have both actinic and metal halide light for their symbiotic zooxanthellae. Provide moderate indirect current from a powerhead. They do not eat supplemental zooplankton. New polyps arise from runners that spread over rocks and even onto the glass. To propagate them, place a rock next to the colony. After the runners spread onto the rock, slice the runner with a single edged razor blade, and remove rock and new colony to a separate location.

Tubiporidae

More difficult to keep is the closely related organ pipe (Tubiporidae: *Tubipora*). The dark red calcareous skeleton is common in shell shops. A slow grower, it fares poorly in captivity because the pieces for sale are fragments, and the torn interconnected polyps seldom heal. Unbroken colonies of the brown polyps need high-intensity (high wattage) metal halide light, moderate current, and supplementary feedings with zooplankton (brine shrimp, mysids, bloodworms, small euphausid shrimp).

Helioporidae

At first glance, blue coral might be mistaken for fire coral but for its color. *Heliopora coerulea* uses iron salts to construct a blue calcareous skeleton hidden by the overlying dull brown polyps. This shallow and quiet water hermatypic coral has symbiotic zooxanthellae, and is the only octocoral contributing to calcareous reef structure. It is seldom in commercial supply.

Alcyonaceans

Most of the soft corals in the hobby are leather corals or Alcyonaceans, fleshy animals with tiny polyps on the top (the capitulum) that withdraw into the body mass (basal stalk), leaving behind a shiny surface above. The polyps may

The polyps of Sarcophyton glaucum *resemble miniature anemones.*

Sarcophyton elegans is an easy soft coral to keep and propagate through cuttings.

Lobophyton planaflorum *has finger-like processes.*

be nocturnal, diurnal, or oblivious to light. Most have symbiotic zooxanthellae, but grow better when fed brine shrimp and iodine is added to the water. Alcyonaceans compete for space by sending out stinging sweeper tentacles, discharging mucus, and by emitting noxious allelopathic terpenes and other chemicals that prevent hard coral larvae from settling nearby. Terpenes and other chemicals also discourage overgrowth by algae, may be distasteful or poisonous to fishes and to other corals, or protect against invasive bacteria. Some Alcyonaceans move and may migrate over *Acropora* and *Pocillopora* leaving a trail of dead stony coral in their wake. Many will multiply in captivity by dividing from the base of the main and branch stalks, none more prolific than the beautiful pulse corals (*Xenia*). Many alcyonaceans brood embryos in their bodies, with the minute offspring migrating a few inches from the parent to start a new colony.

Alcyoniidae

The Alcyoniidae contain the hardy leather corals *Alcyonium, Lobophyton, Parerythropodium, Sarcophyton* and *Sinularia,* and the colt coral *Cladiella.*

Sarcophyton feeds on products of its zooxanthellae by day, and captures zooplankton at night. It has large polyps for prey capture and smaller polyps (siphonozoids) that aid water circulation over the surface. Its powerful toxins kill hard corals in nature, and can also kill other soft corals and prevent the settlement of larvae of hard corals nearby (allelopathy). Killing competitors of its own kind and of larval hard corals allows it to spread and colonize a large area, keeping out reef builders. It reproduces by budding, and is readily propagated by cuttings.

The similar *Lobophyton* has finger-like processes instead of mushroom-like folds in the margins, and ridges radiate from its center. It has different kinds of polyps for feeding and circulation.

Sinularia is distinguished from the others in having a single type of polyp. *Cladiella* species are difficult to identify, requiring examination of the spicules under a microscope. Most of us hope the exporter or breeder has done that.

All need a moderate indirect current from a powerhead, and a mix of actinic and full-spectrum fluorescent, VHO, or metal halide light when more than two feet from the light source. Feeding brine shrimp nauplii, copepods, or rotifers with a food baster just before the lights go off is beneficial to corals and other invertebrates such as feather duster worms. Always rinse live brine shrimp and resuspend in clean water so you never add pollutant laden hatch water to the aquarium. For directed feeding of a single coral at a time, use airline tubing to suck up the cleaned and resuspended brine shrimp and squirt them onto the coral's tentacles.

Sinularia *corals also have finger-like processes.*

Nephtheidae and Siphonogorgiidae

The Nephtheidae (*Dendronephthya, Nephthea, Lemnalia, Litophyton*) and Siphonogorgiidae (*Catagorgia, Scleronephthya*) are the tree corals. Some are hermatypic (reef builders with symbiotic zooxanthellae in their tissues) and others ahermatypic (not reef builders). The spectacular *Dendronephthya* is spiny to the touch, requires light for its symbiotic algae, and doesn't last long unless it gets supplementary feeding with live phytoplankton (microalgae), which you can grow or purchase. The jury is still out on bottled preparations

Sarcophyton may grow mushroom-like folds.

Litophyton arboretum, *a tree coral, requires feeding, but can be fragmented after a few months.*

Dendronephthya rubeola *is difficult to keep, and not for beginners.*

and algal pastes. In general, beginners should avoid *Dendronephthya*. The similar (and smooth-skinned) *Scleronephthya* is easier to keep and even propagate from cuttings, but it needs currents, moderate but not bright light, supplemental iodine, and feedings of zooplankton such as baby brine shrimp or Cyclopeeze. It does not have symbiotic algae, hence the suitability of low lighting. *Scleronephthya* produces unique metabolites, including 19-norpregna-1,3,5 (10), 20-tetraen-3-*O*—fucopyranoside, whose antimalarial activity has important human medical value.

Xeniidae

The Xeniidae (*Xenia, Anthelia, Efflatounaria*) or pulse, pom-pom, or waving hand corals are as beautiful and inexpensive as they are popular. *Xenia* grows from a massive central stalk, individual polyps breaking away and starting new colonies. The similar *Anthelia* forms a spreading mat. Both may pulsate and rapidly multiply under metal halide light supplemented with actinic and full-spectrum fluorescent. They tolerate strong currents, but not directly on the colonies. Ravenous feeders on supplementary zooplankton, they can survive on bright light alone.

Gorgonacea and Pennatulacea

The Gorgonacea are the mostly shallow water sea fans, sea plumes, and sea whips. The Pennatulacea or sea pens occur from near shore to the abyss. The gorgonian *Holaxonia* has a skeleton of horny gorgonin (a keratin or complex protein, in this case also containing iodine and bromine). It resembles dark twigs attached to rocks by a short holdfast.

Xenia, *the pulse corals, multiply profusely and then divide at the base to release polyps that are carried to new locations.*

Anthellia *or pom-pom corals grow by multiplying at the base of the colony, but do not fragment as often as pulse corals.*

Scleraxonia is supported by calcareous spicules. A few gorgonaceans are encrusting rather than twig-like. In sea pens, the stalk is the lower end of a large central polyp embedded in the sediments and strengthened by calcareous spicules; there is no horny keratin. Smaller polyps grow along the sides of the main polyp. Some sea pens retract into the sediments when disturbed. Sea pens even grow in the cold, black abyss of the deep ocean.

The sperm are shed into the sea from a male colony, caught by a female colony, and the fertilized egg incubated within until it develops into a ciliated larva. The planula larva hatches and swims about until it finds a settling location, and then settles to metamorphose into the adult form and divide asexually to form a colony that will be male or female.

All gorgonaceans require strong current and surge, strong light for shallow

Polyps are extended in this Atlantic gorgonian.

Plexaurella *is a common Caribbean sea whip.*

Pseudopterogorgia *sea whips form large forests in the Caribbean and are harvested by lifting the rock to which the holdfast is attached.*

water forms, blue light for deepwater forms, calcium additives, iodine, mixed trace elements, and supplementary feedings of zooplankton such as brine shrimp, bloodworms, copepods, and daphnia squirted directly at the polyps with a food baster. Healthy, well-fed gorgonians and their relatives grow rapidly, but are sensitive to ammonia, which causes the polyps to retract if anything has died. Because polyps are connected, damage anywhere may kill the entire coral. In poor water or light, they decline fast and may not recover. High nitrate, phosphate, and too much iodine can lead to algal overgrowth.

Zoantharia

Zoantharia (= Hexacorallia) polyps are divided into six radial segments, from tentacles to gut. The 5,300 species include solitary and colonial forms with an external calcareous skeleton or none at all.

Actinaria

The sea anemones (Actinaria) are solitary, fleshy polyps with no skeleton, few-to-numerous tentacles and a mobile foot for gliding over hard surfaces. In aquariums, they usually reproduce by binary fission or multiple budding. *Nematostella vectensis*, an estuarine anemone with peculiar nematosomes in its gut (coelenteron), is one of five anemones that divide transversely (as you would cut down a tree); all other anemones divide longitudinally (as you would split logs). Anemones often adhere to rocks or shells. Many Actiniidae (*Actinia, Anemonia, Anthopleura, Bunodactis, Bunodosoma, Condylactis, Entacmaea, Macrodactyla, Physobranchia, Tealia*) require gravel or sand in which the foot is buried. Others do well on rocks. *Stom-*

Making Cuttings (Frags) from Soft Corals

You can make cuttings of mushroom anemones and leather, colt, pulse, and other soft corals that have been established a long time in the same tank. You'll need a sharp single-edged razor blade or fine-point scissors, and toothpicks, thin rubber bands, or a cyanoacrylate adhesive. First, find a rock to be the new base for the cutting. If using a toothpick to nail the fragment in place, make a small hole in the rock and mark it. Although you can often cut a soft coral completely through its main stalk, it is better to take a short branch or lobe. Slice or cut in a single quick motion (do not saw). Insert the toothpick through the wall and out the cut end, and stick it onto the hole in the rock. Or, slip the rubber band around the base of the fragment and then around the rock. Lean a small piece of rock near the coral fragment to keep it in place (the rock should be light enough so as not to squash the fragment, which then would disintegrate). The raw tissue of the fragment should heal and attach to the rock within three weeks, after which you can remove the leaning rock, cut the rubber band, or ignore the toothpick, which will disintegrate. The wounded donor, after a sharp reaction, rapidly recovers. Some coral breeders add vitamin C to the cut surfaces and tank water in the belief it aids wound healing, but there is no evidence to support this practice. Commercial coral farmers put the cuttings in pots with gravel or shell hash as an attachment base.

Another method in commercial use is to cut the soft coral into multiple (often six) longitudinal segments, but not completely through, and then return the sliced animal to the aquarium for recovery. After three weeks of healing, the divided soft coral is removed to a working bowl of seawater, and the segments finally severed from the rock through their bases. The bases are blotted on paper towels, and a drop of adhesive applied to the wound. After ten seconds, the sticky base is attached to a dry rock and held in place for 10 to 20 seconds. You can also attach the coral to a submerged rock, holding the glued end in place for 30 seconds, but success may require more than one attempt. The resilience of soft corals to amputations and chemicals is amazing to us, but many invertebrates have healing capabilities quite unlike anything in higher animals.

---

phia (Actinostolidae) can chemically sense predators, detach from the bottom, and swim away. People living in the cold-water Pacific Northwest or Atlantic Northeast are familiar with tide pool Metriidae. *Metridium* species are prominent, often colorful, large anemones of rocky bottoms, suitable for coldwater aquaria.

The colorful tropical flower anemones (Phymanthidae: *Phymanthus, Ragactis*) are zooxanthellae-containing intertidal anemones with accessory pigments sometimes said to protect against ultraviolet and infrared solar radiation when exposed at low tide. Unlike many intertidal animals that shrink under adverse conditions, these anemones stretch out as though sunbathing. The bright colors might be warnings to gulls or crabs that they taste bad.

Many actinarians have live-in *Periclimenes* or other symbiotic shrimp.

Large anemones need gravel to anchor the large foot.

Atlantic anemones may wander around the tank.

Getting Rid of *Aiptasia*

Methods for removing *Aiptasia* include picking them out with tweezers or using a hypodermic syringe to inject them with concentrated calcium chloride, brine solution, or vinegar. Biological control is easier. Peppermint shrimp (*Lysmata wurdemanni*) and at least one kind of nudibranch prey on *Aiptasia*. If you have an elegance coral, copy a trick from the tool-bearing crabs that use *Telmatactis*. Lift your elegance coral by its base and press the tentacles against those nasty *Aiptasia* anemones. One sting from an elegance coral should kill them.

Bartholomea (Aiptasiidae) is a white-ringed, brown anemone often symbiotic with *Alpheus* snapping or pistol shrimps that emit loud noises to frighten predatory fishes. Some anemones, such as *Telmatactis* (Isophelliidae), are carried as tools by crabs that use them to pick up food or sting enemies. *Adamsia* and *Calliactis* (Hormathiidae) occur on snail shells carried about by *Dardanus* and *Petrochirus* hermit crabs.

Quite a few anemones are clownfish hosts. *Entacmaea,* the bubble tip anemone (Actiniidae), is a fast grower that multiplies in captivity after first retreating to a dark area, shrinking its tentacles, and subsequently dividing to form two daughter anemones; it may be the hardiest clownfish host anemone available. *Stichodactyla* and *Heteractis* (Stichodactylidae) are carpet anemones requiring bright light, including actinic for their symbiotic zooxanthellae. *Stichodactyla* can kill and eat fishes other than its host clownfish, and even prey on other anemones. The Stoichactidae

Many Condylactis *require feedings of meat.*

Clownfish adapt to many Pacific carpet anemones.

(*Stoichactis, Homostichanthus, Radi-anthus, Gyrostoma*) carpet anemones also require bright light. *Cryptodendrum adhesivum* is the only member of the Thalassianthidae that is host to a clown-fish, *Amphiprion clarkii*. Its two kinds of tentacles are different colors and shapes, but unfortunately it does poorly in captivity

Other anemones are nuisances in a reef tank. *Aiptasia* (Aiptasiidae) is a small, rapidly multiplying anemone that stings other cnidarians unable to get out of the way and is difficult to eliminate. The Sagartiidae (*Actinothoe, Anthothoe, Sagartia, Sagartiogeton, Cereus*) can

Condylactis gigantea *is a common Caribbean sea anemone that doesn't stay put.*

Rhodactis *mushroom anemones bud faster under bright light.*

Actinodiscus coeruleus *is a readily propagated mushroom anemone.*

have a powerful sting and must be handled with rubber gloves or a net.

Corallimorpharia

The Corallimorpharia are mushroom anemones, not true sea anemones but false (soft) corals. Many species are native to shallow lagoons or bays enriched (polluted) with nutrients. They need minimal light and little current, and may safely be kept in small (10 gallon) aquaria with low-wattage actinic and daylight fluorescent bulbs and an outside power filter. In larger reef tanks, place them away from strong currents (they tear easily) and intense light. Many produce potent toxins so don't put them in close proximity to other corals. Some of the elephant ear mushrooms will eat small fishes, but supplemental feeding isn't required.

The most popular mushrooms are *Corynactis* (Corallimorphiidae) and the Actinodiscidae genera *Actinodiscus, Amplexidiscus, Rhodactis* (protuberances with small points), and *Ricordia* (with rounded protuberances and sold as colonies on live rock called Florida mushroom rock). *Actinodiscus* are inexpensive, often blue, brown, or reddish, and usually sold in groups with many individuals to a "mushroom rock." They reproduce by budding at the edges or dividing at the base, faster under brighter light. You can transfer a small budded mushroom anemone recently separated from its parent to another rock, where it might start another colony. You can also propagate them by cuttings. Some mushroom anemones eat fish, and can be fed guppies, mollies, or minnows on a stick of rigid airline tubing. Corallimorphs also absorb nutrients from the water (doing especially well in heavily fed tanks containing fishes). These are colorful, hardy soft corals, the colors largely the result of their symbiotic zooxanthellae. They don't undergo "bleaching," but fading in color intensity could indicate zooxanthellae elimination and a water quality problem.

Zoanthinaria

The Zoanthinaria (= Zoanthidea) or sea mats are hardy, fast-growing, usually inexpensive colonial anemones forming clusters on rocks, shells, sponges, mangroves, brown algae stalks, and other firm substrata, even overgrowing filamentous algae. Many have green, red, yellow, or rust-colored pigments and symbiotic zooxanthellae. A few have powerful toxins (*Palythoa* palytoxin) that protect them from predation.

Sea mat rock is a commercial name for zooanthid-encrusted rubble rock. The two families of sea mats are the Epizoanthidae with *Epizoanthus* and *Parazoanthus*, and the Zoanthidae with *Palythoa* and *Zoanthus*. Some sea mats cannot live away from the sponges upon which they are found in nature, and the sponges cannot yet be kept alive in mini-reef aquaria. Individual polyps are not connected except during gemmation (see below), so damage to one polyp does not spread through the colony. Whether or not they have zooxanthellae, all do better if given live brine shrimp nauplii or live copepods, frozen adult brine shrimp, copepods, or bloodworms, and macerated shellfish. Native to nearshore or reef top habitats, sometimes exposed at low tide, they do best in smaller aquaria with strong light close to the surface in moderate to strong currents.

They reproduce by dividing near the base (gemmation). A small rock or shell placed against a colony will eventually be overgrown, and you can then cut the connections at the base with a single-edged razor blade and move the colonized rock or shell elsewhere. For large-scale propagation, chisel the colony into rocky fragments with a substantial base to protect the runners, and glue the fragments to new locations with cyanoacrylate (Super Glue) or other adhesive.

Scleractinia—Stony Corals

The Scleractinians are the major group of stony corals. Most are colonial reef-builders, their massive exoskeletons a honeycomb of calcareous cups with sharp ridges pressing in from the sides, and thin plates below walling off chambers of the colony's earlier polyps. The majority gets almost all their nutrition from symbiotic zooxanthellae; others are denizens of caverns and shaded ledges that feed by stinging or sticking zooplankton in the passing currents.

Shallow water stony corals exposed to the sun at low tide must possess protective substances to prevent the zooxanthellae and coral tissues from heating and burning under the sun's ionizing UV and hot IR irradiation.

Corals of the blue depths have supplemental pigments of unknown function, but that may be used in energy shifts. These deep corals absorb high-energy short-wave blue light, and somehow transform the rays to lower energy red waves (where solar red rays don't reach) to drive supplemental zooxanthellae photosynthesis. Red algae of great depths may also use this shifted blue radiant energy to drive photosynthesis.

About half the stony corals and a few other invertebrate groups of the Great Barrier Reef, and undoubtedly elsewhere in the South Pacific, shed gametes into the sea at night about two to five days after the full moon in October, November,

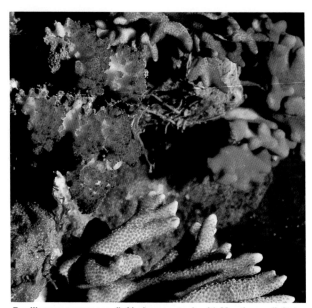
Pocillopora verrucosa *(left) shares a tank with* Montipora digitata.

The small polyp stony corals (SPS corals) are fast-growing photosynthetic hermatypic species with branches often tipped with red, blue, or purple pigments produced in response to intense lighting with 10,000K or 20,000K metal halide lamps. The pigments are unrelated to UV, and are not UV protective. Maintain the calcium concentration at or above 400 mg/L, alkalinity at 7–12 dKH or 2.5–4.5 meq/L, use strontium and iodine supplements, aragonite as a base, powerful surging currents, and carbon filtration plus skimming to keep DOC low. Because the small polyps are easily damaged, new specimens should be transported submerged under a Styrofoam float.

These corals ideally should have their own all-SPS tank. They are at considerable risk when placed with soft corals. Damaged SPS corals take a long time to recover, the wounds becoming foci of infections and polyp withdrawal. *Acropora* is especially vulnerable to protozoan infections from which it rarely recovers. Algal grazers (snails, tangs, pygmy angelfishes) help prevent algal overgrowth.

and/or December. Lunar and temperature periodicity has been replicated by some reef aquarists to induce spawning using artificial moonlight and temperature oscillation controlled by 30-day and longer timers.

Almost all species within the four families of the Astrocoeniina have zooxanthellae. They also are hermaphroditic, releasing sperm in the water that is taken up to internally fertilize the eggs, the zygotes then brooded well into the planula larval stage. This brooding is unique among scleractinian stony corals. (In many invertebrates, hermaphrodites fertilize each other, not themselves.) All four families have small polyp stony (SPS) corals, which is a descriptive, not a taxonomic, term.

Pocilloporidae

The Pocilloporidae (*Pocillopora, Seriatopora, Stylophora, Palauastrea*) are mostly corals of shallow upper reef slopes. *Madracis*, with zooxanthellar and non-zooxanthellar species, contains deepwater forms. *Pocillopora damicornis* is a fast grower that has been induced to spawn with an artificial lunar and temperature cycle that induces bursts of planula larvae every one or two months settling on the glass to begin new colonies. Also fast growers, *Stylophora* can be propagated by cutting its branches, the fragments doubling in size in three months. The red-polyped *Pocilloporida* species are not recommended for beginners.

Acroporidae

The closely related Acroporidae (*Acropora, Montipora, Anacropora,* and *Astreopora*) require intense VHO or metal halide lighting, strong alternating currents to wash particles from the polyps restricted to the stiff corallum, protein skimming, carbon filtration, and a constant, drip-wise addition of rapidly depleted calcium, magnesium, and strontium or an all-in-one supplement. Feed *Artemia* nauplii sparingly, if at all. Acroporids can be kept with soft corals, but far apart to avoid their terpenes and mucus, and might even get important nutrition from the DOC compounds secreted by soft corals, but that's not

Thin Acropora *branches break in violent storms and contribute to reef rubble at the base of the reef.*

Acropora digitifer is a Pacific species of this large genus.

Varying in body form by species and depth, this bulky Montipora *will adapt to powerful surges.*

Live elkhorn (Acropora palmata) in foreground contrasts with rubble of staghorn coral (Acropora cervicornis) on a Caribbean beach.

Montipora digitata *(left) branches profusely.*

Making Cuttings (Frags) of Hard Corals

Fast-growing branching corals like *Acropora*, popular Caryophylliidae like *Plerogyra* (bubble coral), and even massive brain corals like *Favia* can be snapped, cut, or broken and the fragments moved to another location. Broad-based brain corals should be cut with a diamond-edged power saw blade, and smoothed with a regular saw blade. Heavy stainless steel shears or simply snapping will suffice for thin branches; make the break or cut close to the base of the branch. Branch coral cuts should be quick or they will crush the tissues. Caryophylliids can also be placed in water in a plastic basin on their sides and broken at narrow points with a broad-bladed screwdriver struck with a hammer. The exposed end of the fragment is smeared with cyanoacrylate (Super Glue) or other underwater adhesive and pressed against a rock or shell until it holds; complete hardening takes more than a day. The coral fragment should not be placed in a reef tank until it shows recovery and even, in the case of branching corals, some growth, which can take a month or more. Fragments not affixed, but allowed to rest on shell hash or rubble, will attach by themselves over time.

settled. *Acropora*, with strong light and excellent water quality, has sexually reproduced in reef aquaria.

The most abundant of reef-building corals, Acroporids can be branching, encrusting, massively boulder-like, finger-like, or table-like. Many dominate the crest of the reef where, battered by waves and storms, their fast-growing branches break off and become hard substrata for hard and soft corals at all depths. *Acropora* is the largest genus of all corals with some 400 species. Atlantic snorkelers are familiar with abundant staghorn (*A. cervicornis*) and elkhorn (*A. palmata*) corals at Caribbean resort islands, but the Indo-Pacific has most of the species. *Acropora formosa* is a spectacularly fast grower. Cuttings originating with Dieter Steuber are widely distributed in the hobby. *Acropora* must be trimmed to keep them from spreading over the entire water surface where they shade the remaining corals.

Montipora is the second largest genus with about 100 species. *Astreopora* has 15–30 species with encrusting colonies resembling plates or toadstools. The half dozen *Anacropora* are small corals not associated with reefs.

Agariciidae

The Agariciidae are a mixed group from sheltered areas, some hermaphroditic, some with separate sexes, and some that brood zygotes to the planula larva stage. The colonies are leaf-like, plate-like, massive, or club- or finger-shaped. *Pavona* (cactus coral) are leaf-like (foliar) or plate-like and easily broken. Some colonies resemble toadstools and others mimic hammer corals. *Leptoseris* are delicately leaf-like colonial corals of protected waters, some forming overlapping plates with complex ridges and whorls. *Pachyseris* are typically leafy, forming massive colonies that can cover large areas of deep reefs. *Gardineroseris* is massive or encrusting and widespread. There is one massive species making up *Coeloseris*. *Agaracia* is strictly Atlantic and forms leaf-like or encrusting plate-like colonies, horizontal or vertical, mostly in protected waters up

Cactus coral, Pavona decussata, *is easily broken by falling rocks.*

to 80 meters (250 feet) deep. Members of the group require gentle to moderate currents and strong light provided by metal halide and VHO lamps, but do not need supplemental plankton.

Siderastreidae

The Siderastreidae are reef-building zooxanthellar corals requiring metal halide or VHO lighting and calcium, magnesium, and strontium supplements. Colonies consist of a single sex, are dome-shaped, finger-like, encrusting, or plate-like. *Psammocora* (usually massive or fingerlike) and *Coscinaraea* (usually plate-like) dominate the family. *Coscinaria* is cold tolerant and extends into the temperate zone. *Siderastrea* has the most widespread species with *S. radians* worldwide in the tropical Atlantic and Indo-Pacific, including the Red Sea. *Pseudosiderastrea* has only one species *S. tayami,* which ranges from Asia to northern Australia. *Anomastrea* and *Horastrea* are restricted to the western Indian Ocean.

Psammocora contigua requires metal halide or intense VHO light, and calcium and strontium supplements.

Fungiidae

Fungiidae or mushroom corals are distinctive in their radial symmetry and stand-alone habit. Some are elongate, but most are circular and flattened. They are entirely Indo-Pacific, and there is only one non-zooxanthellar genus (*Fungiacyathus*). These mostly non-reef-building (ahermatypic) stony corals usually consist of a single giant polyp on its own large corallite; those with several mouth openings are considered colonial. Despite massive size, many can right themselves if tumbled by a storm and climb out of the sand if buried. Moving like sea anemones, fungiids travel across sandy areas by gliding on ciliary hairs below or inflating and pulling forward with the tentacles above.

Sexes are almost always separate, the females brooding or not. They can also multiply by budding or dividing. Minute juveniles called acanthocauli develop from planula larvae or by budding from a buried or damaged parent. The acanthocaulus is a small stalked polyp that develops its calcareous plate at the end of the basal stalk, the skeleton forming from within the polyp rather than secreted from its base.

Fungia have a furrowed plate-like skeleton holding a single animal. *Cycloseris* are similar, but with a concave bottom. *Diaseris* has distinctive radial fractures signifying ongoing fragmentation, this mode of asexual reproduction often producing large aggregations on hard or quiet bottoms. *Halomitra pilaeus* is the Neptune's cap coral, its helmet-shaped colony plastered with longitudinally grooved platelets. *Sandalolitha* is similar, but the species have curved grooves and the platelets are more flattened than stacked. *Herpolitha, Polyphyllia*, and *Herpetoglossa* are colonial (more than one mouth), often longer than round. *Herpolitha* has two species, one angular at the tips (*H. weberi*), the other rounded at the tips (*H. limax*), both often

Underwater Cements

Underwater epoxies form inert, rock-hard products from the reaction between the amine of a polyamide resin and the epoxide of an epoxy resin. Epoxies are harmless to marine animals, inert after they react, and wonderful for adhering live animals to rocks, or rocks to one another. Hot-melt glue sticks are good for joining rocks, but must be used above water and allowed to dry before immersion. Super Glue cyanoacrylate adhesive is effective in air or water, on rocks, or live animals, but the bond between heavy rocks is fragile. Don't worry about the "cyano" in cyanoacrylate. It is not toxic like potassium cyanide. You can get most of these products at a hardware store.

massive and the heaviest of the Fungi-idae. Of the slipper corals, *Polyphyllia* has long tentacles providing a shaggy appearance, whereas *Herpetoglossa simplex* differs in skeletal structure.

With its long, white-tipped tentacles, *Heliofungia actiniformis* looks like a sea anemone until you discover its stony, *Fungia*-like skeleton below and notice that it doesn't have symbiotic clownfish or damsels among its tentacles. This largest of coral polyps can be 20 inches across with a mouth over an inch wide. It may be the only hermaphroditic fungiid. Because it moves around, it is easily damaged and may suffer infections lead-ing to death.

The leaf-like colonial reef-building (hermatypic) forms (not typical of fungi-ids) include *Lithophyllon* and *Podabacia*. *Lithophyllon* are uncommon to rare. *Podabacia crustacea* is similar but its grooved platelets are recurved at the ends as if withdrawing.

Fungiids should be placed on arago-nite sand with room to move about and feed on detritus and microbes gathered from the sand and water. They require little current, but in most tanks their zooxanthellae need intense light from metal halides and VHO bulbs capable of delivering energy to the bottom. In small or shallow aquaria, less light suffices, but fungiids are then vulnerable to shock from fluctuating water quality.

Poritidae

The Poritidae are zooxanthellar and with separate sexes. Sperm released into the water is gathered by females, and the fertilized eggs are retained and brooded through the planula stage. The predominant genera are *Porites* (with 12 short tentacles) and *Goniopora* (with 24 elongate tentacles).

The plate corals like **Fungia** *are not reef builders. When the tentacles are fully expanded, they mask the corallum plate so the coral resembles a sea anemone.*

Polyphyllia *has long tentacles and more than one mouth.*

Goniopora *are flowerpot corals of the Poritidae. These long-tentacled corals are often isolated by stinging competitors in their territory.*

Goniopora, the flowerpot corals (*G. stokesi, G. stutchburyi,* and *G. fructicosa*) have polyps and tentacles that sting other corals to maintain large territories, and neither have, nor need, sweeper tentacles. *Goniopora* often waste away after a few months, and are not recommended for beginners. They need intense light (metal halide and VHO) and moderate current. Their requirement for supplemental large zooplankton (especially frozen euphausid shrimp) and sensitivity to water quality changes make them troublesome to manage.

Porites are usually massive and lobed, but can be finger-like, branched or not. *Stylaraea* is probably a sub-genus of *Porites*.

Alveopora has some of the largest polyps known among colonial corals, those of *A. gigas* up to 10 cm long and

Colonies of Porites astreoides, *yellow porous coral, on rock at St. John, Virgin Islands.*

Porites lobata *holes are home to these blue* polychaetes.

Large Polyp Stony Corals (LPS Corals)

LPS corals refer to those stony coral species, in many families, that have large fleshy polyps, such as bubble or grape corals and many others. It is not a taxonomic, but a descriptive term. Many LPS corals have sweeper tentacles, which make them nasty neighbors to other corals. LPS corals in general are harder to propagate from cuttings because the large amount of tissue that must be damaged during fragmentation is especially susceptible to infection and healing is more difficult. Many LPS corals are otherwise hardy, but not easily propagated.

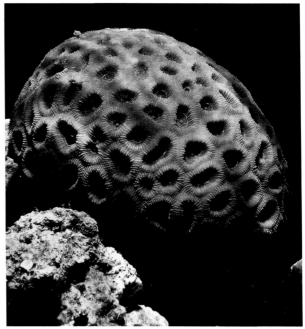

Favites *corallites share common adjacent ridges in this genus of about seven species.*

2 cm thick when fully extended. Reproduction is not known, and if different than described above, they may have to be removed from the Poritidae.

Faviidae

Zooxanthellar with a need for intense light, the faviid brain corals require metal halides supplemented with VHO actinic fluorescents and anything else you can throw at them; most important, keep them close to the light source. Almost all are massive forms that do well in moderate or strong currents. Supplemental plankton are not necessary, but basting the tank with *Artemia* nauplii just before the lights go out may be beneficial to these nocturnally active corals. A thin film of mucus indicates a healthy specimen. A few types need larger foods like meats placed at their tentacles just before dark.

Colonial and social hermaphrodites, the Pacific species shed eggs and

Mancinia mayori *is the Caribbean rose coral.*

Boulder coral, Montastrea, *has elevated corallites.*

Caulastrea furcata *has tall conical corellites, and one of just four species of this genus of Faviidae.*

sperm into the water during the night about five days after the full moon in October, November, and December in synchrony with the spawning of other lunar-triggered corals.

Newly imported faviid corals may not survive shipping and final transfer to a home aquarium. The damage might be the result of shipping, heat on the tarmac or in the hold, bouncing against container sides, or ammonia toxicity from too much time in the bag (the ammonia cannot be used by the coral's symbiotic algae in the dark package). In aquaria, they need supplemental strontium without which they cannot build new skeletal compartments for descendent polyps.

The Faviidae has more genera and the second largest number of species of any hard coral family. The majority are massive brain or boulder corals with multiple high-ridged corallites packed closely with circular, subcircular, or elongate meandrine corallites. A few faviids are plate-like or foliaceous (leaf-like), others arborescent or branched, and one is termed phaceloid (having tall corallites).

The Atlantic genera are *Diploria, Colpophyllia, Solenastrea, Cladocora,* and *Manicinia. Montastrea* and *Favia* have species in the Atlantic and Indo-Pacific. All other genera are strictly Indo-Pacific.

Diploria, Colpophyllia, and *Manicinia areolata* (rose coral) form massive colonies with meandroid ridges and valleys. *Favia, Favites (*closed brain coral), *Cladocora, Solenastrea, Plesiastrea, Leptastrea, Diploastrea,* and *Montastrea* (star and boulder corals) have elevated and circular corallites. *Caulastrea* have tall and conical corallites that jut from the massive corallum; the thick fleshy polyps extend even further and may be smooth, ridged, rounded, or branched. *Barabattoia* are shorter, with massive tubular rather than conical corallites.

Favia occur mostly on shallow back reefs where staghorns do not dominate. Their conical corallites and rounded, massive corallum are typical of Faviid brain corals. The colorful *Favites* species are similar, but the corallites share common ridges and these corals might occur anywhere. *Goniastrea* (honeycomb corals) are typically massive, the corallites with single centers (monocentric) or multiple centers (polycentric), rounded or curved (meandroid). They occur in estuaries, on reef tops, in full seawater or out of it at low tide, on rocks, corals, sand, and mud. Photographs of brilliant green faviids sometimes fail to mention that the brilliant colors are exceptional rather than the rule. Among the hardiest of corals, they're ideal for beginner tanks with intense metal halide and VHO actinic light.

Similarly variable but more beautiful are the species of *Platygyra* (squiggle brain coral) with corallites usually meandroid, sometimes rounded; *P. daedalea* and *P. verweyi* are common, the former with a meandroid pattern and the latter between meandroid and circular. *Oulophyllia* are equally varied. *Leptoria phrygia*, with meandroid channels, is massive and often elevated rather than broadly rounded; it is the only species in its genus (monotypic). *Cyphastrea* has protruding circular corallites, and may occur in massive or branching forms.

Echinopora is usually leaf-like, but can be encrusting, tubular or branching.

Most striking of all faviids is the monotypic *Moseleya latistellata* of muddy inshore bottoms. Its sharply angular corallites have six or seven straight walls resembling a honeycomb instead of rounded or meandroid ridges.

Favia is the popular pineapple coral.

Trachyphyllia are open brain or sand corals of the Faviidae.

Goniastraea paluensis is a massive honeycomb coral of the Faviidae.

Two other monotypic genera, *Trachyphyllia* (sand or open brain coral) and *Wellsophyllia*, are sometimes placed in a separate family Trachyphyllidae, but their close relationship to *Moseleya* supports inclusion in the Faviidae. *Trachyphyllia geoffroyi* when alive resembles *Catalaphyllia* (elegance coral) or *Lobophyllia* (tooth or open brain coral), with large, contorted, meandrine valleys surrounding one to three mouths, and colorful fleshy polyps extended at night. It is free-living on soft bottoms, and predaceous on small fish. It does well with supplemental meat and strong metal halide and VHO light. *Wellsophyllia radiata* is known only from a few small museum specimens with great similarity to *Trachyphyllia*, and the name may not be valid.

Faviid corals are susceptible to black band disease in the wild, an infection with the cyanobacterium *Phormidium corallyticum*. The infection follows an injury, and is self-limiting in cool water. It is not highly contagious. Faviids cut by sharp rocks in reef tanks or by shipping may succumb to Gram-negative bacterial infections or invasive protozoa feeding in the wounds.

Oculinidae

The Oculinidae form single species colonies. They may be zooxanthellar, thickly branched, and fast-growing in clear, shallow water or non-zooxanthellar, thin-branched, and slow-growing at great depths where no light penetrates. They are not strictly tropical, but worldwide into temperate and colder waters. Oculinids are either hermaphroditic or female brooders in different areas.

Galaxea consists of tubular corallites extending from massive or plate-like basal skeletons, sometimes the only species on a fringing reef, and most common in turbid water. In all the species, the beautiful, large, colorful polyps extend from the tips of the widely spaced tubular skeletons to feed in the surrounding plankton. *Acrhelia horrescens* is a shallow zooxanthellar coral of outer reefs in the western Pacific with masses of branches supporting elongate corallites whose polyps come out at night. *Archohelia* and *Cyathelia* are also zooxanthellar oculinids of shallow Indo-Pacific waters.

Oculina diffusa and *O. valenciennesi* are bushy Atlantic corals with widely spaced corallites along thin branches. In shallow waters off the Bahamas, ivory bush coral, *O. varicosa,* is zooxanthellar and occurs mixed with other corals. At lightless depths of 200 to 300 feet along a 90-mile stretch off eastern Florida, 4–5 foot-high individual colonies of non-zooxanthellar ivory bush corals cap 100 foot-high hills of rubble and sediments, the sole species of corals on these banks. These 400–500 year old single-species reefs formed when a solitary coral settled on a rocky outcrop and began to grow at just 16 mm/year, living solely on captured plankton and sediments snared from the strong surrounding currents. Even deeper are coral mounds of *Lophela pertussa* and *Enallopsamma* (=*Dendrophyllia*) *profunda* and the other corals sometimes hundreds of feet high. Some of the live corals are 1,800 years old, the world's oldest animals, living above dead coral rock 5,000–44,000 years old. These plankton and sediment-eating litoherms (rock-forming corals) are worldwide, seven types making up virtually single-species reefs up to 2,000 meters deep.

Galaxea *commonly make up an entire fringing reef in shallow, turbid water. Oculinids are often the only corals in their habitats.*

Meandrinidae

Among the Meandrinidae, *Dendrogyra* are the pillar corals, and *Meandrina* a brain coral. *Dichocoenia* is also in this family.

Merulinidae

The Merulinidae are zooxanthellar, colonial, hermaphrodites of the Indo-Pacific with every conceivable body plan, but distinguished by high ridges or mounds formed where adjacent corallite walls fuse, most prominent in *Hydnophora* where they are given the name hydnophores. Picture a collection of dominoes placed flat side to flat side and extending a great distance, and you'll understand the shape of the ridges characterizing the family. The forms described below may not be true in all cases. It is likely that early settling larvae form encrusting plates that only later

Galaxea astreata *uses digestive tentacles to eliminate competitors on a reef. Other oculinids in deep water also make up entire reefs.*

Merulina *are leafy corals with ridged plates.*

Hydnophora exesa *is an Indo-Pacific staghorn coral in the family Merulinidae, unlike Atlantic elkhorns, which are acroporids.*

arise to form leaves, or grow protuberances that develop into stubby branches, with a couple of species specialized into highly branched, reduced plate, forms.

Merulina are leafy spectacular brown or bright pink corals with flaring or concentric plates having rows of prominent high ridges perpendicular to the ridge lines. *Scapophyllia cylindrica* has stubby branches arising from a flat plate, and elevated ridges of perpendicularly fused corallite walls. *Hydnophora* are either staghorn-like branched (*H. rigida*), plate-like or with stubby branching (*H. pilosa, H. exesa*), or they are massive (*H. microconos*). They're brittle, but grow well under bright light. *Paraclavarina triangularis* is also highly branched, but the branches are not sharply angular and the white polyps provide a soft surface appearance.

Merulinids are zooxanthellar corals requiring intense metal halide and VHO fluorescent light, and supplementary feeding with *Artemia* nauplii or copepods. Place them in a moderate flow out of the direct path of a powerhead effluent. Activated carbon filtration helps protect other corals from noxious merulinid aromatic secretions.

Pectinidae

Massive, encrusting or leaf-like, the pectinids are zooxanthellar, with colorful, thick, polyps that come out at night. *Echinophyllia* have lumpy encrusting colonies, each polyp within a moderately spaced, large, protruding corallite with almost beaded, longitudinal ridges. *Mycedium* are encrusting corals with protruding and angular corallites each resembling a bent nose with a single nostril extending off the plate. *Oxypora* has leaf-like plates covered with widely spaced corallites appearing as blisters on the hard, thin base. The coral can be encrusting or the flat plates raised in a whorl to resemble a head of lettuce. *Pectinia* (elkhorn corals, not to be confused with *Acropora* elkhorn) is fully leaf-like. It contains the hibiscus and carnation corals, species with closely packed upright plates that may be smooth, lumpy, or even branched, and brown, green, or (most beautiful) red. The plates can resemble a smooth- or rough-edged head of lettuce, the closely packed petals of a flower, or clumps of branches arising from a diffuse base (thickly knobbed modified leaves). *Physophyllia ayleni* may be a form of *Pectinia* based on its leafy appearance.

Mussidae

Among the most distinctive and popular corals in the hobby, the Mussidae include a dozen genera of green and brown corals with polyps sometimes more than an inch wide. All are zooxanthellar but also eat zooplankton. Some are solitary and resemble fungiids while others with multiple centers resemble brain corals. At least some are hermaphrodites with external fertilization.

Scolymia is a solitary (monocentric or single center) form with Indo-Pacific and Atlantic species, the only mussid genus in both basins. (The Indo-Pacific *Lithophyllia vitiensis* has been moved to *Scolymia*.) *Cynarina* (meat polyp) is a delicate monocentric species of the Indo-Pacific, its polyps swollen with water and translucent during the day when tentacles are withdrawn, shrunken at night when extended. It lives on rocks or soft bottoms, just like fungiids. Tolerant of many water conditions, *Cynarina* are good selections for beginners.

Blastomussa is polycentric, Indo-Pacific, and red, brown, green, or purple with contrasting centers. The similar

Pectinia aeonia *is a leaf-like Pacific elkhorn coral, not to be confused with Atlantic elkhorns, which are acroporids.*

Scolymia vitensis, *is one of about a half dozen species of this Atlantic and Pacific genus.*

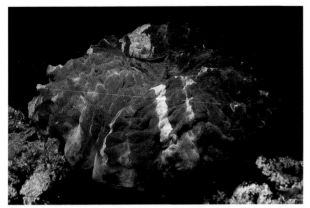

Cynarina lacrymalis *polyps swell with water during the day when the tentacles are withdrawn.*

Lobophyllia hemprichii *is a Mussid with colonies having elongated, abutting centers.*

Mussa of the Atlantic may be solitary when young, but more often is polycentric; *M. angulosa* is the large flower coral of the hobby. The species of *Acanthastrea*, all Indo-Pacific encrusting corals, are also polycentric (each center with its own distinct rim) and variably colored. *Australomussa rowleyensis* of the Indo-Pacific has rims coalescing into what isn't quite a meandroid pattern.

Symphyllia valenciennesii *is in a small Mussid genus having the largest and deepest valleys of all meandroid corals.*

With few species, the Indo-Pacific *Lobophyllia* can have rounded centers abutting one another (*L. corymbosa, L. diminuta*), elongated abutting centers (*L. hemprichii*), or meandroid arrangements of polycentric colonies (*L. hataii*) in green, yellow, or red.

The Indo-Pacific *Symphyllia* (modern brain coral) are fully meandroid, with prominent fused ridges and the largest, widest, and deepest valleys of all corals, even deeper than in the meandroid favids. They are often markedly circular rather than uneven in outline as in the related *Lobophyllia*. In the rare *S. valenciennesii*, the meanders radiate from a central point.

Strictly Atlantic genera are *Mussismillia, Mycetophyllia, Isophyllastrea,* and *Isophyllia*. *Isophyllia* is meandroid, *Mycetophyllia* meandroid but with low ridges and shallow valleys so that it appears almost encrusting.

Caryophyllidae

Probably the hardiest of the stony corals, Caryophyllidae collected from shallow shores with variable light, turbidity, and temperatures usually adapt well to reef tanks, but those collected from deep water are more sensitive. They all do best with metal halide and VHO actinic and full-spectrum lights, moderate indirect currents, regular additions of calcium, magnesium, strontium, and iodine, and daily feedings of zooplankton or weekly feedings of small dead forage fishes (you can buy smelt or silversides and "popcorn" shrimp at a seafood market) or seafood meats. They may starve and decline without supplemental foods. All require intense metal halide and VHO light, and carbon filtration and water changes to deal with the abundant TOC metabolites resulting from heavy feeding, and to dilute and remove nitrates.

Euphyllia contains the popular hammer (C-shaped tip) and frog's spawn (rounded tip) corals from the Pacific. *Euphyllia ancora* and *E. fimbriata* are the hammer corals, *E. cristata, E. divisa*, and *E. glabrescens* the frog's spawn corals. From a stony base, elongate tan or white worm-like polyps with inflated rounded or hammer shaped, white or green tips roll back and forth with the currents, exposing their symbiotic zooxanthellae to the light. Given sufficiently strong current, a healthy colony extends elongate sweeper feeding tentacles from the corals' guts far out from the colony seeking to digest competitors.

The zooxanthellar *Euphyllia* require metal halide or VHO lighting, but can survive in a shallow tank under strong actinic and daylight fluorescent wattage. They need supplementary animal prey that they capture with adhesive mucus, then deliver to the mouths with cilia. The polyps never scrunch up during the day unless the coral is sick. Sexes are separate, but not distinguishable. *Euphyllia* can be propagated by breaking the stony base from below with wire cutters,

Symphyllia species are Mussids and generally called brain corals.

pliers, or a hammer and chisel and separating the daughter colonies. Some colonies form buds at the edges that can be cut off with scissors and attached elsewhere with epoxy or acrylic cement.

Catalaphyllia jardinei (elegance coral) is among the largest and most beautiful of daytime corals, swelling to great size to capture light for its zooxanthellae, and shrinking its body and tentacles at night. It also captures prey by stinging, and

Euphyllia ancora, one of the popular hammer corals, is a reef favorite.

Euphyllia parancora, *another popular hammer coral.*

does best with supplementary brine shrimp or zooplankton. It needs metal halide or strong VHO lighting and current to wash away metabolites. Several mouth areas dot the large central portion, and the entire colony is ringed with prominent sometimes pink-tipped tentacles that fluoresce green at the base. Not a reef builder, it frequents diverse habitats, often on murky mud or silt bottoms where it inflates above the substratum like several mobile sea anemones. Its sting is strong enough to kill *Aiptasia*

Plerogyra sinosa *is a popular bubble coral with inflatable tentacles.*

anemones blotted and obliterated with this coral, but it is easily handled, feeling merely sticky to the touch.

Sexes are separate. Elegance coral also reproduces by gradual fragmentation from within. The vast fleshy body produces new skeletal material inside to be eventually extruded, the weight of the flesh and skeleton (accompanied by water current pressure on the mass) assisting separation of the masses. Elegance often divides this way in reef tanks. You can propagate elegance corals by cutting through a break in the corallum, although in general these large polyp stony corals (LPS corals) are more difficult to "frag" than other corals.

Physogyra and *Plerogyra* are the bubble or grape corals with dual-phase polyps. During the day, the polyps inflate vesicles with water to expand surface areas for zooxanthellar photosynthesis, the vesicles reaching the diameter of a grape in some species. The stinging tentacles are below the vesicle and obscured. At night, the vesicles deflate and extend to sting and capture plankton and small fishes. The genera differ in details of skeletal structure, the species in details of the vesicles. *Plerogyra sinuosa* bubbles are opalescent with clear, longitudinal streaks and are not retractable. *Physogyra* vesicles are smaller, pimply tipped, and somewhat retractable. Colonies bud from the edges, and the thin, stalked, stony plates can be broken off for transplantation elsewhere. *Plerogyra* needs strong light, moderate current, and feedings with fresh clam, mussel, or fish meats. It has a strong sting. Under good conditions, bubble corals reproduce sexually in reef aquaria. When *Plerogyra* tissue recedes showing the teeth of the corallum, it is a signal of decline from poor water quality, stings of other corals, or predation.

Eusmilia fastigiata or flower coral, the only Atlantic caryophylliid, is small with short, thick yellow to tan branches and an oval cup at the end. In the Caribbean, it is commonly found at the base of brain (*Colpophyllia, Diploria, Meandrina*) and boulder (*Montastrea*) corals.

Nemenzophyllia turbida (fox coral) from the western Indian Ocean and western Pacific is closely related to *Plerogyra* but looks like a green or brown mushroom anemone. It has broad, flat plates with thin white longitudinal streaks, but no bubbles nor obvious tentacles. The trade name is fox coral, which is probably due to an importer who listened to "...phyllia" on the telephone but heard "fox." (In the same way, the tropical fish *Rasbora kalachroma* was first imported into the hobby as *Rasbora "kodachrome,"* a name that has stuck.)

Plerogyra sinosa *is a popular bubble coral.*

Dendrophylliidae

The Dendrophylliidae contains *Astroides, Balanophyllia, Turbinaria* (yellow scroll, plate, or pagoda coral), *Tubastrea* (orange cup coral), *Leptopsammia, Heteropsammia, Dendrophyllia,* and *Enallopsammia.*

Tubastrea is an abundant, ahermatypic bright orange to yellow coral common in shaded waters on reef slopes or in caves. It is indifferent to light, and does well in strong alternating surges that mimic wave action. *Tubastrea* should be fed copiously with live or frozen adult brine shrimp, frozen mysid shrimp, or shredded mussel or clam meat placed onto the tentacles; if the food doesn't stick, disconnect the powerhead, but restart the strong current after feeding. Carbon filtration is important to deal with wastes. With lots of food and strong current, *Tubastrea* will sexually reproduce in aquaria, releasing planula

Turbinaria peltata, *pagoda coral.*

Tubastrea coccinea *in the Atlantic.*

larvae that settle on the glass. Stick your *Tubastrea* in a strong current close to the surface where you can reach it for hand feeding; light doesn't hurt.

Turbinaria are hermatypic and need light. They do well in moderate to gentle currents with supplemental feedings of *Artemia* nauplii and the small organisms disrupted from the gravel surface with a powerhead flow. Note that *Turbinaria* is a generic name for both a coral and an alga.

The Evolution of Corals

Coral relationships can be confusing. Corals of the Atlantic appear closely related to those of the eastern Pacific, but corals of the western Pacific appear to be a separate group. How can that be? Equally surprising is the constancy of corals all across the Indian and Pacific Oceans. They differ only in the extreme north and extreme south where the water is colder. And even that's not true when the cold region is invaded by

a warm current. Most confusing is that, at least in the laboratory, corals separated in the wild and that look nothing alike can form fertile hybrids. Does that mean they are the same species?

J.E.N. Veron (Veron, 1995, *Corals in Space and Time*) proposed that coral evolution has been controlled through the millenia by sea level changes associated with ice ages, themselves induced by periodic alterations in the planet's orientation to the sun (up to 100 million-year Malenkovitch cycles), plate tectonics (the riding of the continents on a liquid rock interior), and alterations in the paths of oceanic warm currents such as the Gulf Stream in the North Atlantic and the Kuroshio Current in the North Pacific.

Most of us are familiar with the uplifting of the Central American isthmus to cut the connection between the Atlantic and Pacific oceans. The isthmus was the latest consequence of the uplifting of the continuous North and South American mountain range at the edge of the eastern Pacific ring of fire. As the final piece of mountain range finally blocked flows between the Atlantic and Pacific, it also broke a continuous coral community that freely exchanged genes across two oceans. After that separation, corals in the Atlantic and the eastern Pacific could no longer exchange genetic material that had previously moderated evolutionary trends. With Pacific and Atlantic coral communities now behaving as new founder populations (isolated from a previously larger population), differentiation proceeded quickly. Today the corals of the eastern Pacific off Central America have their nearest relatives in the Caribbean basin of the western Atlantic.

What about Indian Ocean corals? Are they all related to Pacific corals or were they one time related also to

Atlantic corals? Yes to both. The Tethys was an ancient sea that connected the Indian and Atlantic oceans. The Tethys Sea was short-lived, and gradually was squeezed almost completely closed as plate tectonics carried the African landmass northward into Eurasia. The remnants of the Tethys Sea remain as its western arm, the Mediterranean Sea, and an eastern fragment, the Persian Gulf. Only the frigid cold of the Mediterranean has interrupted continuity between corals of the Indian Ocean and of the eastern Atlantic.

The ages of the closing of the Tethys Sea, the uplifting of the Isthmus of Panama, and the fossil record of reefs all explain modern coral family distributions. What the closing of the Tethys Sea does not explain (but which Veron embraces) is the limited diversity of coral forms over the central Indo-Pacific, the variation associated more with depth than distance, the repetition of species across great distances, the slow pace of coral evolution (as shown in the fossil record), and the ability of so many corals to form hybrids even among species that look nothing alike.

Corals in general often discharge eggs and sperm into the water on the same day of the year. That a single species might synchronously spawn makes sense for a species that ranges over a large area. But why would unrelated species over wide ranges of ocean spawn on the same day of the year? And why can vastly different corals from great distances apart hybridize to produce fertile offspring? Does this mean that despite the differences, they are the same species? If corals can (a) hybridize in the lab and (b) have an opportunity to hybridize in nature through synchronous spawning, Veron argues, then what can happen must in fact happen eventually.

Tubastrea aurea *in the Indo-Pacific.*

Richard Dawkins makes the same point in *The Ancestor's Tale* (2005, Mariner Publications): over the enormous period of the Earth's history, anything that statistically could happen, eventually happens.

Thus, the ability of corals to hybridize, changing ocean currents, the stability of ocean temperatures between ice ages, and the opportunities to reconnect their gene pools following ice ages, all led Veron to conclude that most of the reef building corals of the Indo-Pacific are complexes, rather than genetically distinct species. These complexes are called syngameons. Individuals and populations of syngameons may look different, but genetically they can and do interbreed.

Not all corals exist as syngameons. Many species are unique and do not hybridize with other corals.

In the aquarium, corals occasionally release eggs and sperm, but seldom all spawn synchronously. Instead, their main method of growth and reproduction is asexual.

Chapter Fourteen
Diseases of Corals

The best continuing source of coral disease information is the CRC Coral Disease Page of McCarty and Peters (*http://ourworld.compuserve. com/homepages/mccarty_and_peters/ coraldis.htm*).

Corals are subject to parasites, infectious diseases, and extreme environmental changes. They may respond to stress by loss of zooxanthellae, tissue necrosis, abnormal growths, and die-backs. Around the world, large-scale loss of scleractinian corals is associated with many biological (infections) and physical (excessive heat) causes.

Extreme weather may damage corals. Unrelenting heat that raises seawater temperatures is known to cause bleaching that, if extended, can cause coral death. But ultraviolet exposure at low spring tides, or unusual tidal events generally have no effect on corals. Even the Christmas 2004 Indian Ocean tsunami did not destroy the nearshore reefs off Sumatra, and soft corals of Australia's Great Barrier Reef are regularly exposed to the sun at low tide, yet are not killed by the heat or UV or IR radiation. Perhaps combined with other stressors (salinity changes, pollutants, turbidity, sedimentation), the lethal threshold can be overcome, but generally pollution rather than natural events kills corals. Cyclonic mega-storms may tear away macroalgae, stir up the bottom, and smash the outer branches of hard corals, but often the worst damage (and surely that most likely to be seen) is soil in runoff from developed tourist islands.

Changes in predator-prey relationships can reduce coral populations. The population explosion of the crown-of-thorns starfish has devastated Pacific reefs. In the Atlantic, die-offs of the algal-grazing *Diadema* sea urchin contributed to algal overgrowth of corals. Commercial fishing on reefs that decimates tangs and parrotfishes also removes algal control, and Caribbean corals in many areas are being overgrown by macroalgae everywhere you look, although the worst algal overgrowth is invariably associated with storm runoff of soils.

Everything is connected. With fewer herbivores (fish and sea urchins) cropping macroalgae, settling sites for larval corals become sparse, and the start (recruitment) of new coral colonies is reduced. The earliest coral colonies to get a foothold are abraded or shaded by adjacent calcareous macroalgae. This slows growth, exposes bare rock that the algae invade, and confines the young cnidarians so they have no rock space in which to expand. The reef becomes dominated by macroalgae rather than corals. And for that problem, so far there is no answer.

Coral Reef Bleaching

Bleaching is a generalized response to heat stress, but can be induced by other stressors. It develops in days but may go on for months. The longer it continues, the less likely the corals will recover. Bleaching results from the expulsion of the zooxanthellae that give corals their brown or pastel hues. With the algae gone, the corals seem to be white as the skeleton shows through the now translucent tissue. It affects both hard and soft corals, *Millepora* fire corals, sea anemones, sponges, and other invertebrates that rely on photosynthetic symbiotic dinoflagellate microalgae.

Bleaching results from the expulsion of dead or dying zooxanthellae and their accessory pigments (chlorophyll *c*, peridinin, diadinoxanthin). What looks like partial bleaching results from localized UV stress or microbial infections, or bleaching may be incomplete because the zooxanthellae in one part of the coral are susceptible to heat stress but not the zooxanthellae in other parts. Heat-resistant strains of *Symbiodinium* with different mixes of highly unsaturated fatty components in their chloroplast membranes can reinvade where the common, heat-sensitive form of *Symbiodinium* has been expelled by bleaching. Bleaching is neither contagious nor infectious, but can affect all the corals in a large area. Occurring worldwide, bleaching is a response to prolonged elevated water temperatures as happens during mid-summer in El Niño years. Prolonged mid-summer temperatures just two degrees above normal may trigger bleaching.

Coral algal symbionts are adapted to the temperatures of their region, and those from different locales will have different temperature tolerances. The interaction of temperature and time sufficient to kill the microalgae and induce bleaching of the corals can be calculated in degrees heating weeks (DHW).

DHW developed for Belize and Jamaica reefs predicted that 26 DHW would induce mass bleaching. Cold upwellings and reduced salinities can also induce localized bleaching.

Mortality rates of 95 percent of coral colonies have been recorded following mass bleaching, with whole reefs affected in the eastern Pacific, but seldom are entire reefs killed. More often, reinvasion by stress-resistant zooxanthellae allows the corals to recover. *Montrastrea* and other corals often recover from a few weeks of bleaching, but many corals cannot survive more than a month without their zooxanthellae. Partial and short-term bleaching is not unusual and not lethal to the corals.

Bleaching in other invertebrates is also caused by the loss of *Symbiodinium* and other symbiotic microalgae, or by toxins in the water resulting from blooms of noxious microalgae (e.g., red tide dinoflagellates), fungi, or noxious cyanobacteria. It is not uncommon for any animals to shed symbionts and parasites during stress, but some symbionts are more important to the host than others.

Corals fade or change color in reef aquaria as a response to different light regimes; this is not bleaching but adaptation of the zooxanthellae to the new light regime, which they accomplish by a change in the density of their chloroplasts and/or pigments. True bleaching can occur in aquaria when the corals are stressed by, for example, high temperature in the 80°s F rather than the low 70°s F, sufficient to kill their symbiotic microalgae.

Infectious Coral Bleaching

The spiral bacteria, *Vibrio*, are implicated in bleaching and worse. Some coral bleaching is spread by amphinomid polychaete (annelid) vectors that feed on corals. *Hermodice arunculata* carries *Vibrio shilio* in its gut, and transmits this pathogen from an infected coral to uninfected corals while feeding. Vibrios are common in fresh- and marine water. *Vibrio comma* causes human cholera. Frequently fatal human infections with *Vibrio vulnificus* are often acquired by eating or being cut by Gulf Coast oysters harvested in summer. How many other cases of bleaching are vibrio-induced is unknown at this time.

White-band Disease, White Plague, and Stress-related Necrosis

These may be separate diseases, or the same disease given different names. In white-band disease the polyp tissues die and slough away starting from the base and working to the tips of the branches, leaving the white corallum exposed. Primarily affecting acroporids, it has been seen in other corals. Two types (WBD I and WBD II) have been described, the first associated with ordinary bacteria in the callicoblastic epithelium (the tissue that secretes calcium), and the second associated with *Vibrio* bacteria in the sloughed dead tissue, but the linkage of the bacteria with the disease has not been proven, and they may just be scavenging dead tissues. White pox may be the same disease reported from elkhorn corals in Florida. As with many coral conditions, names are applied even when no pathogen is identified and, more importantly, none is ruled out. Many coral disease names will disappear as the hyperbole is replaced with good science. White Plague I and White Plague II may be the same or different. The causative agent of White Plague II has been identified as *Aurantimonas*

coralicida, a bacterial species that affects more than 40 kinds of coral, advancing and killing the tissues at over an inch per day.

Stress-related necrosis (SRN) and Porites Pox are two names for a sloughing condition observed in acroporids, faviids, and poritid corals where no bacteria were seen. Tissue sloughing in hard corals is sometimes reversible by moving the coral to another aquarium, suggesting it's a response to poor water quality.

White Pox

White pox of elkhorn corals in the Caribbean is caused by *Serracia marscencens*, a common bacterium of the human intestine that probably occurs in other mammals. This disease is caused by fecal contamination of coastal waters.

Black-band and Red-band Disease

Black-band disease is an infection of faviids and gorgonians (and perhaps other corals) caused by a biofilm-like community dominated by the cyanobacteria *Phormidium corallyticum* and *Spirulina* and sulfur bacteria plus several other microbes. The cyanobacteria-sulpher consortium acts like a biofilm that eats everything, dividing the food, consuming oxygen, and emitting noxious wastes that kill adjacent coral tissue that is then also consumed. The mass of microbes, looking like an oil-soaked rope, advances around and over the coral and kills it entirely unless stopped by cold weather. It is a summertime disease. *Platygyra* and *Goniastrea* are most often affected, but it was also reported from *Montrastrea, Siderastrea, Diploria*, and *Colpophyllia*. Diseased faviids may be adjacent to uninfected faviids, but an outbreak in the Florida Keys simultaneously affected many corals. The gorgonians *Pseudopterogorgia* in Florida and *Gorgonia* in Costa Rica also were found infected with a community of *Phormidium corallyticum* and other bacteria. *Phormidium* is susceptible to antibiotics and intolerant of cold. Outbreaks in a mini-reef aquarium are rare. Try removing the infected coral to a separate, 70°F aquarium and treating the water with 10 mg/L of oxytetracycline hydrochloride, with a new dose in new water every two days and continued low temperatures until the disease clears.

Red-band disease is also the result of a multispecies biofilm dominated by a cyanobacterium. It affects *Diploria strigosa, Montastraea annularis, Montastraea cavernosa, Porites astreoides, Siderastrea radians, Colpophyllia natans* and gorgonians in the western Atlantic and occasionally on the Great Barrier Reef, so it's probably worldwide.

Nemenzophyllia turbida, *the fox coral, resembles some of the unrelated mushroom corals.*

Skeletal-eroding Band Disease and Brown-band Disease

Previously thought to be different biofilm diseases endemic to the Caribbean, Red Sea, or Great Barrier Reef, these are all protozoan diseases caused by the parasitic ciliates *Helicostoma nonatum* and *Halofolliculina corallasia* (family Folliculinidae). In the Caribbean, *Halofolliculina* affects no less than 25 scleractinians of the Acroporidae, Agaricidae, Astrocoeniidae, Faviidae, Meandrinidae, and Poritidae, from inshore habitats to oceanic reefs. They concentrate in bands at the border of dead and living coral tissue, are large enough to be seen with an inexpensive microscope, and resemble rotifers in the ciliated area around the "mouth" and in seeming to be sessile. The vacuoles (digestive pockets) in the protozoa contain zooxanthellae probably acquired in their feeding. It is possible these ciliates are saprophytes feeding on corals dying from other causes, but not likely. The mode of transmission isn't known.

Yellow Blotch and Yellow Band Disease

Yellow blotch and yellow band occur in corals of the Caribbean and the Arabian Gulf. The causative agents in the Caribbean are four species of *Vibrio* that affect several corals and spread faster at high temperatures. The vibrios infect the zooxanthellae, killing many of them and causing them to swell with

Gracilaria *is ubiquitous in reef tanks and readily removed by hand.*

tible to 10 mg/L of nitrofurazone and other drugs. Treatment should always be in a separate aquarium as many antimicrobial drugs, especially neomycin (250 mg/gallon), chloromycetin (80 mg/L for 25 hours), and erythromycin (any dose) may kill non-target nitrogen cycle bacteria, red algae, and cyanobacteria.

The bacteria of coral diseases are not like the Gram-negative short rods that cause fish diseases, but members of different bacterial groups associated with sulfur products. *Beggiatoa* is a member of the gliders, sulfide-oxidizing filamentous bacteria that live in sediments at the interface of anoxic and aerobic zones. *Desulfovibrio* is an anaerobic sulfate reducer shaped as a curved rod, sometimes a spiral. *Beggiatoa* and *Desulfovibrio* have been found in corals, but whether they are primary or secondary invaders is not always clear. They may be most important when they contribute to the biofilm in black-band disease.

vacuoles, an indication of pathology. As the zooxanthellae degenerate, the corals decline and exhibit symptoms of the infection. Vibrios are pathogenic bacteria that afflict humans, fishes, and corals, plants, and apparently now even symbiotic zooxanthellae. Why the corals don't simply emit the sick and dying zooxanthellae and bleach isn't known.

Other Bacteria

Corals injured by rocks, crabs, fish bites, boring snails, or rough handling may die if the polyps are interconnected, and survive if polyps are separate. Tissue tears become open sores when invaded by bacteria. Under the microscope, the bacteria are usually Gram-negative short rods that may be suscep-

Aspergillosis

Aspergillus is a fungus genus. You've seen it as black spots on white bread. *Aspergillus sydowii* is common in soil. When shorelines are developed and the soil is disturbed, wind blows the dust into the air to settle in nearshore waters. Airborne dust has been suggested as the cause of a "blackening" disease affecting sea fans and gorgonians in the Caribbean. In sea fans, it forms spreading black circles, and in gorgonians, the whole animal blackens.

Rapid Wasting

It's not clear if Rapid Wasting is a fungal disease or the result of parrotfish damage to corals, with the scrapes invaded by fungi. Still under study, the phenomenon is so far restricted to the Atlantic.

Growths and Tumors

True tumors or neoplasms are known from acroporid corals, and appear as raised, white calcareous nodules. The tumor is in the underlying tissue that produces calcium. As the tumors enlarge, the covering tissue loses its mucus secreting cells and the whole tumor becomes ulcerated. The corrallum becomes exposed and invaded by filamentous algae or other organisms. This neoplasm or true cancerous condition is called calicoblastic epithelioma. Its cause is unknown.

Pink Grub and Pink Spot

Pink spot is the swelling of a tip of coral tissue by the walling off (an immune reaction) of an invasive second stage larva of a parasitic flatworm called a digenetic trematode. There are thousands of species of digenetic trematodes, which mature in all vertebrates and use all kinds of animals as intermediate hosts. In the case of pink grub or pink spot, the adult parasite lives in the intestine of a butterflyfish, and its eggs are shed with the feces. In the sea, the egg hatches into a ciliated larva that chemically detects a specific type of snail, bores into the snail, loses its cilia, and undergoes several rounds of multiplication and change. By the final stage, that ciliated larva has multiplied to become hundreds of tailed swimming larvae (cercariae) that bore out of the snail and, again by chemical attraction,

seek a certain coral in which to encyst. The coral tissue tries to wall it off, but the parasite is protected by its cyst. Eventually the infected part of the tentacle swells and changes color, making it attractive to that same species of butterflyfish, which picks at and swallows the infected tentacle piece. Inside the butterflyfish, the cyst hatches and grows up in the fish's intestine, and the life cycle is complete. The parasitic trematode, *Plagioporus* or a relative, whose host is the coral-eating butterflyfish, *Chaetodon multicinctus*, has a larval form that eventually penetrates *Porites* corals to induce nodules selectively eaten by the host fish, which completes the parasite's life cycle. In Australia, the parasite is *Podocotyloides stenometra* and the affected coral is *Porites compressa*. The encysted stage is called the metacercaria, and you can see it by mashing the cyst and observing the squash under the microscope. *Plagioporus* adults occur in marine and freshwater fishes. In some species the life cycle is abbreviated with one of the hosts doing duty as two or even all three hosts.

Algal Nodules

Gorgonians parasitized by algae also develop tumor-like nodules. A filamentous green alga, *Entocladia endozoica*, is an endoparasite of the gorgonians *Pseudoplexaura* and *Pseudopterogorgia*. Its algal filaments irritate coral tissues that subsequently wall them off. Another endosymbiont of (usually) stony corals (probably the alga *Ostreobium*) induces hyperplasia (cell multiplication) followed by walling off with gorgonin when the alga infects the sea fan, *Gorgonia*.

Chapter Fifteen
Sponges

The sponges arose from choanoflagellates, a group of about 150 types of flagellated protists (protozoans). Each looks like a sponge choanocyte (see below) but, more to the point, these choanoflagellates form clusters, foretelling the evolution of sponges.

The sponges, phylum Porifera, consist of 10,000 species of mostly marine animals at the lowest level of multicellular organization, without any recognizable tissues or organs. They are primitive, but not simple. Some sponges build elongate tubes above the bottom, others beautiful branching trees, some latticed clumps, and others huge bowls. Many form beautiful encrusting growths such as the bright red patches on Gulf of Mexico live rock. Many sponges are home to commensal fishes, shrimp, crabs, and lesser-known invertebrates. Sponges are eaten by some angelfishes, sea turtles, and gastropods.

Sponges are organized as a cellular layer or skin inside and outside, with a mostly acellular layer called the mesohyl between the skins. The body plan is like a punctured vase, with water containing planktonic food entering multiple holes in specialized cells (porocytes) and leaving through the open top of the vase (osculum). The inner skin surrounds a hollow space (spongocoel) lined with flagellated cells (choanocytes) that create the current through the pores and out the osculum. The choanocytes also capture bacteria, phytoplankton, and particles too small to be identified with an ordinary microscope. Brightly pigmented ameboid cells (archaeocytes) then engulf and digest this food. The mesohyl layer consists of loosely spaced cells separated by proteinaceous collagen (sometimes fibrin) and other cells specialized to secrete silicious (silica-based) or calcareous (calcium-based) spicules. Is this another example of a multicellular organism that owes its existence to incorporation of earlier symbionts? Perhaps symbiotic diatoms were ancestral to the cells that provide silicious spicules and perhaps millions of years before or since, symbiotic foraminiferans were incorporated and now provide calcite spicules.

Sponges As Chemical Factories

Some sponges produce unique toxins, antibiotics, and even anti-HIV and anti-tumor chemicals. Some of these chemicals include calyculins, pokepola phosphate ester from *Spongia* (with minor anti-HIV activity), laulimalide toxin from *Hyattella*, and the kalhinol family of antibiotics from *Acanthella*. Some nudibranchs and fishes bioaccumulate sponge toxins and use them for defense. (We have already seen that some nudibranchs accumulate cnidarian stinging cells for defense.)

Keeping and Propagating Sponges

Some sponges have photosynthetic symbionts, and all require minute foods. Daily feedings of green water (unicellular algae) or liquid suspensions used to feed corals may support sponges introduced on live rock. Sponges grow in a reef tank when adequate microalgae (phytoplankton), microzooplankton, and/or particulate nutrients are provided as a supplement or through the metabolism of other reef inhabitants. Translucent yellowish white sponges often cover the hard surfaces in fish-only marine aquariums that get heavy feedings of blended fish and shellfish meats.

Sponges can be propagated by cutting them into small pieces and moving them to another part of the aquarium, or even fragmenting a large piece in a blender and pouring the slurry into the tank. The particles include specialized ameboid cells that start new sponges where they settle, provided food is available.

The Caribbean has many kinds of encrusting sponges. Some can be propagated by fragmentation, but there are no rules for success.

Most sponges are more complex than a simple vase. The insides are convoluted or subdivided, increasing the surface area for choanocytes and amoeboid feeding cells. Like corals, sponges adapt to surrounding surges, those growing in strong currents squat or rounded to expose minimal surface area. Sponges in quiet water are elongate, extending well off the bottom, even branching. No matter how complex the sponge, it usually has just one osculum.

Sponges are mostly hermaphrodites that expel gametes through the osculum, the egg fertilized in the surrounding ocean, and developing into a ciliated or flagellated larva. (Cilia and flagella are the same structures, differing in size but not complexity. In the choanocytic flagellates, what looks like a collar around a flagellum is a closely organized collection of cilia that beat so quickly they resemble a contiguous collar of tissue.) The larva settles on an appropriate substratum and develops into a vase-shaped sponge at first, then into its more complex structure.

Demospongia

Ninety percent (9,500 species) of sponges are of the Class Demospongiae, with gelatinous interiors that may or may not contain horny fibers of spongin or of silica spicules, and that grow as simple, encrusting, or branched bod-

Wrasses explore a Caribbean tube sponge.

Sclerospongea

The Class Sclerospongea are cavern dwellers with a gelatinous mesohyl containing calcium carbonate, silica, and spongin in a complex arrangement.

Hexactinellida (Hyalospongia)

The Class Hexactinellida (formerly the Hyalospongia) or glass sponges (450 species) don't have a gelatinous mesohyl, but a loose arrangement of six-pointed silicious spicules arranged in long fibers, the spicules even penetrating the outer skin. The skin and latticework are so loose that water flows through with little need for choanocytes. These colorless but complex sponges resemble crystals.

Sponges for Reef Tanks

Some attractive sponges for reef tanks are *Haliclona permollis*, *Verongula* sp., *Clathrina coriacea*, *Siphonochalina* sp., *Raspailia hispida*, *Cliona* spp., *Hippospongia* sp., *Tethya, Suberites, Pseudsuberites* spp., *Lotrochata purpurea,* and *Spirastrella cunctatrix.* Trade or common names aren't standardized, and not useful.

Some beautiful sponges offered by commercial collectors, such as purple vase and orange-red clump types, are difficult to maintain without feedings, yet those feedings can induce nuisance algae blooms. Yellow and brown sponges that arrive on live rock often take hold and spread.

ies. Some large members of the family Spongidae were collected for bath sponges before industry provided synthetics. The family Clionidae are borers, with special brightly colored ameboid cells that etch holes in mollusc shells or in corals. Several are bright yellow and common on live rock.

Calcarea

The Class Calcarea, about 50 species, have well separated, 3- or 4-pronged calcium carbonate spicules, and no spongin in their gelatinous mesohyl. These are among the simplest sponges.

Chapter Sixteen
Molluscs

The 150,000 species of the Phylum Mollusca include turbo and astraea snails and tridacnid clams popular with reef aquarists, nudibranchs and octopus familiar to snorkelers, and more. Only about 10,000 species are terrestrial, the rest aquatic.

All molluscs have a large organ called the foot, used for locomotion (snails) or anchoring (clams), and a membrane (mantle) enveloping the viscera that secretes calcium carbonate and proteinaceous shell material. Many molluscs have a band of rasping tissue (the radula) in the mouth. In some the radula is a moveable belt of tiny hooks. The blood system uses copper at the center of the heme molecule instead of iron, making the blood blue instead of red; molluscs are also quickly killed by copper.

Molluscs can be male, female, or hermaphroditic, but always reproduce sexually to produce miniature juveniles (as in freshwater snails) or a planktonic larva. If the planktonic form is an early stage ciliated larva, it is called a trochophore. (The same name is used for the larva of polychaete annelid worms and, indeed, molluscs and annelids have a common ancestor.) In most species, the molluscan trochophore changes into a later stage larva called a veliger.

Malacologists (mollusc scientists) divide the Phylum into seven Classes. The Gastropoda, Bivalvia, and Cephalopoda all have species important to marine aquarists. The Polyplacophora or chitons commonly arrive on live rock and multiply in reef tanks. The remaining three Classes, of negligible interest to reef aquarists, include the deepwater Monoplacophora, the Aplachophora with wormlike forms including some living on cnidarians, and the Scaphopoda or burrowing tusk shells.

Gastropoda

The Class Gastropoda (*gastro-poda* = stomach foot) contains 125,000 species of snails. Snails extrude mucus from the foot bottom to assist in gliding and pulling themselves forward over any hard surface. The slime can be instantly liquified for ciliary gliding (common in smaller snails) and just as quickly gelled for muscular pulling. Larger snails use waves of muscular contractions to pull themselves forward.

The radula within the mouth may be mounted on a cartilaginous rod like the base plate of an electric sander. The radula scrapes like sandpaper, in some snails in a rotary motion and back-and-forth in others. The radula can be everted onto the food source (algae, dead plants and animals, live animals, including other molluscs). Oyster drills do not drill with the radula. Instead, they have an accessory boring organ that secretes a chemical to chelate calcium, separating it from its carbonate and dissolving a hole in the shell of the victim; the radula is then inserted into the hole to grind up prey tissues.

A few marine snails produce masses of fertilized eggs that hatch as miniatures (juveniles) of the adult. Most gastropods develop partly in the capsule and hatch to start life as planktonic veliger larvae.

The three groups of gastropods are the prosobranchs, opisthobranchs, and pulmonates. The pulmonates are mostly freshwater and land forms of no interest to marine aquarists.

Prosobranch Gastropods

The three groups of Prosobranchs are archaeogastropods, mesogastropods, and neogastropods.

Archaeogastropods: The archaeogastropods include limpets, abalones, and topshells, omnivorous/herbivorous grazers that feed on diatoms and soft algae. Keyhole limpets also graze on sponges and corals. All have external fertilization, and the male has no need for a penis. The most important reef tank archaeogastropods are the herbivorous topshells, turbans, and starshells of the superfamily Trochacea, especially *Turbo*, *Clanculus*, *Margarites*, *Gibbula*, *Astraea*, and *Calliostoma*. Every mini-reef aquarium should have at least one or two trochid snails per 10 gallons to control diatoms and soft algae on glass and rock. Several species are better than one to accommodate food preferences; *Astraea*, for example, feed mostly on diatoms while *Turbo* feed mostly on hair algae. Most *Astraea* in the hobby are collected from the Caribbean (Atlantic), the *Trochea* from the Sea of Cortez (Pacific).

Trochaceans shed a gelatinous mass of eggs that adheres to rocks or plants. Sperm shed into the surrounding water penetrate the mass to fertilize the eggs, which hatch to release planktonic larvae. Keyhole limpets and the trochids *Turbo* and *Astraea* often spawn in reef tanks during the summer. Prosobranchs can be induced to shed gametes by placing them in a 10-gallon aquarium at high temperature (80°F), draining most of the tank, and adding cold (60°F) water. Alternatively, place a snail upside down in a small container with warm water, then decant and replace with cold water. Some will emit sperm and others egg masses. Add the sperm water to the egg container and then watch the eggs develop into swimming larvae.

Mesogastropods: The mesogastropod snails (*meso* = intermediate) include herbivores and carnivores with an elongated proboscis that can capture and engulf prey. Aquacultured queen conchs (*Strombus gigas*) are excellent detritus and algal feeders for tanks with aragonite gravel; wild conchs are protected and may not be collected. Most mesogastropods are colorful nuisances, such as the Ovulidae that graze on live soft coral, the Cassidids or helmet shells that prey on echinoderms and some molluscs, and the Cypraeidae or cowries that eat almost anything. Some cowries eat sponges, but egg cowries (which differ in the radular teeth) feed on gorgonians and other soft corals, and even mimic their prey. Other cowries feed on black corals. Cowries and their nudibranch mimics toxic to mollusc-eating fishes often carry the same aposomatic (warning) colors or patterns. Cowries in reef tanks eat sponges and soft corals in addition to algae and detritus, and should be limited to fish-only marine aquaria.

Cerithium are valuable algal grazers collected from south Florida sea walls and bridge stanchions, and common on Atlantic and Pacific live rock. *Vermetus* are sessile, with elongate, worm-like shells cemented in large colonies on rocks, and confused with worm tubes. Lacking a planktonic stage, they rapidly multiply in reef tanks. Both types are popular with reef tank aquarists.

Neogastropods: The neogastropoda (*neo* = new) include whelks, tulips, volutes, olives, and oyster drills. Most are predators, the cone shells (*Conus* spp.) among the most venomous marine animals known. In some, a protrusile proboscis has a modified radula enlarged into a hollow harpoon that anchors in flesh and injects a neurotoxic venom. Specialized feeders on invertebrates and bottom fishes, they inject, instantly paralyze, and consume the prey whole. Some predators on fish (*C. striatus, C. geographus*, others) have venoms lethal to man. Cone shells have occasionally been collected and sent to dealers who didn't recognize the danger. All cone shells should be avoided as potentially dangerous.

Opisthobranchs

The major groups of the 5,000 kinds of non-parasitic opisthobranchs are the sea hares (with lateral respiratory parapodia), nudibranchs or sea slugs (many with a circle of gills appended at the rear), bubble snails, notaspids, sacoglossans, shelled sea butterflies, and naked sea butterflies.

The slug-like opisthobranch body has a pair of oral tentacles in front and secondary tentacles called rhinophores immediately behind. Some have a normal shell. In others, a reduced shell is hidden by the mantle or lost entirely, while in a few the body is encased by a pair of shells resembling a clam wrapped on a snail's body. Some opisthobranchs have a gill inside a respiratory cavity, in others the gill is located on the top rear of the body, and in others still, beautiful mantle outgrowths called cerata provide gas exchange. Many opisthobranchs travel on plants, rocks, or corals on a

Casella albimarginata is a Pacific nudibranch that's as attractive as it is difficult to keep in good health.

broad, undulating foot, while others have expanded the foot edges into swimming wings. Hermaphrodites, they deposit strings or masses of fertilized eggs that produce planktonic larvae often not difficult to raise.

Nudibranchs: Nudibranchs that arrive on live rock sometimes live and grow in reef tanks, finding their requirements in the diverse communities. Feeding may be generalized or specialized. *Sacoglossa*, the Anaspidea, and some Cephalaspidea are herbivores, but may specialize on certain macroalgae. The herbivorous sea hares *(Aplysia)* and sacoglossans (*Tridachia*) have a planktonic stage of weeks or even months. Aquarium propagation is time-consuming. Their larvae require antibiotics to protect from bacterial attack, drops of alcohol in their culture containers to keep them from sticking to surface film or become abnormal with inadequate strontium, and they must be fed microalgae.

Philinopsis gardineri *is a Philipinne nudibranch. Most nudibranchs are specialty feeders that die if their specific food is not available.*

The most brightly colored nudibranchs, the Doridacea, recognized by a ring of retractable gills around the anus, are predators on sponges, sea squirts, corals, crustaceans, bryozoans, or anemones; in the reef tank they starve if their specific food is not available. Common genera are *Chromodoris, Phyllidia, Glossodoris, Gymnodoris, Casella, Tambja, Peltodoris, Platydoris, Polycera, Spurilla,* and *Pteraeolidia.*

Dirona albolineata, the white-lined nudibranch, is a generalized feeder from the northeastern Pacific and eats tissues of some cold-water reef tank inhabitants, but dies if the temperature exceeds 59°F.

Some nudibranchs have a toothed radula, but a few (*Melibe, Dendrodoris, Doriopsilla*) eat their prey whole. Aeolids have few radular teeth and use them to cut, rather than rasp, tissue from their prey. Sacoglossans have long, hollow, sharp-tipped teeth that puncture prey and suck out symbiotic algal cells.

Some nudibranchs that feed on cnidarians transport unfired cnidocysts to their own skin to be used for protection. Other nudibranchs save and transport chloroplasts to their own skin where they photosynthesize and provide nutrients to the nudibranch.

Nudibranchs Can Use Chemical Weapons. Some *Hexabranchus* feed only on the sponge *Halichondria,* concentrating the sponge's dihydrohalichondramide to deter predation. The same nudibranchs concentrate other toxins called uapualides in their egg masses, protecting the eggs from all predators except for some species of the nudibranch *Favorinus* that are immune. *Phyllidea varicosa* concentrates isocyanopupkeanane, a predator inhibitor, from its sponge prey. *Chromidoris* concentrates the cytotoxin laulimalide from its sponge prey, *Hyattella.* The sea hare *Stylocheilus longicauda* concentrates the tumor promotor aplysiatoxin from blue-green cyanobacteria. The nudibranch *Phestilla melanobrachia* feeds on the coral *Tubastrea coccinea,* selectively concentrating its chemicals to produce a new toxic alkaloid the coral itself doesn't have.

Bivalvia (Pelycepoda)

Clams, mussels, and oysters are sessile molluscs of rivers, lakes, estuaries and oceans. Some attach to structures by burrowing into a small space and growing to imprison themselves, by secreting silky byssus threads to withstand surge and crashing waves, or by secreting a calcareous cement. Some do not attach at all, remaining free of the bottom and capable of rapid escapes by flapping their valves to create jets of water.

Many unattached bivalves move by extending the muscular foot forward into the sand or mud, pumping blood to swell the tip into an anchor, and then pulling themselves forward by retracting the muscle. Scallops (*Pectin, Aequipectin, Caribachlamys, Nodipectin, Argopectin*) can open and then shut their valves suddenly to leap forward or upward, jet propelled; they often have light-sensitive eyes on the rim of the mantle that can form images and detect predators.

Bivalves may be hermaphroditic or have separate sexes. Most shed gametes into the water, but in some species the sperm are taken in with filtrate water and the fertilized eggs brooded until hatching. The larva is a ciliated trochophore, which transforms into a veliger larva that seeks out by chemical cues a suitable substratum for settling. Many bivalves can be induced to shed gametes by injection with the hormone serotonin or with 0.1 N potassium hydroxide, both available from laboratory supply houses.

The bivalves can be divided into seven subclasses. Two are important to marine aquarists.

The Subclass Pteriomorphia: This group contains bivalves that live on the surface, usually attached by cement or byssus threads. It includes the mussels (*Mytilus, Modiolus*), scallops (*Pecten, Argopecten, Aequipecten*), ark shells (*Arca*), pen shells (*Pinna*), file shells or flame scallops (*Lima*), and oysters (*Ostrea, Crassostrea, Spondylus*). *Lithophaga* is a mussel that bores into corals.

The Subclass Heterodonta: This group contains bivalves with siphons and without a shiny nacre layer. It includes the common edible clams (*Venus, Mercenaria*), cockles (*Cardium, Dinocardium*), razor clams (*Ensis*), coquinas (*Donax, Tellina*), exotic zebra mussel (*Dreissena*), exotic Asian clam (*Corbicula*), rock-borer (*Petricola*), wood-borers (*Teredo, Martesia, Xylophaga*), and Indo-Pacific giant clams (*Tridacna*).

The flame scallop, Lima scabra, *has eyes at the tips of its tentacles and will leap and jet propel away to safety if a shadow passes overhead. Scallops cannot be kept with sea stars.*

Rudist Bivalves

The rudists are extinct Heterodont bivalves that formed reefs long before coral reefs existed. One valve (shell) was larger than the other, and many forms, upright, flat, thin, and massive lived in huge colonies with other invertebrates and macroalgae, building up large mounds over time. Today, those mounds or fossil reefs are sometimes erroneously called ancient coral reefs, but should simply be called ancient reefs or ancient precoral reefs. The 65–450 million-year-old rudist reefs are comprised mostly of rudist shells, other nautilus-type molluscs, and the deposits of red calcareous algae mixed with calcareous and silty sediments.

Tridacnid Clams

Indo-Pacific clams of the family Tridacnidae live in shallow, often intertidal, well-lit tropical waters where they are adapted to intense sunlight, ultraviolet light, desiccation, infrared heat, and nutrient-poor water. The giant clams *Tridacna gigas* and *T. derasa* are common in exposed reef tops where they exceed three feet

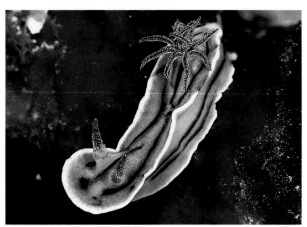
Chromidoris *is a large genus of nudibranchs. This one was collected in the Philippines.*

near the surface but far enough away from metal halide lamps to prevent UV burn; VHO lamps are not strong UV-emitters. Tridacnids have valuable functions in a reef aquarium. They absorb ammonia and nitrates, and are a simpler alternative to the complex and labor-intensive algal scrubber.

As with reef-building corals, tridacnid clams should be provided calcium for their shells, iodine for their algae, and intense light (preferably metal halide, but VHO may be sufficient) close to the animal at least six hours a day.

Tridacnid clams farmed in the Pacific include *Tridacna derasa, T. gigas, T. squamosa, T. crocea, T. maxima, Hippopus hippopus,* and *H. porcellanus.* The clams are induced to shed gametes, and two days later the veliger larvae collected, transferred, and exposed to zooxanthellae. Later, the pediveliger settles on the bottom for growth in raceways. Growth is accelerated by supplementary ammonia or nitrate, especially in daylight; nitrate is only taken up as ammonia is depleted, and all uptake activity is depressed after dark. Young clams are sold to other farmers for a three-year grow-out period to 5 or 6 inches market size. Called vasua in Fiji, clams are propagated throughout the Indo-Pacific for sushi, sashimi, cooking in coconut milk, or salt-dried. The aquarium market is small.

The smallest and most beautiful species is *T. crocea* with its blue iridophores, but other tridacnids with green or yellow pigments are also beautiful and rarely outgrow an aquarium. The narrow end is open and vulnerable, so predatory crabs should not be kept in a reef tank with tridacnids. This narrow end produces the byssal attachment threads and chemicals that erode rock to give the clam a tight fit.

across and 400 pounds. *Tridacna, Hippopus,* and certain cockles are the only clams known to harbor symbiotic algae. Tridacnid veliger larvae, already containing symbiotic *Symbiodinium* zooxanthellae, settle on coral rocks where they soon attach with byssus threads and eventually burrow into the rock by excreting acids. They filter the water for plankton, but get most of their nutrients from symbiotic zooxanthellae. The zooxanthellae in tridacnids are extracellular, lining the outer edge of the mantle and digestive tract where they are exposed to sunlight. Tridacnids provide the zooxanthellae with waste phosphate and ammonia and a platform awash in seawater and sunlight. In turn, the algae provide the clam with amino acids and carbohydrates. The clams harvest and swallow excess algae, which have been found deep in their digestive tract and in their wastes. Even though lacking the enzyme cellulase, the clams are able to digest algal cells because the cellulose cell walls of these algae are leaky.

Tridacnid clams have fluorescent pigments that may protect them from ultraviolet radiation. Situate the clam

Mark Gervis, Manager of the ICLARM Coastal Aquaculture Center in the Solomon Islands, had these recommendations for mini-reef aquarists:

"Purchase a clam that isn't gaping with a mantle nicely spread out over the shell edge and not torn. In *T. maxima, T. crocea,* and *T. squamosa* the byssal gland should be visible. Reject clams with flatworms or the small white snails that look like sand grains near the byssus or in the scutes of the shell. Make sure there are no dead organisms attached to the shell. Place the clam horizontal, not vertical, on a hard surface, and shorten the metal halide exposure from the normal 8–10 hours down to just 2–4 hours until the clam adjusts to the light level. In fact, small clams don't need so many hours of metal halide light, doing just fine as long as they get 12 hours of fluorescent. Small clams need less light than large clams. Tridacnids also like warmer water than corals, so place them high up where they'll be warmed by the metal halide light. They do best at close to 80.6°F, pH 8.3, calcium 400–480 mg/L, and salinity 32–35 ppt. High quality skimming is essential for water quality. Don't place the clam directly in a strong current. Tridacnids don't do well in heavily fed tanks and should not themselves be fed."

Because they occur in tropical shallows, tridacnids do not require blue actinic (420 nm) light but do require intense light. Thus, they may thrive under aged 5500–6500 K lamps that have color shifted but retained intensity. The same is true for VHO lamps. Ordinary fluorescent lamps have insufficient intensity for tridacnids.

The colorful tridacnids sometimes lose bright pigments in a reef tank, the mantle becoming brown. The problem is caused by excessive light and nutrients resulting in overgrowth of zooxanthellae

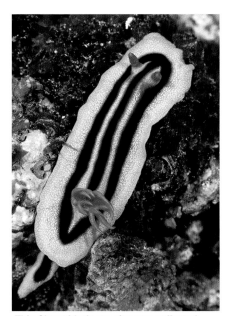

This Chromidoris species was collected from the Pacific. Nudibranchs are beautiful but hard to feed.

in the clams, which then mask the iridescent pigments. The solution is to cut back on feeding. Tridacnids retain their colors in reef tanks kept nutrient-starved. Tridacnids are susceptible to boring molluscs (*Cymatium*, Pyramidellids), many shrimp and crabs, and some fishes that pick at the mantle. They have few defenses beyond inserting themselves deeply into a rock, and that takes time. Chemicals also affect them. Strontium supplements may be toxic to tridacnid clams, and should be avoided.

Manuals on tridacnid clam aquaculture are available from Bibliotech, Australian National University, Canberra ACT 0200, Australia.

The remaining five subclasses of the Bivalvia (the Palaeotaxodonta, Palaeoheterodonta, Analodesmata, Cryptodonta, and Solemyoida) are small groups of little interest.

Chapter Seventeen
Crustaceans

The predominant land arthropods are insects (estimated at 30 million species), while those most important in the sea are crustaceans (52,000 species total for freshwater and marine). Marine crustaceans include crabs, shrimp, lobsters, barnacles, amphipods, isopods, fish lice, and copepods. Copepods are the most important of all zooplankton, and the most abundant animals on earth.

Crustaceans have an outer skeleton of chitin, a mucopolysaccharide (complex carbohydrate combined with a peptide). They possess two pairs of antennae. As they increase in size and advance in development, crustaceans develop a new cuticle under the hard skeleton, molt (split and shed the old skeleton), swell with water and salts, and harden the new cuticle to protect the soft body. A crustacean has several larval stages, each accompanied by a molt, and one last molt to mature and breed. Many crustaceans only mate during the brief period before the new cuticle hardens. Molting (ecdysis) is under hormonal control.

The crustacean body has 15 segments apportioned among a cephalothorax or head and chest region (8), abdomen (6), and telson or tail (1). The front of the cephalothorax carries antennae for sensing and filtering, or claw bearing chelipeds for feeding; behind them, still on the cephalothorax, are chewing appendages (maxillipeds); and the remaining appendages are the legs

for locomotion. The abdominal appendages (pleopods) are used for swimming, respiration, carrying the eggs, copulation, and digging into the sediments. Behind the abdomen is the telson or tail (a single segment) that may be covered by additional narrow or flattened abdominal appendages.

Crustaceans feed by filtration, grazing, or predation. Copepods, cladocerans (daphniae), barnacles, and anacostracans (brine and fairy shrimp) sweep algae, protozoa, and other zooplankton from the water column with bristles on their antennae. Crabs and shrimp chew or macerate detritus, algae, leaves, and other animals with still more modified appendages behind the antennae, placing the macerated food into the mouth opening.

Some crustaceans feed on corals. A few can be propagated as live food (brine shrimp, copepods). Others are ideal tank inhabitants that can be collected or propagated.

Barnacles

The Cirripedia are bizarre crustaceans living inside a double shell or carapace reinforced with calcium deposits. Most are free-living and abundant on rocky shores (*Balanus)* or attached to drifting flotsam and seaweeds (*Lepas);* others are parasitic on crabs (*Sacculina)* or other fishes (*Lernaeodiscus). Balanus* frequently occurs on live rock, *Lepas* on sargassum weed and driftwood, and both are sometimes sold in aquarium shops. Feed barnacles frequently with brine shrimp nauplii, which they filter from the water with their antennae-like legs. *Lepas* (gooseneck barnacles) do well when fed regularly; if feeding is interrupted for as little as a week, they die.

Copepods

Of a half-dozen major groups of copepods, the harpacticoids and cyclopoids are the most abundant in marine water. In general, harpacticoids live on surfaces as adults (benthic) and have larval and naupliar stages that occur in the water column, while the cyclopoids are almost always in the water column at all stages of life. You would think that cyclopoids would then be better live foods, but in fact they are more difficult to rear. The harpacticoids have many species of tide pools, estuaries, and other coastal waters that vary daily in salinity, temperature, and water quality. Because harpacticoids are well adapted to these conditions, their culture is relatively easy. For example, the harpacticoids *Euterpina, Nitokra, Tigriopus,* and *Acartia* are all grown in culture and used as food for larval marine fishes. These and others have also been collected with plankton nets and used to feed baby fish, and that's a lot easier than cultivation, provided you live on a coast.

Copepods are cultured on the same microalgae used to grow rotifers, such as the green algae *Chaetoceros, Tetraselmis, Isochrysis, Nannochloropsis,* and dinoflagellates such as *Gymnodinium.* Some algae are better than others because of the mix of fatty acids in the membranes of their chloroplasts. Commercial microalgae paste eliminates the need to culture live microalgae. The

1. telson
2. abdomen
3. cephalothorax
4. antennae
5. cheliped
6. pleopods
7. uropods

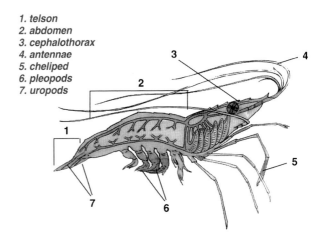

Typical decapod crustaceans, shrimp and prawns are divided into three body areas, the cephalothorax in front, the abdomen in the middle, and the telson or tail area. The cephalothorax appendages are modified into sensory antennae, chewing mouthparts, and sometimes grasping appendages. The abdomen has appendages for walking, swimming, and delivery of sex products (eggs and sperm). The tail has a fanlike array of flattened uropods for simple flipperlike swimming.

copepod goes through six naupliar (larval) and five juvenile (miniature adult) copepodite stages, before the final molt to the adult stage. The nauplii are about the size of rotifers, but have a different motion that attracts larval fishes and, more important, a high concentration of HUFAs critical to larval fish survival. Copepods can be cultured in screened cages (37 micron mesh Nitex) suspended in water enhanced with algae, and the smallest larvae harvested from outside the screens. Or the copepods can be cultured in bare tanks with aeration, screening out the adults first and then using the remaining green water (larval copepods and algae) to feed young fish. In either case, breeder copepods should be fed new live algae or prepared algae paste as the copepod culture water lightens from slightly green to clear. The chloroplast membranes of

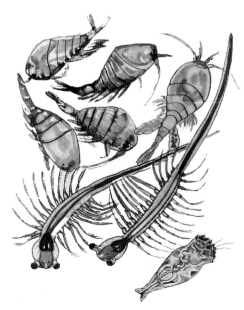

Copepods (top), the most abundant plank-tonic animals in the sea, are the principal nutrition for almost all fishes and larger sea creatures at early ages. Brine shrimp, (center), are salt pond variants of a fresh-water group of crustaceans. The nauplii or larvae are ideal for aquaculture and feeding marine fishes and invertebrates. Rotifers such as the brackish water Brachionus plicatilus, (lower right and not to scale), are cultured to feed marine fish babies too small to eat brine shrimp nauplii.

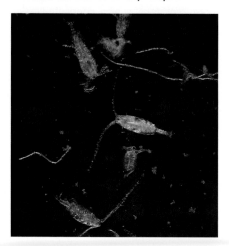

the microalgae provide copepods with omega 3 highly unsaturated fatty acids (HUFA), and that is why copepods are so nutritious. Copepods accumulate and store HUFAs. You could also purchase commercial HUFA preparations such as Selco, but algae paste is an easier way to the same ends.

We can expect more kinds of Harpacticoids to be cultured and offered to the hobby. The families of Harpacticoids include Canuellidae, Cerviniidae, Ectinosomatidae, Darcythompsoniidae, Tachidiidae, Harpacticidae, Tisbidae, Peltidiidae, Tegastidae, Thalestridae, Diosaccidae, Metidae, Ameiridae, Paramesochridae, Tetragonicipitidae, Canthocamptidae, Cylindropsyllidae, Cletodidae, Laophontidae, Ancorabolidae, and Latiremidae.

Many kinds of parasitic copepods occur on marine fishes. The most common types are described in Chapter 23.

Crabs

Small hermit crabs of the genera *Paguristes, Clibanarius, Phimochirus,* and *Calcinus* are harmless to corals and eat algae and detritus; very popular are blue-legged and red-legged hermits (*Clibanarius tricolor, Paguristes cadenati*). Sally lightfoot crabs (*Grapsus, Hemigrapsus*) of coastal mangrove forests are excellent algae eaters. Small reef crabs such as *Stenorhynchus, Percnon, Melybia, Neopetrolisthes, Lybia, Carpilius, Mithrax,* and *Peresphona* even help control predaceous bristleworms (carnivorous annelids with powerful biting

Calanoid copepods viewed under the microscope. The culture of copepods has completely changed the success rate of breeding and raising marine fishes, but wild ones (like these) are still used by coastal aquarists.

jaws). Porcelain crabs (*Porcellana, Pachycheles*) are free-living or symbionts of corals, anemones, and hermit crabs unlikely to damage corals. However, other tiny symbiotic crabs found in *Acropora* coral sometimes stress the corals during shipping. Sponge crabs (*Dromidia, Macrocoeloma*) are attractive when small, but untrustworthy when more than an inch in carapace (upper shell) width. Crabs can be propagated in the same manner as shrimp (see below).

Crabs to avoid include the spectacular shamefaced and box crabs (*Calappa*) and coral crab (*Carpilius),* which eat anything they catch, including sleeping fishes. Large hermit crabs (*Pagurus, Dardanus, Petrochirus*) may graze corals, but are relatively safe in clownfish breeding tanks, where they eat algae and leftover food, but don't seem to pursue the incubating eggs. All swimming crabs (*Portunus, Arenaeus, Callinectes*) are predators to be avoided. The rock and mud crabs (*Carcinus, Menippe, Panopeus, Rhithropanopeus*) are omnivores difficult to remove from rock cavities. Fiddler crabs (*Uca*) often climb out of the aquarium.

Shrimp

Recommended reef tank shrimp are the small, colorful *Periclimenes, Stenopus, Lysmata, Gnathophyllum, Hippolysmata, Hymenocera, Stegopontonia, Pontonia, Pinctada, Conchodytes, Rhynchocinetes, Saron, Tozeuma,* and some colorful species of *Palaemon.* Some are symbionts or predators that need cnidarians, sponges, gobies,

Neopetrolisthes, *the porcelain crabs, live in several kinds of cnidarians, where they receive protection and conduct housecleaning.*

Stenorhynchus sellcornis, *the arrow crab, is common throughout the Caribbean and the Florida Keys. They are inexpensive, and not difficult to propagate, and are a good reef tank inhabitant, safe with corals.*

Periclimenes yucatanicus *is symbiotic with Atlantic sea anemones, but often overlooked.*

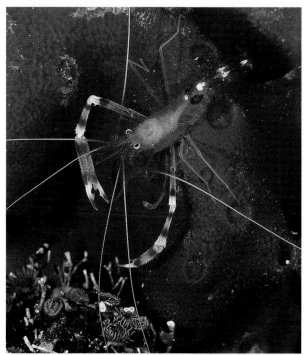

Stenopus tenuirostris, *the golden coral shrimp, is often overlooked by collectors and aquarists. Not yet commercially aquacultured, it will probably become available as techniques improve.*

starfish, sea urchins, or clams. *Periclimenes* should be provided with their host cnidarians in a reef tank. *Lysmata wurdemanni,* the peppermint shrimp, normally a symbiont of sponges, does not require them, and will eat anything, including stinging anemones, *Aiptasia.* Snapping or pistol shrimp (*Alpheus, Synalpheus*) may prey on other shrimp, although some are symbiotic with burrowing gobies and do well in tanks with deep gravel and a goby partner. Mantis shrimp (*Squilla, Gonodactylus, Odontodacytlus, Lysosquilla*) are capable of slicing a fish, a soft coral, or an aquarist's finger with the efficiency of a razor blade and should never be placed in a reef tank. Reef tanks with decorative shrimp should not have large tangs or pygmy angelfishes, which sometimes forget their mostly herbivorous habits.

Because crustaceans molt as they grow, even after they are adults, they are vulnerable to attack by fishes or other crustaceans, even of the same species. If your pretty crustacean has disappeared, do not assume disease. It probably molted, and was attacked during the 24-hour period often required for the new shell to harden.

Breeding Shrimp

Lysmata and *Stenopus* have been bred in aquaria. *Lysmata* are hermaphroditic, and almost any two can be a breeding pair. Within hours of a molt, one shrimp delivers a packet of sperm to another before its cuticle hardens, the latter shrimp then carrying the fertilized eggs attached to abdominal appendages or pleopods. While carrying its own fertilized eggs, this shrimp can also deliver a sperm packet to the other shrimp when the latter molts.

Either capture an egg-laden shrimp from the reef tank for removal to a

Molting in Crustaceans

Crustaceans increase in size by shedding the chitinous exoskeleton, and growing into a new and larger exoskeleton. The molt is called ecdysis, and is identical in crustaceans and insects. The inactive form of the molting hormone is called ecdysone, secreted by the crustacean Y-organ, located in two glands in the lower front part of the chest or thorax (in insects it is called the prothoracic gland). Other tissues in the body change a single hydrogen atom ($^-$H) on the ecdysone molecule to a hydroxy group ($^-$OH) at the 20th carbon in the chain, altering the molecule to 20-hydroxyecdysone, the active form that initiates ecdysis (molting).

The eyestalk of crustaceans contains a bundle of secretory neurons called the X-organ, which produces a molt-inhibiting peptide that is stored in a nearby sinus or cavity. In lobsters the X-organ is a 1 mm light blue spot on the upper side of the stalk. When the molt-inhibiting peptide is released from the sinus into the circulatory system (the hemolymph), the Y-organ slows its production of ecdysone. Snipping off the eyestalk can initiate molting.

Stenopus hispidus is a common and popular Caribbean shrimp, suitable for reef aquaria. During molts, shrimp are tasty morsels for every other predator in the aquarium.

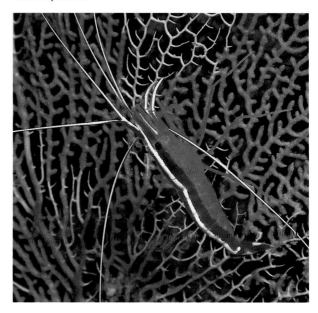

hatching tank, or devote a small tank to breeding. Place one egg-laden shrimp or two or more non-ovigerous shrimp in a well-illuminated 10-gallon aquarium with a sponge filter, aragonite sand for

Lysmata grabhami, the most popular decorative shrimp, perches on a sea fan. Most of the Lysmata species in the hobby have been propagated, but not commercially. The nauplii require enriched HUFAs and frequent water changes.

137

Lysmata wurdemanni *is commercially propagated for the marine market, and inexpensive. It is not difficult to breed them yourself.*

Lysmata debelius, *the fire shrimp, is the most difficult of the genus to propagate. At press time, about 10 percent of the larvae were being raised at the University of Texas using a diet of enriched rotifers supplemented with a slurry of peneid (supermarket seafood) shrimp.*

pH control, and live rock with macro-algal growth for nitrate control. The shrimp will mate after a molt induced by heavy feeding. It takes two weeks from mating until the night the eggs hatch. The zooea early stage larvae are larger than brine shrimp nauplii, and move with slow up-and-down jerks.

After hatching, remove the adults, turn off the aeration so the water is still, and add rotifers, copepod nauplii, or brine shrimp nauplii enriched for a couple of hours with microalgae. Most zooea die within days from starvation, competition, predation, or ammonia toxicity. The larval shrimp and the live food move toward light in the absence of current, so you can use less food and deliver it to them with a baster. Nothing will kill baby shrimp faster than overfeeding, with the excess food decaying and degrading the water with ammonia and microbial wastes.

Lysmata takes 2–9 weeks to grow from first naupliar to the quarter inch juvenile stage. The adults produce clutches every 10–12 days. *Lysmata amboinensis* and *L. debelius* larvae are large at hatching, while *L. wurdemanni* are small. Space, adequate food, and high quality water are all important. Commercial production requires constant flow-through water changes and almost constant feeding, but home aquarists can raise small numbers with a little effort.

Lobsters

The rock lobsters (*Panulirus, Enoplometopus*) and slipper lobsters (*Evibacus, Scyllarides, Scyllarus*) have several species attractive when small, less interesting as they grow. All are carnivores that may attack tridacnid clams, snails, tubeworms, and even resting fishes at night.

Chapter Eighteen
Echinoderms

Sea stars, brittle stars, sea urchins, crinoids, and sea cucumbers live on the bottom of all the seas in the world. Of almost 7,000 species, several are kept by marine aquarists because they graze algae and rocks, clean the gravel, or provide larvae for feeding newly hatched marine fishes. Many echinoderms are too large for reef tanks, require cold water, eat red algae, or kill other reef creatures. All are intolerant of drastic changes in salinity, and some cannot tolerate trapped air. The Atlantic coast of the United States has few species, the cold Pacific Northwest many more. The greatest diversity is in the tropical Indo-Pacific.

Echinoderms don't have blood. Their water vascular system serves the same purpose of delivering nutrients and removing wastes, and is also used for rigidity, respiration, and mobility. The system contains a saline fluid often with a small amount of hemoglobin that enables echinoderms to move by filling and depleting tiny sacs arranged in five rows around the body. These sacs continue into tiny tube feet on the bottom of the animal. Fluid pumped into the tube feet causes them to elongate. Tube feet are used for motility, capturing food, and cleaning the skin.

Echinoderm skin contains particles or ossicles of calcium and magnesium carbonate. These ossicles are loosely connected (sea stars, brittle stars), fused to form a rigid test (sea urchins,

sand dollars), or minute and almost irrelevant (sea cucumbers).

Most remarkable is the ability of echinoderms to instantly transform from limpness to rock-hard rigidity. In this way, an urchin can lock itself into a crevice, a sea cucumber can suddenly change from limp to solid, or a sea star can exert enough force to open the valves of a clam. They accomplish this change from limp to turgid (which can be generalized throughout the body or localized) by forming calcium ion bridges among specialized macromolecules in their connective tissue. The calcium bridge, turned off, can instantly liquefy the tissue connecting an arm or parts of the gut or respiratory systems, breaking off a body part. Sea cucumbers break off and release pieces of their intestinal tracts or respiratory systems to eliminate unneeded tissue, and sometimes to smother or to poison a predator.

Echinoderms can regenerate lost parts. New England oystermen years ago discovered to their dismay that cutting up oyster-killing sea stars only resulted in more sea stars when the parts grew into whole animals.

Similarly strange chemistry is employed by the tube feet of sea stars. Although tube feet on an aquarist's hand may feel like suction cups, in fact the sea star secretes an instantly bonding adhesive, and just as instantly can secrete a chemical that dissolves the bond.

Himerometra robustipinna, *a feather star, requires zooplankton fed with a baster, or it dies of starvation.*

Feather stars (crinoids), this one from the Indo-Pacific, all require direct feeding using a baster of zooplankton such as brine shrimp.

Echinoderms are usually separate sexes, shedding eggs or sperm into the water, where they form a zygote inside the egg membrane that will soon hatch into a bilaterally symmetrical, ciliated larva. The swimming larva settles on the bottom to form the new echinoderm and quickly becomes radially symmetrical. In some larval forms, it first forms clones of itself before developing into the juvenile and then adult form. So one settled larva may become many settled larvae that each becomes an adult. In some echinoderms, the fertilized egg is brooded inside the female, and a completely formed juvenile is released from the mother.

Feather Stars

Feather stars (Crinoidea) are available through mail-order suppliers, but they don't ship well. If handled, they go rigid and may fragment. Feather stars have the basic complement of five parts divided into 10, 20, or even 200 branches or arms. The arms have comb-like teeth and tube feet that capture suspended planktonic tintinnid protozoa, bacteria, and detritus, wiping them off with cilia and rolling them into packets carried to the mouth. Feather stars begin life attached to the bottom by a stalk, but soon break free and move about on mobile arms; some can even flap the arms to swim. A single large group, the Order Comatulida, is of recent origin and radiating out of the tropics. Many live on or below coral, rocks, and rubble, and a few associate with gorgonians. Most are active after dark. I've frequently found them in the Caribbean in deep cracks and holes in shallow water rock walls (from which they were impossible to extricate). *Comatula, Comaster, Comissa, Comanthina, Comantheria,*

Amphimetra, Heterometra, Himerometra, Oligometra, Oxycomanthus, Oxymetra, Pilometra, Stephanometra, Petasometra, Liparometra, and *Lamprometra* are Indo-Pacific; *Analcidometra* and *Nemaster* are Caribbean.

In mini-reefs, feather stars eat blended fish-shrimp particles or brine shrimp squirted onto the arms with a food baster. Few aquarists report success with crinoids, and I don't recommend them for beginners.

Holothuroids

The Order Holothuroidea (sea cucumbers) contains over 900 species of elongate echinoderms with reduced ossicles resulting in a rubbery or leathery skin. The ossicles have distinctive shapes useful for identification. Sea cucumbers may be an inch long to three feet or more, and squat to wormlike. Of the five rows of tube feet, the two on top are bare eruptions, and the three on the flattened lower side provide mobility. There are no arms. The tube feet around the mouth are enlarged as feeder tentacles that gather food and push it into the pharynx. The pharynx contracts around the tentacles to squeeze out the food.

There is a rather odd respiratory arrangement. Sea cucumbers swallow water at the cloaca, pump it through the body into blind compartments making up a respiratory tree, and then discharge it back out the cloaca. If starved or attacked by a predator, the sea cucumber can release calcium ions in the rear connective tissue macromolecules, liquifying the connections to its viscera, and expel the viscera from the cloaca to distract the predator. The new viscera are regenerated in weeks. Some sea cucumbers, converting defense to offense, emit sticky white strings

Some sea cucumbers use poster-warning colors to protect against predation. Many sea cucumbers discharge the intestine when threatened, and grow a new set within weeks.

(Cuvier's tubules) with the expelled respiratory tree that stick to and strangle the predator, and in still others the Cuvier's tubules contain a toxic saponin called *holothurin.* This toxin also occurs in sea cucumber skin. Crushed sea cucumbers are used by some Asian fishermen to poison and kill food fish in tidal pools. Other sea cucumbers are delicacies in Asian countries.

Sexes are generally separate, the single gonad expelling eggs or sperm into the water. A few sea cucumbers retain and brood fertilized eggs, releasing fully formed juveniles. Breeding can be induced by putting at least a dozen individuals together on a deep sand bottom and rapidly changing temperature.

Eggs and their larvae may be large or small; smaller larvae may require a month or more of planktonic care, including feeding with microalgal culture, until they are large enough to settle; large eggs and their large larvae may store food, not need supplemental feeding, and settle out of the plankton much faster (less than two weeks).

Sea cucumbers are scavengers, detritus feeders, and grazers in mini-reefs with aragonite sand or gravel, but less likely to find adequate detritus in bare-bottom tanks. The burrowers churn gravel, recycle detritus, and control infaunal worms and crustaceans. Others sweep detritus from the surface, and still others collect material from the water column. Generally, particles are collected by a sticky substance on the tentacles, and the sea cucumber wipes the tentacles in its mouth as though licking its fingers of candy. Most require no special foods, but all should only be introduced to well-established aquaria with accumulated detritus in the sand. Using a powerhead to blast detritus into the water column is beneficial to sea cucumbers, and much of the uneaten detritus can be captured by a filter or protein skimmer.

Holothuria and *Stichopus* occur in the Atlantic and Indo-Pacific. Atlantic genera include *Actinopyga, Euapta, Astichopus, Isostichopus, Pentacta*, and *Parathyone*. *Ceto, Neothyonidium, Psolidium, Synapta, Synaptula, Cucumaria, Cholochirus, Pseudocholochirus, Thelenota, Pseudocholochirus, Bohadschia*, and *Opheodesoma* are Indo-Pacific genera. The most attractive sea cucumbers are the purple *Pseudocholochirus violaceus* from the Philippines and the red and white striped *Thelonota rubrolineata* from deep water in Indonesia and the Solomon Islands. The Caribbean five-toothed cucumbers (*Actinopyga floridana, A. agassizi)* can be identified by the teeth surrounding the cloaca. This back end pore is the hole through which symbiotic pearl fishes (Carapidae) enter and exit the cucumber's respiratory tree, used as a biological cavern.

A few swimming sea cucumbers (*Pelagothuria*) occur in deep Atlantic waters from the surface to the bottom. Many others (*Cucumaria, Actinopyga, Thyone*) burrow, swallowing sand and digesting the small benthic animals within. Still others sweep surface detritus. Some sticky species live among rocks (*Euapta, Synapta*), grazing attached algae and other marine life, and a few are plankton feeders. Still others are surface forms always out and about, either plain (*Stichopus, Astichopus, Actinopyga, Holothuria, Isostichopus*) or beautifully colored (*Brandtothuria*, and the sea apples, *Pseudocolochirus*). The brightly colored surface forms are most likely to contain holothurin, but seem to be safe for mini-reef and marine fish aquariums as it takes considerable trauma to generate release of toxin.

Echinoids

The Class Echinoidea (sand dollars, sea urchins, heart urchins) lack arms, and their ossicles are joined providing a solid case or test. The lower body has tube feet enabling them to move over rocky surfaces. Sea urchins have two sets (occasionally one) of elongate movable spines used for defense and movement. The spines are connected through holes in the test with a loose mesenchyme, and can lock the body in place when the macromolecules are stimulated to form calcium bridges. Some urchins also have barbs and irritants on their spines. Pedicillariae are tiny jaw-like structures on short stalks located all over the body and used for catching particles or cleansing the skin. Sand dollars and heart urchins have tiny spines and burrow through sand feeding on detritus. Sea urchins have a powerful five-part calcareous jaw structure (Aristotle's lantern) that scrapes algae from rocks and coral. One species grinds a personal cave, then becomes sessile and captures planktonic microalgae for food. The majority are grazers. Grazing urchins are among the most important algal controls on the coral reef. When an Atlantic epidemic almost wiped out longspine black sea urchins (*Diadema*) years ago, algal overgrowth severely damaged coral reefs from Florida to South America, and recovery of the urchins and coral reefs is still incomplete.

Most echinoids have separate males and females that release gametes into the seawater; a few are brooding species. Sea urchins can be kept sexually ripe with a summer-like 18/6 photoperiod, and induced to shed gametes by touching the shell with electrodes connected to a 12 volt transformer for 30 seconds, injecting 0.1 M acetylcholine, or

Eucidaris tribuloides, *an Atlantic pencil urchin, is sensitive to air, and should be transported completely submerged.*

injecting 0.3–0.5 ml of 0.5 M potassium chloride (dissolve 9.32 grams of granular KCl in 250 ml of distilled water to make a 0.5 M solution). Urchins are stimulated while upside down on a beaker of seawater, the red eggs and white sperm mixed, and the zygotes used in biology classes to study cell division through larval formation. Aquaculturists use the minute echinopluteus larvae as live food for marine fish larvae that don't accept rotifers. *Strongylocentrotus intermedius* is raised in China, and the gonads sold for the sashimi market in Japan. Growth is accelerated at high temperatures and with prepared foods instead of its normal food, brown algae or kelp.

The common pink, black, and purple long and short spine or pencil urchins (*Arbacia, Colobocentrotus, Lytechinus, Echinometra, Eucidaris, Diadema, Strongylocentrotus, Heterocentrotus*) are good algal grazers in reef tanks, but large ones may knock over rocks and even small ones may eat right through everything. Watch for bald patches

Coldwater Echinoderms

Echinoderms of the Pacific northwest are diverse, beautiful, and popular in public aquaria. They require refrigerated aquaria with live rock and less intense light than tropical reef aquariums. Among the most popular species are the sea cucumbers *Parastichopus californicus* and *Cucumaria miniata*, the urchin *Strongylocentrotus franciscanus*, and the spectacular sea stars *Pycnopodia helianthoides, Solaster stimpsoni,* and *Pteraster tesselatus*.

Lytechinus of the Atlantic is popular in high school science classes, since its gametes are readily emitted under electrical or chemical stimulation. The zygotes develop rapidly, and you can see it all under the microscope in a few hours. The larvae are live food for baby marine fishes that don't take rotifers. The adults are good algae cleaners, but might scrape your red coralline algae as well, and must be watched.

Ophiurioids

The brittle and basket stars are the most successful echinoderms with 2,000 species everywhere from muddy estuaries to abyssal trenches.

Brittle stars are abundant in holes among rocks, avoiding light during the day, coming out to forage at night or whenever they sense food. They'll eat almost anything small, and some are noctural planktivores. Brittle stars are harmless to corals, and do a great job of cleaning beneath rocks and within gravel. Five long, thin, and mobile arms radiate from a central disk. Any arm can coil snake-like to lay a loop and rapidly pull the body forward; tube feet are hardly used. Each arm has a single row of articulated ossicles, providing incredible mobility in certain planes, like a vertebral column. The mobile arms encircle food and carry it to the jaws, dig in sediments, climb rocks and tank walls, and wrap around structures to provide stability in current. The arms can immediately stiffen (calcium bridges among macromolecules in the mesenchyme) and break off when attacked, but soon regenerate. Most brittle stars release gametes into the water where fertilization occurs and a swimming ophiopluteus larva develops, but female brooding to fully formed juveniles is also common, and brittle star multiplication in reef tanks is not unusual. Some of the prettiest species are in the genera *Conocladus, Ophiomyxa, Ophioderma, Ophiomaza, Ophiolepis, Ophioactis, Ophiomastix, Ophiocoma*, and *Ophiothrix*, but it's hard to find a brittle star with a bad reputation. Some brittle stars luminesce upon stimulation.

The basket stars are a small family (Gorgonocephalidae) with divided arms and large disks requiring considerable

where the coralline algae have been eaten down to the rock; in that case, you've too many urchins or they're too large. Sea urchins are useful glass cleaners for marine tanks generally.

Sea urchins should be moved while submerged to avoid air trapped inside the test that might oxidize their tissues and kill them. Avoid *Toxopneustes* and *Asthenosoma*, whose poisonous spines are painful or lethal if they penetrate human skin.

Sand dollars and heart urchins are deposit feeders. Heart urchins like *Culcita* and *Echinoneus* are attractive, but clumsy and tend to hide. Sand dollars (*Clypeaster, Echinodiscus, Encope*) are valuable subterranean gravel stirrers, and don't need to be attractive.

food. They are carnivores and plankti-vores of deep reefs that climb up onto a structure and capture small crustaceans and worms drifting by, trapping them with both mucus and microscopic hooks on the arms for delivery to the endlessly hungry jaws. They shouldn't be kept with small shrimp or crabs. The common tropical reef genera are *Astroboa* from the Indo-Pacific and the hardy *Astrophyton* of the Caribbean. Basket stars require daily feedings of frozen adult brine shrimp, shredded fish or shrimp, or frozen euphausids. They climb air lines and tubes to the top of the tank, going where they wish. Basket stars emit gametes that develop into ophiopluteus larvae that drift through the ocean until they sense and settle on adult basket stars. At one time these newly settled larvae were thought to be the adult basket star's brooded off-spring. There is no information on whether they can be propagated by fragmentation of arms.

Asteroidea

With 1,500 species from the tropics to the poles, from rocky shores to the silty abyss, the sea stars (starfish) are almost as numerous as brittle stars, and more prominent. One of the richest areas in the world is the Pacific north-west of the United States, with 70 species, but the tropical Indo-Pacific has far more species.

Sea stars usually have five or more stiff arms with little mobility except at the tips. Sea stars glide by first sticking to the surface with an adhesive from tube feet beneath each arm, and then dis-solving the adhesive with a second secretion. The arms continue into the central body, with no demarcation setting off a separate disk.

Ophiocoma echinata, *the Atlantic harlequin brittle star, is fine in reef tanks where it scavenges the sand and rocks for edibles. All brittle stars are excellent reef tank residents, and effective cleaners.*

Creatures of grass beds, sand flats, rocks, and reefs, sea stars are preda-tors of bivalves whose shells they force open by gently crawling over them and suddenly freezing their arms in place to maintain a vise-like grip that prevents the bivalve from closing. The sea star then extrudes and inserts its stomach into the gap between the valves and onto the flesh of the clam or oyster. Sea stars eat other animals as well.

Indo-Pacific genera include *Acanthaster, Archaster, Iconaster, Stellaster, Pentagonaster, Tosia, Bothriaster, Choriaster, Culcita, Halityle, Mithrodia, Monachaster, Pentaceraster, Pentaster, Pateriella, Protoreaster, Radiaster,*

Sea stars use their abundant tube feet to move about and to exert hydraulic force on prey. The sea star Linckia *at the Great Barrier Reef.*

niles. One group attaches eggs to rocks. The Mediterranean *Echinaster sepositus* lays fertilized eggs that hatch as fully formed baby starfish, bypassing the larval stage. A *Henricia* species may have similar reproduction. Smooth-skinned sea stars have a reputation for safety in reef aquaria. That may be true regarding predation on corals, but the generality is risky in aquaria containing tridacnid clams and a sea star that hasn't eaten in a few days. Blue and red species of *Linckia* are popular with mini-reef aquarists.

The Pacific crown-of-thorns starfish, *Acanthaster*, a predator on scleractinian corals, has undergone a population explosion over parts of its range, leaving some reefs practically bald of living hard corals.

What's In a Name?

Many sea stars are planktivores, scavengers, or omnivores, while others are predatory on corals, snails, clams, sponges, tunicates, other starfish, and even fishes. What's in a name? Unfortunately, there are no standardized names for sea stars. You need to look at the animal and match it with a picture to get a correct identification. If you don't recognize the sea star, then avoid warty or multiple arm species as they're frequently predaceous on bivalves. A scallop might escape predatory sea stars, but tridacnids, which have no defenses, are a sea star delicacy.

Recommended: *Linckia, Pharia, Phataria, Fromia, Othilia.*

Not Recommended: *Protoreaster, Pentaceraster, Acanthaster, Astrometus, Heliaster, Pisaster, Astropecten, Echinaster, Choriaster, Culcita, Oreaster.*

Euretaster, Ferdina, Fromia, Gomophia, Leiaster, Nardoa, Neoferdina, Ophidiaster, Tamaria, and *Thromidia.* Atlantic sea stars are less numerous, and include *Coscinasterias, Hacelia, Ceramaster,* and *Oreaster.* Genera common to both the Atlantic and Indo-Pacific include *Asterina, Astropecten, Echinaster, Luidia,* and *Linckia.*

Sea stars can divide through the disk to form two individuals from one, but normal reproduction requires shedding gametes into the water where they meet and develop into bipinnaria and then brachiolaria larvae that later become juve-

Chapter Nineteen
Annelids

The Phylum Annelida contains 15,000 species of segmented worms, usually with a hemoglobin-based blood circulatory system, a coelom or fluid-filled body cavity with respiratory and excretory functions, a straight gut, complex nervous system, and vast diversity of habitats. The major groups are the oligochaetes, poly-chaetes, and leeches.

Oligochaetes are terrestrial (earthworms, white worms, grindal worms) or aquatic (red tubifex, blackworms) hermaphrodites that lay eggs in capsules called cocoons. Oligochaetes are important live foods for aquarium fishes. Leeches are parasitic all or part of the life cycle, and also are hermaphrodites that lay eggs in cocoons. In nature, leeches may transmit protozoan diseases from infected fish to naïve fish during feeding, but they are not serious pests in aquaria or aquaculture. Polychaetes are marine with many species important as fishing bait, fish food, predators on invertebrates, and sometimes as vectors (transmitters) of marine diseases. *Hermodice carunculata*, a polychaete predaceous on *Oculina* corals, transmits the pathogenic bacterium *Vibrio shiloi*, an agent of one type of coral bleaching.

In polychaetes the sexes are usually separate. Males and females shed eggs and sperm through pores or by splitting the body wall (there is no cocoon). The eggs are fertilized and hatch to produce a ciliated trochophore larva that swims or crawls on the bottom. A few poly-chaetes store eggs until larval development transforms them into juveniles.

Polychaetes can be motile and roaming (errant) or sedentary. Each body segment has a branched lateral extension called a parapodium that looks like a tiny oar or lump, and each branch of each parapodium is armed with stinging bristles (setae) used for respiration and defense. The setae in the errant sea mouse covers the entire body, while in sedentary tube worms, setae are reduced. The parapodia (*para-podium* = accessory foot) are used for purchase to push the body forward, and the setae provide additional traction, like cleats on a golf shoe. In the brightly colored fire-worms (Amphinomidae), the calcified toxic bristles break and imbed in any fish foolish enough to attack. Polychaetes also move by sequentially inflating the coelom in each segment and then pulling themselves forward through sand or mud, or by extending the pharynx, everting the jaws to grab onto something, then retracting the pharynx and pulling the body forward. Polychaetes can also sinuously twist their bodies snakelike for rapid traverse.

The head is modified for filter feeding, predation, deposit-feeding, or grazing. Four or more eyes detect light and shadows, and one pelagic form with fully formed eyes (lens, cornea, etc.) and a head reminiscent of E.T. can see images. The mouth cavity leads to a protrusible

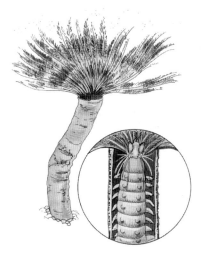

Polychaete marine worms often have complex jaws or other mouthparts in front, or they may have mouthparts modified to function as both gills and planktonic filters. The sides of the body have numerous appendages modified for movement and sometimes to assist in respiration.

Epitokal Reproduction

Indo-Pacific Palolo worms live within coral reefs, and simultaneously swarm in great masses. The non-reproductive worm in the coral is called an atoke. With the reproductive moon approaching, the rear segments transform into a series of short but complete worms with modified heads, enhanced swimming appendages, and a coelom packed with eggs or sperm. This string of dwarf reproductive worms or epitokes breaks off and the individuals swarm at the surface during one night of the year, the male epitokes seeking out female epitokes. Each releases gametes upon sensing the gametes of the opposite sex. The swarming epitokes also emit bursts of phosphorescent light, and the sea is illuminated with blue-green sparks as though millions of fireflies were mating beneath the surface. Epitokal reproduction occurs in many polychaete worms. Epitokes can form by multiple division of the atoke's original body or the growing of additional individuals from the rear of the atoke.

Polychaetes, including epitokal species, are common in live rock. Search your tank with a flashlight after dark, and you may see an occasional half-inch long epitoke arching and flapping its short body this way and that as it swims in the upper reaches of the aquarium seeking a mate.

pharynx armed with 4, 6, or 8 pincer-like jaws that have drawn blood from more than one fisherman trying to put a blood-worm (*Glycera*) on a hook. Some polychaetes don't have jaws, but "gum" the live prey or feed on dead tissues.

The amphinomid fireworms are coral predators and one at least is a vector of a blue-green alga causing a type of coral bleaching disease. The nereids are mostly detritus and algal eaters that occasionally take a nip of a coral, but usually scavenge dead tissue and macroalgae. Errant nereids are among the most abundant and important of live sand infauna, working oxygen and water through the sand as they consume and recycle detritus. You can't have too many polychaetes in the sand and rocks; their housekeeping cleans leftover food, dead plants and animals, and generally reduces the frequency of decomposition

blooms by fungi and bacteria. The sedentary polychaetes are mostly filter feeders or deposit feeders. The deposit feeders (*Terebella, Amphitrite*) live in holes and thrust out long, thin, white tentacles that adhere to food particles on the surface, then bring them to the mouth where they are wiped off the tentacles like a child licking an ice-cream stick.

The most beautiful coral reef filter feeders are the sabellid, sabellarid, and spirorbid Christmas tree worms, feather duster worms, and fanworms (*Sabella, Sabellaria, Sabellastarte, Hydroides*) that may be red, blue, orange, or yellow. Their clusters of filaments at the head are arranged in helical vortices, their bodies buried in the rock or extending above it in a sand or calcareous tube. The vortices of filaments are modified for gas exchange and to filter plankton from the water, just as many fishes have cartilaginous gill rakers to capture plankton arising from the opposite end of the same gill arch carrying the respiratory tissue. Captured plankton and particles are delivered down the vortex to the mouth where the catch is sorted into food, waste, and sand grains to be mixed with mucus and laid down around the top of an ever-growing sand tube (in sabellariid and pectinariid worms), or the sand is discarded in a calcareous tube (spirorbids). Fanworms have primitive photoreceptors to detect shadows of predators and can instantly withdraw into their tubes, closing the walls of the tube to protect the head, or capping the tube with a snail-like opercular lid.

The sabellid and sabellarid Christmas tree worms and other fanworms require zooplankton, and should be fed live *Artemia* nauplii. They are picked on by pygmy angels, shrimp, and wrasses, and do best in a hard coral tank devoid of fishes other than tangs.

Some sedentary polychaetes are easily overgrown by macroalgae and need shade for protection, while others do well in brilliant light. In St. John, Virgin Islands, I saw blue forms in shade below rock ledges, and orange forms in full sun on top of the same rocks.

Sabellastarte, the feather duster worm, is a large filter feeder that is unable to withdraw when threatened, and can be killed by predatory crabs or fishes.

Most polychaetes, including fanworms, can reproduce by fragmentation, each fragment developing into a complete worm. Some polychaetes that fragment or brood eggs and hatch late stage crawling trochophore larvae or even juveniles may suddenly populate an entire reef tank.

Spirobranchius giganteus lives in holes in corals and rocks throughout the tropics. It can instantly withdraw into the hole when threatened by a passing shadow.

Chapter Twenty
Chordata

The 50,000 species of the phylum Chordata are divided among three subphyla, the primitive Cephalochordata and Urochordata, and the advanced Vertebrata. Fishes are in the last subphylum, along with humans and all other animals with backbones. A fourth group, the Hemichordata or marine acorn worms and pterobranchs, was recently removed from the Chordata and placed in its own phylum. Because Hemichordata are not suitable as reef tank animals, they will not be covered in this book.

Cephalochordata

Cephalochordates are the lancelets. The common lancelet in high school biology laboratories is *Amphioxis*, but other lancelets include *Branchiostoma*, *Epigonichthys*, and *Asymmetron*. Lancelets are small, translucent animals living in or under the sand, filtering small particles and microbes, and passing water through gill slits. Their chordate affinities are evident from the embryonic stages in the development of gill slits in a pharynx, the straight gut, the form of the circulatory system, and mostly by the stiffening notochord adjacent to a dorsal, hollow nerve cord. Lancelets are excellent laboratory teaching animals, but otherwise rarely seen unless you know what to look for and where to look. One tropical species, *Branchiostoma caribaeum*, might survive in a reef aquarium devoid of fishes or large hermit crabs.

Urochordata

The Urochordata are divided into the Ascidia (tunicates or sea squirts), the Larvacea (larvaceans), and the Thaliacea (salps and relatives). The larvaceans and salps are transparent, planktonic marine animals occurring singly, in chains, or in clusters, not suitable for reef tanks, and not considered further.

The Ascidians (tunicates, sea squirts) are 1,250 species of sessile invertebrates that attach to hard structures all over the world. The body wall contains tunicin, a tough cellulose-like carbohydrate and protein complex. Coastal residents of colder climates are familiar with the pudgy greenish brown *Ciona intestinalis* (sea grape, sea liver) of rock jetties and pier pilings. Many sea squirts have symbiotic shrimp, are preyed upon by specialized nudibranchs, or require symbiotic cyanobacteria or symbiotic archaeobacteria.

Sea squirts can be solitary or colonial, each zooid resembling a pea or a walnut. Often, the larger the colony, the smaller the zooids. Much of the tunicin-based body is shared by the colony's zooids in a common test (structure) reinforced with calcareous spicules. An inhalent siphon protrudes from the rounded body of each zooid, drawing in seawater. Plankton and drifting detritus pass through meshlike slits in the pharynx and are captured by a sticky exudate for transfer down the gut where it is

Purple sea squirts on this live rock have large exhalent siphons.

digested. The filtered wastewater is excreted through an individual zooid's exhalent siphon or through a common siphon shared by a group with a common test. The worldwide *Pyrosoma atlanticum* forms giant colonies with one exhalent siphon large enough to insert your arm or leg. One wonders how these bags of tissue could be related to the higher animals. It's the larvae that give them away.

Sea squirts are usually hermaphrodites that release sperm, fertilized eggs, or fully formed tadpole-shaped larvae into the water. The larvae look like any other chordate larvae, with a nerve expansion (primitive brain) at the head end continuing as a nerve cord along the back, a stiff notochord just below the nerve cord (a primitive backbone), and the swimming motion of a fish. The larva swims about, eventually locates a site to settle down,

and then attaches to that surface by its head. The head, "brain," nerve cord, and notochord are completely absorbed and disappear, the bilateral symmetry disappears, and the rounded mass of tissue grows into the adult tunicate, a simple bag-like creature without any trace of its chordate ancestry.

Tunicates also reproduce asexually by budding (blastozooid formation) from a specialized zooid called an oozooid, or even from the larval stage. Some colonies of cloned siblings number in the hundreds.

Many tropical tunicates are brilliant blue, green, red, or orange. Many live beneath ledges protected from sunlight, while others thrive in full sun. Green tunicates often have symbiotic algae and transport these algae from generation to generation through the tadpole-like larva.

The Missing Link

Many green tunicates contain specialized symbiotic microalgae, in some cases blue-greens (Cyanobacteria), and in other cases a type of green microbe called *Prochloron*, discovered in 1973. Prochloron is technically a prokaryote (like bacteria and blue-greens) in that it doesn't have its DNA enclosed within a nucleus. Yet its DNA is organized in a manner similar to algae and all other plants and animals (eukaryotes). In 1996, *Prochloron* was proposed as representing a group linking bacteria with higher forms of life. This group is the Archaeobacteria or simply Archaea. They occur everywhere, including extreme habitats such as undersea volcanic vents. One Archaea species from hot springs in Yellowstone National Park is the source of the heat-resistant DNA polymerase used in the polymerase chain reaction or PCR used to grow large amounts of DNA from small pieces.

Tunicates are divided into three orders, the Aplousobranchia with 14 families, Phlebobranchia with 5 families, and Stolidobranchia with 4 families. Among the most important tropical families in the Aplousobranchia are the Clavelinidae (*Clavelina, Oxycorynia, Neptheus, Sycozoa*), and Didemnidae (*Didemnum, Lissoclinum, Diplosoma, Trididemnum*). *Clavelina* is rich in species, many of them beautiful and colorful. Visitors to the Caribbean will see colonies of ice blue *Clavelina* beneath ledges in shallow water, green or white forms coating dead boulder coral surfaces. *Didemnum* is also rich in brilliant red, yellow, or orange species. *Sycozoa* and *Oxycorynia* resemble green macroalgae, with colonies of zooids at the end of a common stalk.

Important Phlebobranchia include the family Corellidae (*Corella, Rhodosoma*). The family Diazonidae is sometimes included in the Phlebobranchia and sometimes the Aplousobranchia. It contains the delicate lacelike *Diazona* and the spectacular blue *Rhopalaea*.

Prominent among the Stolidobranchia are the Styelidae (*Botryllus, Botrylloides, Eusynstyella, Polycarpa, Cnemidocarpa*) and Pyuridae (*Pyura, Herdmania, Microcosmus*). *Pyura* is peach- or lavender-colored and grows as a clump at the end of a stalk up to 2 feet tall. It has sharp calcareous spicules in the body wall.

Sea squirts are tough-skinned and transport easily, but should have large volumes of shipping water and oxygen (not air). Feed sea squirts daily with unicellular algae, rotifers, brine shrimp nauplii, and commercial suspensions based on egg yolk. Iodine is extracted rapidly and must be supplemented as though you were providing for soft corals. Calcium levels should be maintained as for hard corals.

Growth rates depend on species, light, supplemental iodine dosing, regularity and volume of feeding, and predation. A few herbivorous snails (*Turbo*) and many nudibranchs graze on tunicates, but otherwise they have few enemies. The potential combinations of grazers and tunicates from around the world is astronomical. Use trial, error, and cost to determine which tunicates will thrive in your reef tank.

Chapter Twenty-One
Fishes: Foods and Feeding

Many corals require a complete diet from the combination of nutrients from symbiotic algae, plankton, and meiofauna. Once a week, use a powerhead to blast the gravel and rock, dislodging and sweeping surface microorganisms into the water where they can be captured by polyps. These meiofauna consist of protozoa, gastrotrichs, rotifers, annelids, roundworms, and flatworms. In addition, dislodged bacteria, fungi, and algae are also potential coral food. A side benefit is that biofilms are disrupted, regenerating gas and nutrient exchange with the water.

Fishes and crustaceans have additional needs. The propagation of marine fishes and crustaceans requires enriched and attractive foods such as brine shrimp nauplii, rotifers, and copepods.

Brine Shrimp

Brine shrimp (*Artemia)* are the salt pond relatives of fairy shrimp (*Stephanolepis*), crustaceans (Branchiopoda: Anostraca) that occur around the world in temporary, ephemeral, and vernal fish-free pools. The brine shrimp most commonly sold in the U.S. is *A. franciscana* native to California and Utah, but widespread through introductions around the world. Another species, *A. monica*, occurs in Mono Lake, California, but is not in commerce. Other brine shrimp species include *A. tunisiana, A. urminiana,* and *A. salina*. Live *Artemia franciscana* adults are a by-product of commercial salt drying ponds in California and sold widely in the country, but on the east coast, most of the live adult brine shrimp sold in pet stores are grown in greenhouses by a company in Florida.

Brine shrimp reproduce both parthenogenetically and sexually. The dark brown cysts (called eggs in the hobby) are gathered from windblown shores of saline lakes. The aquarium hobby uses less than 5 percent of production, the bulk of the harvest shipped to aquaculture facilities for the production of edible shrimp and fishes. Brine shrimp cyst harvest now occurs worldwide.

Brine shrimp cysts in small plastic packages produce poor hatches because moisture penetrates the packaging and kills the cysts. Most breeders purchase canned cysts, which give excellent hatches and have a shelf life of years. Open the 15-ounce can by puncturing with a can opener, pour a two-week supply into a covered jar, and recover the can with a tight-fitting plastic lid and put it in a freezer. Exposure to water vapor in air damages cysts and reduces the hatch, while storage in a freezer prolongs useful life by drawing water vapor out of the air.

Most of the cans provide hatching instructions directed at commercial inland aquaculture facilities, and call for un-iodized salt in a pan or a hatching cone. Cones are difficult to clean and

Breeding Artemia franciscana *viewed under a low power microscope. You can grow adult brine shrimp in double-strength seawater with bright light over a shallow container, or in white buckets outdoors in the summer.*

unnecessarily complicated, and pans give erratic hatches. You will get your best hatch using regular marine mix salts and a simple gallon jar. I recommend one level teaspoonful of cysts in one gallon of full strength synthetic seawater at room temperature with vigorous aeration and bright light, preferably daylight. This is also a good re-use of seawater removed from your tank during regular water changes.

After 24–48 hours (shorter is better), pour the hatching water through a fine mesh net (or handkerchief cloth), and invert the retained shells and nauplii into a pitcher of cool tap water. Within 15 minutes, the nauplii sink to the bottom and the empty cyst shells rise to the surface and float. Decant the floating shells and excess water as far as you can without losing the orange nauplii, wipe the remaining shells from the walls with your finger, and refill the container with cool tap water. The cleaned nauplii can now be fed to fishes and corals. (By the way, used hatch water can be recycled for reuse with a spare 30-gallon tank or trash barrel supplied with a trickling filter.)

The newly hatched nauplii are rich in essential fatty acids for about 24 hours when they are smallest. Beyond 24 hours, the nutritional value of nauplii drops off as they use up their fatty acids.

If you wish to grow adult brine shrimp, fill a large low container with used seawater or brine shrimp hatch water, and add extra salt to make the salinity super-saline. At normal salinities, brine shrimp do not grow well, but they do well at much higher salinities other creatures cannot withstand. Add vigorous aeration and bright overhead light, and seed the container with live nauplii (not cysts, which don't hatch in super-saline water). Feed the young shrimp lightly with a suspension of algae or baker's yeast in water once a week. Be sure the suspension is well distributed, as dry yeast or algal clumps sink and decay. Algae are the better food, and need not be marine species as all algae are consumed rapidly. Excess juvenile and adult brine shrimp are wonderful foods for marine fishes and filter feeders.

Brine Daphniae

Freshwater *Daphnia* are cladocern crustaceans that quickly die in seawater. *Diaphanosoma, Moina,* and some other cladocerans are native to hypersaline brine ponds and alkaline soda (salt) lakes from the American west to Australia, and can survive for a while in marine water, but at this writing there are no commercial sources. If you live out west, you can search for your own starter culture or call around to university biology departments in western states. If the local faculty expert is not culturing them, s/he can probably direct you to someone who is, or to a nearby pond where you can get your own.

Live Fish

Carnivorous fishes (hawkfish, scorpionfish, lionfish, anglerfish, grouper) are popular because they ignore corals and clams; they will, however, take shrimp (even cleaners) and crabs. Carnivores can be fed mollies or killifishes, which survive indefinitely in marine water, or goldfish, guppies, and minnows, whose short survival time eases capture by weak swimmers like pipefish.

Prepared Foods

Fishes, shrimp, sea stars, and crabs can smell, see, and find non-living foods delivered with a baster, straw, or tweezer. Frozen, thawed, and ground uncooked fish meat, shelled shrimp, and raw mussel are excellent foods. Packaged seafoods are available in pet stores and the raw products from supermarkets. Fresh raw mussel (open the shell with a blade, not by cooking) is a good trap bait for removing polychaetes and noxious crabs overnight from the aquarium.

A paste combining animal and plant ingredients is easily made by combining shrimp, fish fillet, squid and their entrails including gonads, a spoonful of cod liver oil or a capsule of drugstore fish oil, Japanese seaweed soaked in water to soften, cooked fresh (not canned) spinach, yeast, and just a dash of a powdered or liquid multivitamin. The ingredients are blended in a food processor with just enough cool water to make a thick paste, then are stored in zip-lock bags laid flat in a freezer. As needed, a portion is thawed and fed to the inhabitants. Because the oils oxidize over time, sniff the packages for rancidity, and discard any that smell bad. Some people add gelatin and heating to keep the juices from escaping, but heat may degrade

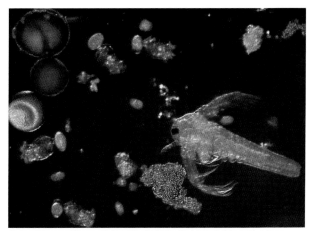

Artemia *nauplii are richest in HUFA oils at hatching, but lose almost all HUFAs by 24 hours of age. Older nauplii should be enriched before feeding them to larval marine fishes.*

important proteins and other nutrients and gelatin has no other particular benefits.

Flaked, pelleted, and liquified commercial preparations release excessive particles or juices not used by the fishes or corals, but which increase the risk of cyanobacterial blooms, resulting in loss of alkalinity and oxidation-reduction potential, depressing pH, and stressing ammonia-sensitive and pH-sensitive animals. Home made pastes and frozen foods reduce this risk if you don't overfeed.

Only experienced reef-keepers with an eye for coral health should use liquified supplements. They are available commercially, or you can make your own with blended raw clam, mussel, shrimp, fish fillet, fish liver (ask your seafood dealer), yeast dissolved in water (not particles), and preliquified cooked spinach. Do not heat. Filter through 300–500 micron nytox or a plastic coffee filter, stir in a drop or two of liquid multi-vitamins, and freeze in 1-ounce packages, thawing as needed. The particles retained by the filter can be rinsed and fed to *Xenia* and other

Pterois volitans, the lionfish, has become established in the western Atlantic from New Jersey to the Caribbean. It's probably an accidental release from ballast water. Stories about accidental release from broken outdoor tanks during a hurricane in Florida are nonsense, but continue to circulate.

planktivorous corals, some fishes, and some decorative shrimp and crabs.

Commercial fish farms use encapsulated dry foods for larval fish and shrimp. These aquaculture products yield improved growth and survival and decrease dependence on expensive brine shrimp cysts. The diets contain cholesterol, phospholipids, xanthophylls, and HUFAs, components that enhance survival and growth. Several suppliers offer these same aquaculture products in small packages through magazines or on the Web, or your pet store can order them for you on request. The feeds are packaged in semibuoyant microparticle sizes of <100 through >450 micron in 50 micron intervals, sizes appropriate for newly hatched lar-val fishes and crabs and for enhancing the nutritive value of live brine shrimp.

Macroalgae

Some herbivorous reef fishes eat tank-grown macroalgae (*Centropyge* angelfishes, Moorish idols, tangs), but when the tank is depleted they require supplemental feedings. Others such as Potter's angel (*Centropyge potteri*) are obligately herbivorous and starve after eating all macroalgae, and do not survive long on substitutes. It's difficult to keep sufficient macroalgae growing in a reef tank, and some of those that do grow well are ignored by the fishes, perhaps because of taste. Many marine red and brown algae are dried and sold in the Oriental food trade as nori, a general term for dried seaweeds. Nori sheets should be fragmented, then soaked in cold water (do not cook) until rubbery and limber. In this form, nori is nutritious and acceptable. For herbivores that cannot deal with the texture, cook the nori until it falls apart. Many kinds of nori are on the market, so try several to determine those acceptable to your fishes. Both dried and canned nori are available from oriental food markets.

Vegetables

Some reef fishes accept leafy green vegetables, but these foods are deficient in iodine. Although fish will eat leafy vegetables, they get little benefit beyond providing food for intestinal microbes. Nutritionally, lettuce and spinach do not enhance health or promote growth, but they can be part of a comprehensive mixed diet for specialized feeders such as large angelfishes.

Chapter Twenty-Two
Fishes: Care and Breeding

Some marine fishes are easily kept with corals, others are not, and still others should never be kept at all because they grow too large, require special foods, damage corals, or excrete noxious chemicals. What looks attractive in a store may prove a headache at home. Of the pet store fishes usually available, several originate at hatcheries and tend to adapt well. Slightly more expensive than wild fish, their survival rate is excellent, making them the better buy.

Most marine fishes in stores are wild fishes often collected and treated harshly through storage and shipping, and you see only the survivors—perhaps 10–20 percent of what was collected on the reef in a far-away country. Excessive stress or hidden injuries may lead to anorexia and death, and there is nothing to be done about it. In general, fishes that grow to less than 3 inches and are not top predators or specialized feeders make the best coral tank inhabitants. Many smaller marine fishes not only survive, but spawn in captivity under the right conditions.

Guidelines for Keeping Fishes in Reef Tanks

What a fish does in nature is the product of adaptation over the eons (evolution) and what happened during each fish's lifetime (experience). Evolution may have adapted a fish's teeth to crop algae, and competition with other species on the reef may restrict it to that food source. From an early age it learns what food it can get and which foods it cannot. In short, competition trains fish to become specialized to a particular food, while evolution has prepared it to be efficient at this activity.

When an older fish (trained by experience) is placed in a new environment, two outcomes are possible. The first is the fish will search for the food it learned to eat and failing that will waste away and die. The second outcome is it will learn from watching other tank inhabitants and adapt to new foods. Examples abound. Before mini-reefs, marine aquarists had little success with butterflyfishes (Chaetodontidae) that mostly feed on corals and worms extracted from crevices. However, if a butterflyfish is captured young, its capacity for learning is great, and it can be weaned onto ordinary fare. It happens even in the wild. On some Hawaiian beaches, swimmers feed local butterflyfishes frozen peas and synthetic cheese spread. It is likely these fishes have given up feeding on corals, or at least are no longer restricted to them.

Any fish in any tank might be induced to behave differently by watching its cohabitants. With this caution in mind, be aware that a fish believed safe with corals may, in fact, learn to be a terror, while another reputed to be a fierce predator might in fact be a pussycat.

The yellow tang, Zebrasoma flavescens, *is abundant in Hawaiian waters, and an excellent nuisance algae remover for reef tanks. The fish is now being investigated in Hawaii for commercial aquaculture.*

You will frequently see a large (trophy) marine fish for sale at a remarkably low price. It was likely brought back by someone whose aquarium or good graces it had outgrown. As with used cars, consider that you may be buying someone else's headache.

A safer approach is to select young fish that can learn from other fishes. Older fish are risky for the bad habits they have learned, including dependence on what the last guy fed them, and their inability to change.

Select reef fishes with good reputations and be wary of others. Any fish can turn territorial or predaceous, may learn to eat corals, or otherwise disrupt a reef tank. Watch your fish.

Acanthuridae

Reef algae are cropped by sea urchins, pygmy angelfishes, parrotfishes, and tangs. Tangs or surgeonfishes (named for the razor sharp bone on either side of the caudal peduncle) are useful for the control of macroalgae in a reef aquarium. Of some 75 species of tangs around the world, several have quite different food preferences (called resource partitioning) reflected in the types of teeth. But evolutionary adaptations can fall by the wayside in reef tanks, where availability determines what is eaten and, tooth structure notwithstanding, tangs become more flexible than anatomy suggests.

Not all tangs are herbivores. Some eat zooplankton in the water column (*Paracanthurus hepatus*). Many are opportunistically coprophagous, eating the feces of other fishes, and providing another round of digestion before the waste fragments sink all the way to the bottom.

The herbivorous tangs control macroalgal succession on the reef, and their populations in turn are limited by the reef's production of (mostly blue-green) algae and fleshy red macroalgae. In places where the tangs (or parrotfishes or sea urchins) are fished for human consumption, the reefs may become overgrown by macroalgae and the corals die.

Herbivorous tangs may be *browsers* that crop algae (in the way cattle crop grass by biting it off above the dirt and root zone) or *grazers* that scrape algae from calcareous rock. In common with parrotfishes (Scaridae), grazing tangs metabolize about 11 percent of the algae and pass 89 percent through the gut as fragments that become detritus and the calcareous sand of the reef. Tangs feed mostly on surface macroalgae, whereas parrotfishes specialize in microalgae growing inside limestone, especially in the rubble zone, but both groups leave distinctive tooth marks on rock and scraped coral.

The most popular and useful reef tank herbivore is the inexpensive yellow tang (*Zebrasoma flavescens*), now the subject of aquaculture investigations in Hawaii. The more expensive sailfin tangs (*Zebrasoma veliferum, Z. desjardinii*) eat fleshy red and green macroalgae in the wild, but in the reef tank will control several kinds of filamentous algae. *Ctenochaetus striatus* and *C. strigosus* (kole or yellow-eye tang and chevron tang) feed on meiofauna in the sediment and on detritus in nature, but are algae eaters in reef-tanks.

Acanthurus nigrofuscus and *A. striatus* eat fleshy red microalgae in nature; *A. triostegus* eats various fleshy macroalgae. *Zebrasoma scopas* prefers small fleshy red algae. Many tangs are large, expensive, and not useful for algal control (*Acanthurus achilles, A. olivaceous, A. aliala, A. leucosternon, A. guttatus, Naso* spp.), but continue to be popular for fish only tanks.

Tangs should be fed supplemental frozen brine shrimp and parboiled or microwaved lettuce or spinach leaves in addition to the general diet given all reef fishes.

Tangs are broadcast spawners. They breed by swimming rapidly upward high into the water column and, near the top, shed eggs and sperm into the water. Some breed in pairs, others in groups, some daily or seasonally, others in conjunction with moon phases. There are no aquacultured tangs at present, although yellow tang aquaculture is being tried in Hawaii.

Zanclidae and Siganidae

The Moorish idol (*Zanclus canescens = Z. cornutus*) is the only species in the family Zanclidae. The family Siganidae contains about two-dozen kinds of milkfishes, popular Asian food fishes.

The yellow-eye tang, Ctenochaetus strigosus, *eats nuisance algae and detritus, making it a popular reef tank inhabitant. None of the tangs is yet aquacultured.*

The Moorish idol and the foxface (*Lo vulpinus*) are both recommended herbivores for reef tanks, harmless to corals. Given abundant algae and live rock for cropping and grazing, they do fine. Moorish idols have bred in a large tank, but the young were not raised. Their acronurus larval stage (similar to the larva of tangs) must reach more than 2 inches in length over many weeks before transforming into an adult.

Siganids or rabbitfishes eat algae and plankton. Some inshore species invade estuaries and even fresh water. A few are aquacultured, injected with hormones to induce spawning, and the young grown in fish ponds on simple foods such as rabbit pellets, then sold live or packaged as seafood. Several siganids will control algae in a reef tank, but few are as attractive as the foxface. The aquaculture literature on siganids is extensive, but marine aquarists are more interested in trying Moorish idols, whatever the difficulties.

Pomacentridae

The 350 species of pomacentrids or damselfishes include the gregories, dascyllus, jewelfish, sergeant and night majors, and clown or anemonefishes. They take all foods, from flakes to meats, yet are rarely predaceous on other fishes or reef tank invertebrates, and seldom fight except as territorial adults. Pomacentrids are among the easiest fishes to keep, and frequently spawn in captivity.

Sergeant majors, jewelfish, and gregories become too large (over 3 inches), too aggressive, and gray-black as adults. They should be enjoyed in the wild, but do not belong in a home marine aquarium.

Stately dascyllus can grow large as adults and lose color contrast, but they remain social and seldom bother coral polyps. Yellowtail and orange-bellied blue damsels remain small (under 2 inches) and hold their colors into adulthood. Some damsels, in the wild, cultivate an algal turf food supply by killing polyps on a branch of hard coral, but this behavior is rare in captivity. Dascyllus are often

Amphiprion clarki, *tending eggs. The easiest clownfish to breed, it's larger and not as popular as the red, pink, and orange species of this genus.*

associated with hard corals in the same manner as clown fishes associate in nature with anemones. All damsels with lyre-shaped tails are midwater plankton-feeders. Jewelfish juveniles, in nature, associate with fire corals.

The most popular damsels are the clown anemone fishes, which readily spawn to produce small numbers of eggs (100 to 200) that hatch into large fry, with a brief larval period of under two weeks. Other damsels often spawn large numbers of small eggs (sometimes thousands) that hatch into tiny fry difficult to raise with rotifers, sifted plankton, ciliates, or green water, and which won't metamorphose for an average of three weeks. Many aquarists successfully raise clownfish, but few raise other damsels.

Most damsels have separate sexes determined at birth, with no sex reversal. In clown anemonefishes, sex is not determined at birth. A group settles among the tentacles of a protective anemone, and the largest becomes a functional female, the second largest fish a functional male, while the remainder remain sexless. Should the female be removed, the male transforms into a female and the next largest indeterminate fish matures as a male. Thus, any group of small fish will yield a pair, but all large fish are irreversibly females. Spawning behavior is induced by excellent nutrition, elevated temperatures (about 80°F), and 14 hours of light and 10 hours of total darkness. In a reef tank, clownfish will take over a host Pacific anemone, sometimes another kind of cnidarian, and sometimes even large Atlantic anemones. Clownfish will also establish a territory if no cnidarian is available, and do not require an anemone for survival or spawning. A pair establishes a territory, in the shade of an anemone if available, on a hard surface that they scrape vigorously over many days. The smaller of the pair is the male, who displays to the female by arching his side and trembling as though in pain or tetanus. After some days the spawning tubes appear. On the day of spawning, the female glides over the hard surface wiping it with her thick blunt ovipositor, leaving behind a line of eggs. Subsequently the male glides after over the eggs with his smaller, pointed spawning tube, emitting sperm to fertilize the eggs. The oblong eggs adhere by filaments and take a few days (most damsels) to two weeks (clownfishes) to hatch, typically an hour after darkness. The pelagic fry are attracted to light (a narrow beamed flashlight is useful to aggregate them), and can be retrieved near the surface after the water and air pumps are turned off. Gather them up with a cup or ladle, as a siphon or food baster will damage some of them.

Damselfish fry cannot capture food in moving water. Keep them in still water with dim light and dark sides and bottom. Feed HUFA-enriched rotifers on the second day for at least ten days. In the absence of aeration, the rotifers aggregate at the oxygen-rich surface where the near-sighted fry easily locate and capture them. Even gentle aeration disperses rotifers and the fry don't get enough to eat. Brine shrimp nauplii can be started on the third day after hatching. The tank bottom should be siphoned to remove dead fry and food every day, and a good portion of the water replaced with reef tank (not newly made) water. Losses are high the first few days, but

Amphiprion ocellaris *has been the most common and popular clownfish in the hobby since long before it was a movie star. It is readily spawned and raised in captivity. Most clownfish sold today are aquacultured rather than wild fishes.*

An Indo-Pacific sea star amid polychaete worms. Sea stars are not safe in reef tanks, but do fine in fish-only aquariums. They should be fed live mussels or small clams from a seafood market.

Juvenile Pomacanthus imperator *being cleaned by a cleaner shrimp.* Pomacanthus *are large angelfishes, the young produced in aquaculture by stripping and mixing the gametes of wild parents, which are then released back into the wild.*

after that you should raise most of the remainder. By day ten, the fry transform and wag against the bottom, and aeration can be started. Continue daily water changes. The fry should be transferred to a grow-out tank when not less than ½-inch long. Use a clear cup in dim light. Netting and bright light can induce panic in which the juveniles go into tetanus, the jaws and gills frozen open, and they die of asphyxiation.

Dascyllus and *Pomacentrus* can be raised on enriched rotifers, copepod nauplii, or sifted plankton, but their long larval period makes this considerable work. In nature, pelagic larval dascyllus use odor to locate a preferred coral species the night they settle out of the plankton. Apparently many coral reef fishes use smell to locate suitable settling sites and even their natal reefs. The Hawaiian endemic *D. albisella* usually settles on *Pocillopora meandrina*. Neither clownfish nor dascyllus species require a host cnidarian in captivity. Genetic studies on mitochrondrial DNA of dascyllus show variation in the number of deletions and

repetitions of the same string of DNA, enabling biologists to use *copy number variants* to map relationships of the populations. It's the same principle used to determine relationships in contested wills and paternity suits.

Pomacanthidae

The 80-plus species of marine angelfishes are specialty feeders. Larger angelfishes (*Pygoplites, Pomacanthus, Apolemichthys, Holacanthus*) feed mostly on sponges and algae, with some crustaceans, and are generally unsuitable, unless weaned from an early age. The intermediate *Chaetodontoplus* tend to omnivory, but need plant matter and fat-soluble vitamins. *Genicanthus* are planktivorous (the forked tail is a dead giveaway), difficult to maintain in good health, and should be fed krill and mysids. The most suitable for reef tanks are the pygmy *Centropyge* with about two dozen species. *Centropyge* are herbivores or omnivores that primarily browse or graze algae, but some pick on coral polyps in the absence of adequate meat (brine shrimp, shellfish, fish) in the diet. Larger *Centropyge* such as *C. bicolor* have poor captive survival records as a result of their need for sponges and algae in the diet. The large *C. potteri* from Hawaii is a strict herbivore that starves after consuming all available algae. It will not eat cyanobacteria and rarely adapts to nori, spinach, or lettuce. Intermediate sized species (*C. bispinosus, C. ferrugatus, C. loriculus*) are omnivorous on algae and small crustaceans, and adapt to an aquarium when filamentous macroalgae flourish. The smallest species, represented by *C. argi, C. acanthops,* and *C. shepardi*, are easiest to keep because of the small amount of food required and omnivory. They do not bother corals.

The majority of angelfishes form a male-dominated group (harem) of one species that will not look kindly on other males or other kinds of angelfish in the same tank. The larger types of angelfishes live in pairs, and may have a life span of more than 15 years. Angelfish species can be mixed if they have dissimilar color patterns, but in general one species to a tank is advised because of territoriality.

Harem types such as most *Centropyge* are sequential hermaphrodites. Young fish mature first as females (protogynous), and (usually) the largest member of a group subsequently changes into a male. (As in clown anemonefishes, if you start with two small fish, you can count on getting a pair.) Harem spawning among *Centropyge* is the rule, with one male herding and spawning with up to several females. Just before sunset, a pair rushes upward into the water column where gametes are broadcast (dispersed into the water). The male *Centropyge* spawns with different females on different rushes or on different days.

At Hawaii's Oceanic Institute, the small, drifting fertilized eggs of captive *Centropyge loriculus* were sifted from the surface and sterilized with 3 percent hydrogen peroxide for five minutes, incubated, hatched, and the fry raised on the cyclopoid copepod *Oithona* together with *Isochrysis* microalgae as the copepod's food source. Survival was limited because of infections and pH alterations common to high-density culture.

Pomacanthus fry have been raised from stripped eggs and sperm, the transformed larvae fed with sieved natural plankton as a first food, followed by rotifers and brine shrimp nauplii. With the availability of cultured *Oithona* and other cyclopoid copepods, and of several kinds of harpacticoids, commercial aquacultured stocks of pygmy and other angelfishes now seem feasible.

Gobiidae and Eleotridae

More than 2,200 species of gobies (Gobiidae) and sleepers Eleotridae) occur worldwide in nearshore ocean waters and adjacent freshwater. In gobies, the pelvics are fused into an adhesive disk that adheres to solid surfaces even in strong current. If the pelvics are not fused, the fish is a sleeper.

Gobies and sleepers are carnivorous on zooplankton and benthic invertebrates, and harmless to corals. They prefer crevices or burrows, sometimes shared with symbiotic snapping shrimp or another species of fish. Bottom-dwelling gobies and sleepers are solitary or occur in pairs throughout suitable habitat. The firefish and related sleepers (*Nemateleotris, Oxymetopon, Parioglossus,* and *Ptereleotris*) are planktivores that hover in the water column, but retreat to a crevice, burrow, or cave when threatened. Hovering sleepers form aggregations, a common defense of planktivorous fishes.

Ptereleotris splendidum *is a hovering, communal planktivore that breeds in caves.*

Gobiosoma oceanops, *the neon goby, and several close relatives are now aquacultured for the marine aquarium market. It's not difficult to breed, but the fry need rotifers for several weeks.*

Easy to breed, gobies and sleepers deposit adhesive eggs inside a burrow, crevice, or shell defended by the male. In the aquarium, they will spawn inside a PVC tube that can be removed and aerated in a separate jar or tank after the embryo eyes appear. The planktonic larvae of neon and related gobies require rotifers as a first food, but many gobies and sleepers have fry too small even for rotifers; a HUFA-enriched dry food or copepods and green water microalgae might be effective. The pelagic stage lasts days to weeks. Upon settling to the bottom, the metamorphosing larvae are difficult to see on gravel and rocks. Continue feeding brine shrimp nauplii and copepods on faith, and you'll be rewarded when the cryptic young become visible. Hovering sleepers metamorphose at a large size (about an inch), and take up their midwater habit right away. Cleaner gobies are safe with many predators, but all other gobies and sleepers will be considered snacks by lionfish, groupers, and other piscivores.

The neon goby (*Gobiosoma oceanops*) and its relatives are commercially tank-raised. Green, blue-spotted, and yellow *Gobiodon citrinellus*, *G. histrio*, and *G. rivulatus* are small, stubby gobies that live outside crevices but spawn inside. Some popular gobies in the reef hobby are the yellow *Quisquilius* from Hawaii, *Ctenogobius* with rusty spots, and the colorfully spotted *Oplopomus* of the Philippines, but the group is huge and new ones constantly imported for the hobby. Gobies are mostly inexpensive, likely to spawn, and hardy.

Grammatidae and Pseudochromidae

The Atlantic grammas (*Gramma loreto, G. melacara, G. linki, G. braziliensis*) and Indo-Pacific dottybacks (*Pseudochromis, Pseudoplesiops, Cypho, Ogilbyina, Labracinus, Lubbockichthys, Chlidichthys*) are mostly small (2–4 inch), colorful fishes that feed on zooplankton, small crustaceans, and tiny fishes. Exceptions are the giant, dark green to brown predaceous dottybacks (mostly genera other than *Pseudochromis*) not imported or bred for the hobby. In aquaria, *Gramma* and *Pseudochromis* take all kinds of live and frozen meats and even dry foods. Protogynous hermaphrodites, any two develop into a pair if you start with *small*

Gramma melacara, *the black-capped basslet, is a deepwater Atlantic cave spawner that can be kept in groups.*

Pseudochromis paccagnellae, the bicolor dottyback, is one of a dozen Pseudochromis *species now aquacultured and sold in pet stores. All of them are territorial.*

Dottyback eggs are numerous, small, and enclosed in a membrane. They should be dipped in disinfectant and hatched away from the parents, who are likely to eat the fry.

specimens and abundant space. Harmless to corals and large shrimp, they are vulnerable to piscivores.

Grammas are few, dottybacks speciose. Some are sexually dichromic, and colors may differ among regions. The Pacific species are territorial and aggressive to conspecifics irrespective of sex, and likely to kill a rival. Several young fish introduced at one time may adapt and divide territories, but later become territorial. Grammas are more sociable than dottybacks.

Dottybacks and grammas spawn in caves, PVC tubes, or shells in the aquarium. The male may guard unattached eggs (grammas) or egg clusters or balls (dottybacks) of different ages from different spawns. The tube of eggs or the cluster can be removed for sterilization in 1 percent formalin for 15 minutes or 3 percent hydrogen peroxide for

5 minutes, then placed in a gallon jar for aeration and hatching in the dark after about a week, generally at night. The phototropic fry accept enriched rotifers as a first food, and are most likely to survive metamorphosis if fed copepods (wild or cultured) as a bridge between rotifers and brine shrimp nauplii.

Clinidae, Blenniidae, and Pholidichthyidae

Clinids, blennies, and engineerfishes are elongate goby-like bottom-dwellers of algae-covered rubble, sediments near reefs, rocks, or wooden breakwaters. They are tropical and temperate, marine and estuarine, and occur worldwide. Most graze macroalgae, but in captivity eagerly take brine shrimp and bloodworms. They eat anything but seldom bother decorative shrimp or corals. The most common genera in the hobby are the engineerfishes (*Pholidichthys*), rockhoppers (*Atrosalarius*), bicolor blennies (*Escenius*), and canary blennies (*Meiacanthus*). Many are colorful (*Runula, Aspidontus*). They will lay eggs in PVC tubes, shells, or burrows in gravel, and the fry can take rotifers. The engineerfish has enormous eggs and large fry capable of

Pterosynchiropus splendidus, the mandarin fish, has been spawned in aquaria, but the fry are difficult and require marine infusoria. Cultures of tintinnid ciliates may soon be available.

eating brine shrimp nauplii as first food. J.R. Shute observed one carrying a mass of eggs in its mouth, and I found a mass of eggs under an undergravel filter plate.

Tripterygiidae and Callionymidae

Triplefins are small, goby-like fishes mostly in the Indo-Pacific, with three species in U.S. waters of the Atlantic. Most live in nearshore rocky pools, at breakwaters, and on coral reefs. The front of the dorsal fin has a few long spines followed by a middle zone with shorter spines, and the rear of the fin has soft rays, hence the common name. Dragonets are similar, again with just three species in U.S. waters in the Atlantic, and many more in the Indo-Pacific. The only common species in reef aquaria are *Synchiropus (=Pterosynchiropus) splendidus* (mandarin) and *S. picturatus* (spotted mandarin). Related species are *S. calauropomus, S. lineolatus, S. ocellatus,* and *Pogonemus pogognathus*. The largest group is *Callionymus*. Mandarins breed in shells or caves

in reef aquaria, and a few fry can be raised on rotifers or copepods, but not easily. Mandarins are sensitive to water quality and fare poorly in small tanks.

Apogonidae

Cardinalfishes occur worldwide, their greatest diversity in the tropical Indo-Pacific. They occur from tide pools to muddy estuaries to shallow coral and deep rocky reefs, and even fresh water. All are mouthbrooders, some producing tiny eggs and tiny larvae, others large eggs hatching to large young that accept brine shrimp nauplii as first food. Most are bright scarlet, some pink or silvery. The popular Banggai cardinalfish is silver and black, easily bred in groups, and produces large young the size of mollies. Cardinalfishes are catholic feeders taking any live, dried, or fresh meat. Giant isopods in the mouth, gill chambers, chin, or head of wild fishes are readily removed with tweezers.

Cardinalfishes frequent caves, cracks, and holes beneath rocks. The conchfish, *Astrapogon stellatus*, lives in the mantle space of the queen conch, *Strombus gigas. Phaeoptyx xenus*, the sponge cardinalfish, lives inside the sponges *Verongia* and *Callyspongia*. Common in the hobby is *Sphaeramia orbicularis*, a social fish often spawned (but not raised). Wood's siphon-fish, *Siphamia cephalotes*, occurs in estuaries, an ecological equivalent of a stickleback. *Mionurus bombonensis* lives in Lake Taal (Bombon Lagoon) in the Philippines.

Spawning follows side-by-side trembling. Cardinalfish lay eggs in a single mass connected by threads or enclosed in a sac that is picked up by the male for brooding. In *Sphaeramia*, the eggs are less than a millimeter, and number 6,000 to 11,000. In the Banggai cardinalfish, eggs number 15–40 and the molly-sized young form midwater aggregations resembling a group of freshwater angelfish.

In the wild, cardinalfishes breed twice monthly, usually during high tide. In captivity, they may spawn repeatedly and within days of releasing the last brood. Brooding males should be isolated and undisturbed. The fry of Banggai and some others do well on brine shrimp nauplii and probably on live copepods. Premature releases of yolk-sac larvae are common, but not invariably lethal. When visiting a pet store, look for any cardinalfish with swollen jaws. It may be a brooding male.

Plesiopidae

The Plesiopidae probably include those that lay eggs on the bottom wrapped in a ball membrane and others that pick up the ball for mouthbrooding. The comet "grouper" or marine "betta" *Calloplesiops altivelis* is a popular reef fish of modest temperament and omnivorous appetite that threatens only small shrimp. It is peaceful, has been spawned in aquaria, and said to spawn like dottybacks. The many *Assessor* species include the beautiful mouthbrooding *A. flavissimus, A. meleagris,* and *A. macneill.* Breeding reports of assessors are uncommon, perhaps because they are often kept in large reef tanks with many other fishes. Other plesiopids include *Plesiops* (longfins), *Belonepterygion* (spiny basslets), and *Trachinops* (hulafish).

Antennariidae

The anglerfishes are worldwide. These bag-like, soft-bodied, seemingly cumbersome predators motionlessly await or slowly stalk their prey. The tax-

Antennarius pardalis, like other anglerfishes, is a master of adaptive camouflage, here mimicking a red sponge.

onomy is based on the shape of the fishing rod-like illicium on the snout and its fleshy and enlarged lure at the tip called the esca. Different species have one or two illisciums, with or without escas, or none at all.

There are about 25 species of *Antennarius. Histrio, Kuiterichthys, Allenichthys, Lophiocharon, Nudiantennarius, Echinophryne, Trichophryne, Histiophryne, Phyllophryne, Tathicarpus,* and *Rhycherus* have one or two species each.

Most antennariids are ambush predators of invertebrates and fishes, including their own kind, luring and waiting for prey to come within striking distance. *Antennarius commersoni* produces a small number of eggs with tiny looping filaments that hook to skin thorns or to other eggs, the entire mass a brightly conspicuous cluster on the flanks of the mother. It's been suggested that piggy-backing the eggs protects them from predators and attracts prey to mama. *Lophiocharon* and *Histiophryne* also brood eggs on the body or in the angle of the pectoral fin. Some anglerfish from abyssal depths are so

Sargassum frogfish, Histrio histrio, *ranges worldwide in sargassum weed, and has been spawned in captivity.*

modified that the male is reduced to a parasitic gonadal sac.

The sargassum frogfish or sargassumfish, *Histrio histrio,* occurs in tropical seas worldwide and is the only antennariid living in floating sargassum weed. The frogfish stalks its prey, so a wiggling esca is not necessary. Its pectoral fins are used as hands to pull it along, to push away, and even to "brush" a partially engulfed meal in the same way a toad brushes its food to align it for swallowing. Frogfish will eat live minnows, guppies, or mollies, or a strip of cut fish on a thin rod. They'll eat all the other fishes and invertebrates in the tank up to their own size and sometimes larger. For spawning, always make sure both your fishes are the same size, feed them well, and hope for the best.

As its ovary ripens, the female swells, changes color, and seems to breathe with difficulty. The male darkens and soon mouths the vent of the female. They lumber about, then dart upward, the female expelling a gelatinous egg raft as the male releases sperm (milt). She seems to lose balance and tumbles down awkwardly, but will eat normally the next day. The male recovers right away.

The eggs are embedded inside that jellylike mass. I've found individual sargassumfish babies in plankton samples that look like tadpoles inside balloons. After hatching the young have bony plates on the head and were once thought a distinct genus (*Kanazawichthys*).

Serranidae

"And the great fish swallowed Jonah..." If you thought that Jonah was a pip to be expectorated by a tasteful whale, think again. Biologists, who know all about such things, assure us that Jonah was slurped up and spat out by a grouper, a member of the family Serranidae. Bohlke and Chaplin, in *Fishes of the Bahamas* (1968, University of Texas Press) mention an Indo-Pacific grouper that attains 12 feet and 1,000 pounds, claiming this is "the fish responsible for the stories of divers being swallowed alive by giant groupers." J.L.B. Smith concurred, noting that *Promicrops lanceolatus* was reputed to "attack men in the water" (*Smith's Sea Fishes,* 1986, Springer-Verlag). But was Jonah in the Indian Ocean, the Red Sea, the Pacific, the Mediterranean, or the Atlantic?

The 400 or so groupers are divided into subfamilies Serraninae, Epinephelinae, Anthiinae, Liopropominae, and some smaller groups. The Serraninae and Epinephelinae are mostly large edible groupers, protogynous hermaphrodites, sexually maturing first as females, and 3–12 years later resorbing ovarian tissue and developing testicular tissue to become functional males. Several kinds of large groupers are seasonal group spawners, migrating to a specific location from other reefs for a once or few times a year orgy.

A few types of smaller groupers (*Hypoplectrus, Serranus*) are simultaneous hermaphrodites. The spawning habits of most groupers are generally unknown.

Groupers are predators. At one time it was believed they ate small fare, their maws creating a suction that drew in their prey. Today we know groupers use those big mouths to ambush or even stalk big prey animals and drag them back into their holes in the rocks. *Grammistes* has toxic skin.

In the Indo-Pacific region, the Epinephelinae contains *Centrogenys, Cromileptes, Anperodon, Plectropoma, Variola, Aethaloperca, Aulacocephalus, Promicrops, Pogonoperca, Dermatolepis,* and *Ypsigramma*, each with one or two species. The largest Indo-Pacific genera are *Epinephelus* (31 species) and *Cephalopholis* (12 species), with additional species along the Pacific coast of South America and in the Red Sea.

Epinephelus akaara, E. awoara, E. bleekeri, E. areolatus, E. fuscoguttatus, E. malabaricus, E. polyphekadion, E. coioides, E. tauvina, Cromileptus altivelis, Plectropomus leopardus, P. areolatus, and *P. pessuliferus* are all collected in the Indo-Pacific for the Asian food market (mostly Hong Kong, Singapore, China, and Japan). The bulk of the collecting is in Indonesia and the Philippines, much of that by cyanide. Juveniles of some species (*Cromileptus,* polka-dot grouper) are also provided to the aquarium market.

Typically, grouper juveniles are collected inshore where they sidle up to palm fronds placed in shallows. *E. coioides* and *E. malabaricus* (epinephelines with giant larvae) are then transported to floating cages where they are fed artificial diets tailored to promote rapid growth, then sold at market size

Hypoplectrus, *the hamlet basses, are hermaphrodites. To date, they have not been propagated for the hobby.*

for the restaurant trade. Juvenile groupers are found in mid-Atlantic estuaries where they aggregate in attached bottom-growing sargassum weed.

Pacific red-spotted groupers (*Epinephelus coioides*) are induced to spawn by hormone injection, the tiny eggs incubated to hatching, and the minute fry cultured with copepods and algae in outdoor vats or pools. Recent advances include growing phytoplankton blooms in coastal ponds, seeding the ponds with small rotifers (*Brachionus rotundiformis*) and copepods (*Pseudodiaptomus annandalei* and

Grammistes *has a chemical in its skin that makes it distasteful to predators. It's a popular reef fish that won't bother corals.*

Chromileptis altivelis, *the polka-dot grouper, is popular both with aquarists and seafood restaurants. You're likely to see them live in windows of Hong Kong restaurants.*

Acartia tsuensis) to form zooplankton blooms, and then placing newly hatched grouper fry in the ponds for grow-out. Some day groupers will be provided to the hobby market, but today all cultured groupers are sold to the food market.

The coney, *Cephalopholis fulva*, is an Atlantic grouper not exceeding a foot long, with a red body and iridescent blue spots. It is an excellent candidate for aquaculture in Florida and the Caribbean, if the aquarium market can support the cost of cultivation.

Small groupers do well in reef tanks, but may eat fish up to half their size, and relish shrimp and crabs. They're harmless to corals and other sedentary invertebrates. Feed them live goldfish, guppies, minnows, and mollies.

Labridae

The wrasses are among the most diverse and abundant fishes of coral and rocky reefs. Their variety in tooth types (many have large, specialized incisors) derives from feeding specializations (resource partitioning), habits

that break down in the aquarium where food is abundant. In most species, diverse color phases characterize the juveniles, females, males, and (in some species) supermales. In species with supermales (e.g., Atlantic bluehead wrasse), one supermale may spawn with one female, while the remaining adults group spawn.

Hogfish have been spawned in a laboratory by manipulating day length, but in general wrasses are not targeted by breeders. These broadcast spawners might be spawned in public or commercial aquaria, but perhaps need too much vertical space for the upward rush to be successfully spawned in home aquariums. A need for height may not apply to all of them.

Many wrasses sleep under the gravel at night and are valuable gravel mixers. The most popular wrasses for reef tanks include *Pericheilinus, Pseudocheilinus, Halichoeres* and *Coris*, which are generally safe with invertebrates, although *Coris* may go after decorative shrimp. *Anampses* are cleaners that pick parasites off other fishes, but might pick at worms and corals.

Many other wrasses popular in fish aquaria are unsafe in reef tanks because of their catholic feeding habits or preference for corals. These include *Gomphosis* (bird wrasse), *Lienardella, Cheilinus, Thalassoma, Novaculichthys* (dragon wrasse) and *Hemipteronotus* (razorfish). In general, if you see a wrasse in a dealer's coral tank, it is probably safe for your mini-reef.

Cirrhitidae

The hawkfishes are about 35 species of ambush predators related to scorpionfishes, but without a particular bone across the cheek. Color variation is often a response to the habitat and not an indication of sex. The genera are *Cirrhitus, Cirrhitichthys, Gymnocirrhites, Paracirrhites, Cyprinocirrhites, Cirrhitoidea,* and *Amblycirrhitus. Amblycirrhitus pinos* (redspotted hawkfish) is common on corals in Florida and the Caribbean. *Paracirrhites arcatus* (arc-eye hawkfish) is widespread in the Indo-Pacific on branches of *Pocillopora meandrina.*

One or a pair of hawkfishes takes up station amid hard corals to ambush small invertebrates within strike range. They pounce on amphipods and isopods, and control predaceous polychaetes. Adapting to frozen brine and edible shrimp, they thrive in reef aquaria but cannot be kept from eating decorative shrimp.

Breeding Reef Fishes

Some marine fishes need no special inducement to initiate spawning (e.g., gobies, cardinalfishes), while others must be induced by injection with hormones or by adjusting the day length in a controlled light cycle and/or manipulating temperature. Marine fish are mostly egg-scatterers, often group spawners, but also include rocky bottom benthic spawners with and without egg protection, mouthbrooders, cave spawners, pit-spawners, and even live bearers.

Most reef fishes (tangs, parrotfishes, angelfishes, wrasses, butterflyfishes, snappers, groupers) are broadcast spawners that release drifting eggs and sperm high in the water column during a spiraling spawning ascent from the bottom toward the surface. The eggs are tiny and abundant, the newly hatched prolarvae (larvae without eye pigments or functional jaws) incapable of feeding for days.

Oxycirrhites typus, the longnose hawkfish, is an ambush predator. It cannot be kept with small shrimp.

In captivity, the pelagic fertilized eggs are collected with a net placed over the outflow from the tank to the sump. These eggs are incubated in large volumes of water with gentle aeration, preferably after a brief bath in formalin or peroxide to sterilize their surfaces of adherent bacteria. After the eyes, mouth, and jaws fully form, the larvae are fed rotifers, copepods, ciliates, or wild plankton (mixed with microalgae and sometimes yeast to keep the tiny feed animals nourished and nourishing) as a first food, followed by larger brine shrimp nauplii, encapsulated diets, or freeze-dried copepods as they become larger and stronger. This process has been successful with hogfish wrasses, *Pomacanthus* angelfishes, jackknife, hi-hat, and spotted drums, porkfish sparids or porgies, and many other fishes.

In addition to skimming or filtering the eggs from the water, there are other means of breeding broadcast species. You can spawn small ones (*Centropyge*) in bare aquariums, removing the adults after spawning and raising the eggs and fry in-situ. Or you can strip large fish

Paracirrhites arcatus, *the arc-eyed hawkfish, is an ambush predator that will eat small invertebrates of any kind.*

(*Pomacanthus*), mixing the gametes, and incubating the zygotes and subsequent larvae in bare containers. Various methods have been used to produce French and black angelfish and their hybrids, several kinds of groupers, foxface rabbitfishes, and other fishes.

Many fishes (clownfish and other damsels, dottybacks, gobies, cling-

Clownfish produce large demersal eggs that hatch into large fry. They require rotifers for only a few days, and thereafter can take newly hatched brine shrimp and other foods.

fishes, grammistids, trypterygiids) are benthic (bottom) spawners, the eggs attached by adhesive filaments to a hard surface or each other, usually inside a cave or open shell, but sometimes in the open. The fertilized eggs may be tiny and abundant, hatching to release partially developed prolarvae in a day or two, or large and less numerous, developing over a week or more into advanced larvae capable of feeding at once. The eggs of benthic spawners like the clownfishes and dottybacks have been harvested for hatching in a separate container, or been allowed to hatch in the breeding aquarium and afterward transferred to a rearing tank. The dottybacks and grammas breed almost weekly, so the eggs within a nest are of varying ages and require selective removal of those ready for hatching.

Filefishes and triggerfishes spawn in a pit dug in the gravel by the parents, and the hatching prolarvae then drift off in the currents. These fishes too have spawned in public aquaria.

Mouthbrooding occurs in jawfishes and apogonids. The eggs are generally abundant and small, hatching into prolarvae, but in a few species like the Banggai cardinalfish are large and so advanced that the fry can take brine shrimp nauplii at once. Cardinalfishes and pearly jawfishes are now commercially aquacultured.

An uncommon breeding mode among reef fishes is livebearing, but it is the rule in almost all elasmobranchs, surfperches, pipefishes, and seahorses, and in cuskeels (family Brotulidae).

The extrusion of a gelatinous egg mass occurs in some antennariids. Encapsulation of the eggs or the egg mass occurs in some cardinalfishes, assessors, and at least one tilefish (Malacanthidae).

Several principles of care can increase success in propagating marine fishes. Foremost is having ongoing cultures of microalgae, rotifers, and copepods before they are needed, so the food is ready when the fry are ready. You also now have the option of ordering a week's supply of live microalgae, rotifers, or copepods from commercial sources. Copepods are the most important of all zooplankton, so their culture or the collection of wild copepods is the most important tool in being successful. Because wild plankton collections include predators (e.g., arrow worms, predatory crabs) not easily removed, cultured copepods are safer than wild copepods. To be nutritious, however, cultured copepods must be fed microalgae rich in HUFAs and, as we shall see, not all algae are created equal.

Live microalgae have long been grown to feed rotifer cultures. Today, concentrated microalgae in packs or jars are used to feed rotifers and copepods. Microencapsulated commercial foods are used for culturing edible shrimp, but are not nutritionally adequate for decorative shrimp larvae, nor attractive to larval fishes. As an alternative to microalgae, you can mix yeast in water (never use simple dried yeast) to feed copepods and rotifers, but always in moderation. Powdered and liquid suspensions in excess induce bacterial blooms that degrade water quality and kill fry.

Careful feeding of baby marine fishes means feeding frequently but lightly. Baby fishes in marine tanks might grow too slowly to suit you, but rarely die of starvation. The most common causes of mass mortality are bacterial blooms from failure to siphon the tank bottom and failure to make adequate frequent water changes.

HUFAs

Highly unsaturated fatty acids (HUFAs) are a group of different long chain oils found in the chloroplast membranes of microalgae. These oils are important in nervous system development and brain health thoughout life. They are concentrated up the food chain, and in the sea start in algae, are concentrated by algal-eating copepods, and through a series of other predators upon predators eventually are highly concentrated in fish liver, which is why you suffered through spoonfuls of cod liver oil as a baby and your physician recommends eating fish regularly or fish oil capsules as a dietary supplement.

Copepods (and fishes and people) cannot synthesize HUFAs from other oils. Instead, they need to be in the diet. That's why we grow microalgae to feed zooplankton (rotifers, brine shrimp naulplii, and copepods), in order to load them with HUFAs that get to the baby fish. But not all microalgae are equally effective.

It's long been known that some microalgae grew better rotifers (lower

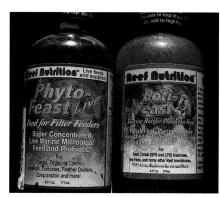

Commercial preparations of algal liquids or pastes are good sources of HUFA oils, and a simpler approach to enriching rotifers or brine shrimp nauplii.

Commercial preparations of HUFA can be used to enrich rotifers or brine shrimp nauplii. You can also make your own preparation.

baby fish mortality) than other microalgae. It was because the microalgae differed in their concentrations of different HUFA oils. As a result, we switched to mixed microalgae, since it wasn't clear which HUFA was important to which larval fish. Now we know the highest concentrations of the most important 3-omega and 6-omega HUFA oils are in the chloroplasts of dinoflagellates and a few other algae. Equally important, we can now purchase concentrates of mixed or single species microalgae to enrich rotifers, brine shrimp, ciliates, or copepods. (Copepods are not the original source of HUFAs, but concentrate them from phytoplankton, so copepods aren't equivalent to a vitamin but to a vitamin capsule.) There are several kinds of HUFA oils, some more important than others.

Today we can grow live copepods in culture, or buy cans of freeze-dried copepods or packages of frozen copepods. We can purchase starter cultures, collect our own from the seashore, or buy a week's worth of feedings through the mail. Copepods concentrate more

HUFAs than other live foods. Also important is that copepods have a jerky movement attractive to baby fishes, so until we come up with encapsulated foods that jump up and down, we need to rely on live copepods to deliver HUFAs to developing baby fish.

Rotifers, ciliates, or brine shrimp enriched with macroalgae are the preferred way to grow marine fish babies. But there is an alternative, and that is the synthetic HUFA preparation.

Synthetic HUFA preparations are more difficult to use but they work. We use them to enrich *Artemia* nauplii or rotifers, and sometimes even copepods or ciliates. Commercial preparations (Selco, Super Selco, Selcon) from Florida Aqua-Farms and other companies are more convenient than mixing our own. The thick, pink liquids must be stored in the dark under refrigeration and have a limited shelf life. When they start to smell rancid, the oils are oxidized, and the preparation should be discarded.

Add a few drops of fresh HUFA preparation to a gallon of marine water with brine shrimp nauplii or rotifers and vigorously aerate for six hours, then filter and rinse in clean seawater before feeding to baby fishes.

You can mix up a HUFA-rich additive by blending fish oil (menhaden, anchovy, or cod liver) with lecithin. The fish oils contain two of the essential HUFAs called DHA (20 carbons and five double bonds in the carbon chain) and EPA (22 carbons and six double bonds). See the glossary for the full chemical names. Cod liver oil is available from pharmacies, anchovy oil from oriental groceries, and menhaden oil from farm supply stores (it is a poultry feed additive).

Lecithin is a phospholipid emulsifying powder available at pharmacies. It is dissolved in water and added dropwise to fish oil in an electric blender until the mixture emulsifies. Before feeding to brine shrimp or rotifers, the emulsion is broken into microparticles by swirling into clean seawater in an electric blender. The rotifers or brine shrimp are filtered from their hatching or culture water, added to the seawater-emulsion mix, and aerated for six hours. During this period, zooplankton (brine shrimp or rotifers) take up the HUFA-enriched microparticles and become little HUFA packages themselves. After six hours the rotifers or brine shrimp are sieved out of the suspension, rinsed, and fed to the larval fish and shrimp. The wastewater, a bacterial soup, is discarded.

HUFA at 2 percent by weight is the concentration required for effectiveness; it is commercially available in dry larval food preparations at 5 percent by weight. Lecithin may have additional benefits besides being an emulsifier.

Which Live Food?

Not all larval fishes take all live foods. Motion is important, and nutritive value affects growth and survival. But the food cannot be too large for the fish to engulf in its jaws. Aquaculturists use 70 percent of the gape width as the maximum size for an encapsulated particle or live food for the fish larva at different stages of development. Aquarists use all the tools at our disposal, including food size, motion, and nutritive value, and we have many tools.

Rotifers

Rotifers are multicellular animals no larger than protozoa. Both small (S strain) *Brachionus rotundiformis* and large (L strain) *Brachionus plicatilus* are cultured as live foods for marine fishes and invertebrates. A healthy rotifer culture consists of diploid females parthenogenetically producing amictic (unfertilizable) eggs that develop into more diploid females. Degraded water quality triggers the production of mictic (fertilizable) haploid eggs. If the mictic eggs are not fertilized, they hatch into short-lived haploid males. Those males that mate then induce the females to produce thicker-walled dormant or resting eggs. These dormant eggs sink to the bottom where they resist pollution and desiccation for days or years, awaiting another environmental cue that triggers them to hatch into young parthenogenetic diploid females.

Rotifer cultures are fed microalgae, usually in mixed cultures as various algal species have different nutritive values.

You can grow cultures of green algae (*Dunaliella, Chlorella, Tetraselmus*), golden brown algae (*Isochrysis, Cricosphaera, Monochrysis*), diatoms (*Skeletonema, Phaeodactylum, Thalassiosira, Lauderia, Nitzschia, Navicula Biddulphia, Rhizosolenia, Coscinodiscus*), and dinoflagellates (*Prorocentrum, Gymnodinium*) in 7 tablespoons of marine salt per gallon of tap water with 2 ml/gal of Guillard's F/2 algal fertilizer. The cultures are aerated and illuminated with cool white fluorescent light from the top and sides, 24 hours a day. Small starters of old dark cultures are subcultured into clean water to produce new algal cultures, and the old, dark green cultures poured slowly into the rotifer containers to maintain the rotifers in a light green density of food. You can, alternatively, feed rotifer cultures with algal pastes or liquid concentrates, yeast suspensions, or enhanced vegetable juices or other mixes.

Living on a coast allows you to collect nutritious wild copepods in plankton nets, but these should be screened to separate vicious predators such as arrow worms and small crabs, which will eat your baby fishes.

The rotifers, also cultured at 7 tablespoons of marine salts per gallon, appear as fine white specks throughout the container, concentrating at the surface if aeration is turned off. *Brachionus* is euryhaline, but is grown best in brackish water. Rotifers excrete toxic ammonia, and whole culture water should not be placed into the larval fish/invertebrate aquarium. The chemical stabilizer EDTA is a component of Guillard's F/2 solution, and it is toxic to shrimp larvae even at low concentrations.

Discarding the culture water, screen out the rotifers through a plastic coffee filter, add them to clean marine water, and feed the cleaned rotifers to the baby fish with a baster. Should the rotifer culture crash, save it, as it contains dormant eggs. Pour off most of the water, and refill with new algal culture water to restore the rotifer culture. Alter-

natively you can store dormant eggs in the dark in seawater in the refrigerator. Rotifer cultures, Guillard's fertilizer, HUFA, and instruction manuals can be purchased from Florida Aqua Farms or Carolina Biological Supply Company and other sources.

Trochophores

Some molluscs produce trochophore larvae, useful as a first food because of their small size and distinctive motion. One company sells live trochophore larvae from the Pacific oyster (*Crassostrea gigas*) frozen in liquid nitrogen, which must be stored in laboratory grade freezers until needed. This product is expensive but used by public aquariums, commercial hatcheries, and research facilities. When thawed, the larvae resume movement and are fed to Nassau groupers and other problem fish, generally with, rather than instead of, rotifers. Aquarists living on a coast can collect and place native oysters in small clear aquariums or shallow outdoor pools, feeding microalgae or dispersed algal paste. Gradually increase the water temperature and some will release trochophore larvae. You can scoop up a gallon jar of water at different times of different days and hold it up to the light. If trochophores (or their later veligers) are present, you'll see them in the water, resembling protozoan cultures. Feed this directly to your larval fishes.

Copepods

Copepods are the largest component of marine zooplankton, nutritious because of their high protein content and especially their high concentration of highly unsaturated fatty acids in the "waxy" portion. Various copepods are benthic when adult, only the nauplii swimming, and other copepods swim at all life stages. Some release eggs while others brood eggs and release nauplii. The nauplii are followed by several stages of copepodites, and finally the sexually mature adult. The three common groups of copepods are the benthic (as adults) harpacticoids, the mostly planktonic calanoids, and the ubiquitous cyclopoids. Only a few species are mass-cultured; starter cultures are commercially available. The culture procedures are similar for the harpacticoids *Tigriopus, Scottolana, Nikotra*, and *Euterpina*. Provide a 10–20 gallon tank with full strength seawater, a light cycle (dark is important for hatching in some species), and microalgae supplemented with powdered flake food. Aeration keeps the nauplii and copepodites from adhering to the surface film and aids dispersion of food and wastes. Copepod adults can be maintained inside screened containers (plastic milk jugs with the bottom cut out and replaced with 50 to 60 micron mesh Nitex) through which the nauplii escape. The nauplii are harvested with a 30-micron mesh net after concentrating them at the surface by turning off aeration. Many aquaculture facilities culture larval fishes in ponds with copepods and don't worry about separating stages. If you prefer not to culture, you can purchase a week's supply of harpacticoids (shipped overnight) to add to your larval fish tank, enough to carry many fry to the stage where they can eat brine shrimp nauplii.

The cyclopoid *Oithona oculata* was grown in 250-gallon and 650-gallon unaerated outdoor tanks mixed with S or small-size rotifers, *Brachionus rotundiformis, Nannachloropsis* and other microalgae, and a yeast supplement.

Live copepods are rich in HUFA oils, but frozen or freeze-dried copepods are a good substitute. Not commonly used, they are among the richest foods you can feed fishes, planktivorous corals, and other invertebrate filter-feeders.

Cultures produced up to 13 copepods per milliliter, a suitable density for larval fish use. An *Oithona* (species not named) has been used to raise the flame angelfish *Centropyge loriculus*.

Ciliates and Mixed Infusoria

Marine ciliates are available from commercial sources and other aquarists, or you can start your own culture in a manner similar to growing freshwater infusoria. Mandarin and damselfish fry have been raised with homemade infusoria cultures. Start the culture by collecting wild sea lettuce, *Ulva,* from the shore and placing it in an aerated bucket of seawater in sunlight. Slow

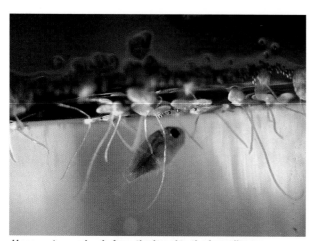

Upon metamorphosis from the larval to the juvenile stage, clownfish fry need an enhanced diet of enriched brine shrimp, copepods, or microencapsulated aquaculture feed and intensified water changes.

above that provides light and concentrates live food and baby fish in the bright beam. Newly hatched larvae not yet able to feed (prolarvae) may be damaged by bright light. Keep all fry under dim light the first week of feeding.

Dissolved oxygen is important. Hatcheries keep fry in wide round black containers with large surface area. In home aquaria, we can't afford the room, so we use tanks with gentle aeration to enhance gas exchange. Currents and scattered lighting interfere with the plankters' tendency to aggregate and the ability of fry to find them. Water quality is maintained by massive water changes and siphoning the bottom.

Marine fry grow faster with higher survival rates if their food is enriched with HUFAs. For fastest growth, use live foods enriched with microalgae, and wean them onto richer microencapsulated or frozen foods early. The diet should be about half-and-half fats and proteins; carbohydrates are not important.

Some marine fish fry are large enough to take brine shrimp nauplii as a first food. These include some cardinalfish, seahorses and pipefish, surfperches, and cuskeels.

Metamorphosis marks the transition between the larval stage and the juvenile (miniature adult) stage. Under a dim (never bright) light, transfer the metamorphosed juveniles to a grow-out tank using jars or cups, but never nets. Netted clownfish juveniles may go into tetanus, their body and gill plates rigid, and they die of respiratory failure because the gills do not ventilate. Do not chase the juveniles; instead move the cup slowly until they drift inside, then lift slowly. The cup should be floated in the new tank to provide temperature equilibration before tipping into the grow-out tank.

decomposition over weeks will yield copepods and protozoa. Turning off the air causes them to swarm at the surface where they are harvested with a plastic coffee filter or food baster, to be fed to your baby fish or used to inoculate a microalgae culture. If you can get live ciliate cultures commercially or from another aquarist, follow the directions of the supplier.

Handling Larval Fishes

Larval fishes vary in tolerance to alterations in water quality, sudden bright light, and handling. You will lose spawns before you learn what they can tolerate. In general, fry to be removed from the spawning aquarium should be moved in ladles or cups, never by baster or eyedropper. Apparent normal swimming after baster transfer is misleading, as injury may not manifest for hours or days. Most aquarists rear the fry in tanks darkened on the sides, bottom, and top, except for a small hole

Chapter Twenty-Three
Diseases of Fish

Pet store fish disease books are far behind veterinary medicine. Textbooks such as Noga's *Fish Disease: Diagnosis and Treatment* (2000, Blackwell Publishing Professional) are more reliable. A few principles of fish diseases will be covered here.

Environmental Stressors

Improper diet, crowding, and poor water quality depress resistance to disease. In nature, fish do not eat soybean-based pellets and flakes. The most nutritious plant materials for herbivores and omnivores are macroalgae and green or red filamentous algae, but you can substitute blanched dark green leafy vegetables. These are all vitamin sources but not sources of HUFAs, which are found in microalgae and in fish liver oils. Omnivores and carnivores should have mixed diets that blend fish and shellfish. All food mixtures should contain a fish meat, fish liver, shrimp with shell, mussels, and squid meat and viscera. Many authorities recommend small amounts of vitamin mixtures to these blends. Other valuable foods are frozen bloodworms, mysid shrimp, copepods (Cyclopeeze), adult brine shrimp, and live brine shrimp nauplii, daphniae, mosquito larvae, whiteworms, blackworms, and red tubifex. Martin Moe first reported that arthropod shells in the diet of brood stock improves survival of their offspring.

Fish foods to avoid are liquids and suspensions, flakes, pellets, freeze-dried worm preparations (but not copepods and zooplankton), beef, pork, and chicken liver, and beef heart. All pollute the aquarium by inducing bacterial blooms, and the tough connective tissue in liver and heart and around gonads can cause intestinal blockage.

Infectious Diseases

Stressed fish have depressed immune systems that allow bacteria to multiply faster than they can be eliminated by antimicrobial white cells and blood substances. Medication should occur in a bare aquarium with aeration but not carbon filtration. Medications placed in balanced aquariums may kill beneficial bacteria, and are seldom effective on pathogens. Medications are ineffective against viral diseases like *Lymphocystis* on angelfish, which goes away by itself, and for which the best treatment is patience.

Bacterial Diseases

Suspect bacterial infection when you don't see white spots on the body and the water appears clear, yet the fish are bloated, listless, disoriented, not feeding, breathing too slowly or too rapidly, hiding in a corner, bleached, or their fins or gill plates seem abnormally stiff. Bacterial infections of the blood, gills, and

Lymphocystis is an infectious viral disease affecting many fishes, but especially large marine angelfishes where it appears as lumps of cottony or fungal-like growths on the skin and fins. Drugs don't work and wholesalers cannot sell such fish until it clears up and the fish returns to full health.

kidneys often start through wounds to the gills, intestine, or skin. They may start after stress from high temperature, low pH, high ammonia, or low oxygen.

There is no universal treatment. A treatment must be specific for the cause of the disease, which is difficult to diagnose without training and the use of laboratory techniques. Hatcheries, fish farms, and dealers consult with a fish-wise veterinarian at once, as the cost of the visit, diagnosis, and appropriate medication (including drugs not available in pet stores) will be less than the losses incurred by taking action too late with the wrong drug.

Bacteria can invade open wounds caused by other fishes (bites) or dashing into sharp rocks and coral skeletons. Bites from territorial competitors are a common cause of skin damage. Wounds on large, easily handled fish should be dabbed with mercurochrome or tincture of iodine. Wounds on small

fish may often be successfully treated by isolation, clean water, slightly elevated temperatures, darkness, and rest.

Antimicrobial Drugs

Our arsenal of antimicrobials includes natural antibiotics and synthetics such as sulfa drugs and quinolones. The most common deadly bacteria infecting marine fishes are Gram-negative curved rods of the genus *Vibrio*. Oxolinic acid, nalidixic acid, the synthetic quinolone sarafloxicin, and the potentiated sulfa drug Romet are all effective against vibrios. Treating the water is useless, and you must get the drug into the fish with food. Oxolinic acid can be put into flake food to treat some bacterial infections.

Acid-fast bacteria (*Mycobacterium*) may cause chronic wasting, with hollow belly, a bent back, and listlessness. Drug treatment is ineffective, but the disease is seldom contagious. Still, any unhealthy fish should be removed as a potential source of infection to other weakened fishes.

Erythromycin is not effective against marine fish diseases and may kill useful nitrifying bacteria and marine algae. Many fish drugs (e.g., those with copper) may kill shrimp and corals. Any drugs effective as a bath should be used in a bare hospital tank. Because tetracycline binds to calcium, it is ineffective in seawater.

Stimulating the immune system may aid the fish in clearing pathogenic bacteria without medication. The immune system works best when the fish is unstressed. An important part of the immune system is the phagocytic white cells that engulf and digest bacteria. They can be stimulated by a special carbohydrate extracted from yeast and

Drug Resistance

Many bacteria are unaffected by certain drugs. Gram-positive bacteria are often unaffected by tetracyclines, while Gram-negative bacteria are unaffected by penicillins and erythromycin. Some bacteria inactivate, block, or fail to take up these drugs, while others quickly excrete it. Some are unaffected by the usual dose, but susceptible to a higher dose. Many of these attributes are genetically determined. Bacteria with genetic resistance to a drug can, over multiple generations, become dominant when the drug has been given at a low dose for a long time.

The genes for resistance are usually not on the circular bacterial chromosome, but on floating genetic pieces called plasmids. Related bacteria can exchange genes during sexual conjugation. But even unrelated bacteria can transfer genes that confer drug resistance. One way is by fragmenting at death, the fragments then absorbed by unrelated bacteria that now carry the other's genes (transformation). A second way is by transfer of plasmids by the viruses that infect bacteria (bacteriophages). These bacteriophages incorporate and transmit the drug resistance genes to an unrelated bacterium (transduction) during the next infection.

called beta 1,3-D glucan. This activator of fish white cells is used in aquaculture as an immersion (bath) or a food additive, and is effective at 0.5 to 1.0 ppt against *Vibrio vulnificus*.

Fungal Diseases

Fungal diseases are usually deep inside internal organs and seldom recognized. If you suspect a mycosis (fungus infection), take the fish to a veterinarian familiar with fish diseases, but keep in mind that fungal diseases are often untreatable. To prevent contagion, remove all dead or dying fish so healthy fishes can't eat their tissues, a common route for spreading diseases.

Protozoal Diseases

Protozoa are common skin parasites of marine fishes. They frequently have a drug-resistant sheath (the cyst) during much of the life cycle, and a brief unprotected stage. The recommended treatments are heat (to speed up the life cycle so the naked stage appears while the drug is still active) combined with up to 5 drops of formalin per gallon, 0.1 mg/L malachite green, or 0.2 mg/L chelated copper sulfate, always in a bare hospital tank, and always with a further two week quarantine after all signs of disease have cleared. Copper will kill shrimp and other invertebrates, so never use it in a reef tank.

Parasitic Worms

Parasitic worms include the roundworms (in any internal organs), tapeworms and thorny-headed worms (in the intestine), digenetic trematodes (intestinal tract, eyes, liver), and monogenetic trematodes (on skin or gills). All these worms occur naturally on wild fishes without causing harm except for the monogeneans. Many monogeneans that multiply to great numbers can damage gills, skin, and eyes. Monogeneans can sometimes be seen by lifting the fish's gill cover with a flat toothpick and looking for minute black spots that are the clusters of worm eggs. The translucent worms are usually all but invisible

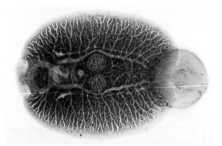

Neobenedenia, a giant monogenetic trematode, causes epidemics in many species of marine fishes. This was one of hundreds taken from a dying Indo-Pacific goby.

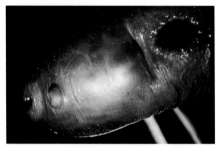

Digenetic trematodes have a mouth and one or two suckers, and usually live in the stomach or intestine. They have complex life cycles, impossible to complete in an aquarium, so they never cause epidemics.

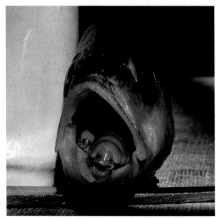

Large isopods in fish throats can be removed with tweezers and generally do no harm despite their imposing appearance.

against the backdrop of a gill. A scraping of gill slime viewed under a microscope will confirm if you have monogeneans. Monogeneans can often be treated with a freshwater dip (five minutes or until the fish becomes stressed), with 5 drops of formalin per gallon of seawater, or anaesthesia (3 drops per gallon of 10 percent quinaldine in absolute alcohol). Some monogeneans are refractory to these drugs. A highly effective treatment is a 1–2 ppm praziquantel bath for 24 hours. Sold under the brand name Droncit, it is available through veterinarians and normally used to treat tapeworms in dogs. Intestinal parasites (roundworms, tapeworms, digenetic trematodes, etc.) rarely do harm and should not be treated.

Parasitic Crustaceans

The important parasitic crustaceans include isopods, copepods, and fish lice. Large isopods occur on the throat, head, or in the mouth or gill cavity of many wild marine fishes, do not multiply in aquaria, and can be removed with tweezers or forceps. Tiny parasitic copepods can multiply on the gills and cause severe damage. Copepods are killed with Dylox or other organophosphates used for pond fish infected with anchor worms. Fish lice cause minor damage, multiply in aquaria, and should be removed with tweezers as soon as they are seen, well before their numbers increase to the point of requiring Dylox.

Non-infectious Diseases

Fish can be sickened by ammonia or nitrites, drugs, metals and other chemicals, cold, low dissolved oxygen, high concentrations of carbon dioxide, and

Cyanide

Cyanide can be used as an anaesthetic, but its anaesthetic dose is close to its lethal dose. Cyanide widely used in the Indo-Pacific to stun fishes for the restaurant and aquarium markets is dispensed with a squirt bottle, so the dose is uncontrolled and many fishes are killed. It is more toxic to invertebrates. Squirting cyanide over a reef destroys non-target fishes, corals, and other invertebrates.

Aside from acute toxicity that causes asphyxiation, other pathologic effects of cyanide are associated with long-term, sublethal (chronic) exposure. Chronic exposure from mine drainage and electroplating causes sublethal pathologic changes in liver and gonad. These changes are potentiated (increased) when combined with stressors such as ammonia, hypoxia, and other metals.

In the laboratory, fishes that recover from a single anaesthetic (acute) exposure to cyanide appear normal with no pathologic changes in their tissues. Fish collected with an anaesthetic dose of cyanide on reefs also have no visible pathology.

Unexplained delayed deaths are often blamed on cyanide. However, these deaths are likely caused by stress leading to irreversible, ammonia-induced gill and perhaps kidney damage and/or starvation. Exposure to stress capable of inducing such damage and leading to delayed death might occur in dirty, hot, acidic, hypersaline, unaerated, or ammonia-rich holding facilities where water is added but never changed. Or it may occur in shipping from overheating on the tarmac, or from oxygen deprivation and carbon dioxide buildup in a shipping bag with too little water and air space. Perhaps the fish was starved between the time it was collected and the time it arrived at a retail store.

The so-called syndrome (group of clinical signs) of cyanide poisoning is said to be heavy feeding with continual wasting away and a mucoid exudate from the gut, but there is no evidence for this urban myth.

degraded water quality associated with rotting materials leading to bacterial blooms. Bacterial blooms often follow feedings with liquid or suspension food supplements, which fish cannot consume and which have no useful purpose.

Eroding lateral line pores on the head and sides are generally caused by poor water quality, high nitrates, low pH, and/or dietary deficiencies. Swollen bodies are a sign of bacterial infection of the kidneys or gills, kidney damage, or intestinal blockage. Any sick fish should immediately be quarantined so it cannot infect other fishes. You can decide what to do with it afterward.

Parasitic copepods on gills typically have a lateral pair of egg sacs. Copepods can multiply rapidly in a captive environment and produce severe gill erosion.

Appendix

Relationships

watts	=	volts×amps
amps	=	volts/watts
1 amp	=	120 watts at 120 volts
30 amp line capacity	=	3,600 watts (30×120)
20 amp line capacity	=	2,400 watts (20×120)
15 amp line capacity	=	1,800 watts (15×120)
1 gallon	=	3.785 L (liter)
	=	3,785 cc (cubic centimeter)
	=	3,785 ml (milliliter)
1 liter	=	1,000 ml
	=	1,000 cc
	=	0.264 gal
	=	35.28 oz (weight)
	=	33.8 fluid oz
	=	2.25 lb
	=	1 kg water
cc	=	ml
drop	=	1/20 ml
ml	=	20 drops
tsp	=	5 ml
tbsp	=	15 ml
fl.oz	=	30 ml
aquarium capacity (gal)	=	L×W×H (inches) /231
(liters)	=	L×W×H (cm) /1,000
(liters to gal)	=	×0.264
parts per thousand (o/oo or ppt)	=	ml/L (liter)
	=	3.8 ml/gal
	=	3.8 gm/gal
	=	gm/1,000 gms
	=	gm/kilogram (Kg)
	=	gm/2.2 lbs
part per million (ppm)	=	mg/L
	=	3.8 mg/gal
	=	gm/cubic meter of water
	=	ml/1,000 L

1 percent solution	=	38 gm/gal
	=	38 ml/gal
	=	1 oz/3 quarts
	=	1.3 oz/gal
	=	10 gm/L
	=	1 gm/100 ml
	=	10 ml/L
1:1,000 solution	=	1 ml/L
	=	0.1 gm/100 ml
	=	3.8 gm/gal
	=	3.8 ml/gal
	=	0.13 oz/gal
Centigrade or Celsius	=	$(F - 32) \times 5/9$
Fahrenheit	=	$(C \times 9/5) + 32$
Oxygen in ppm x 0.7	=	O_2 in cc/L or ml/L
Oxygen in ml/L or cc/L $\times 1.429$	=	O_2 in ppm
CO_2 in ppm $\times 0.509$	=	CO_2 in ml/L or cc/L
CO_2 in cc/L or ml/L $\times 1.964$	=	CO_2 in ppm

Logarithm to the Base 10 Prefix Terms

billion	10^9	(G)	giga	1,000,000,000
million	10^6	(M)	mega	1,000,000
thousand	10^3	(k)	kilo	1,000
hundred	10^2	(h)	hecto	100
ten	10	(dk)	deka	10
(tenth)	10^{-1}	(d)	deci	0.1
(hundredth)	10^{-2}	(c)	centi	0.01
(thousandth)	10^{-3}	(m)	milli	0.001
(millionth)	10^{-6}	(μ)	micro	0.000001
(billionth)	10^{-9}	(n)	nano	0.000000001
(ten billionth)	10^{-10}	—		0.0000000001

References

Abbott, R.T., and P.A. Morris. 1995. *Shells of the Atlantic and Gulf Coasts and the West Indies*. Peterson Field Guide 3. Houghton Mifflin Company, New York, 350 pp.

Adey, W.H., and K. Loveland. 1991. *Dynamic Aquaria, Building Living Ecosystems*. Academic Press, Inc., San Diego, 643 pp.

Allen, G.R. 1991. *Damselfishes of the World*. Mergus Publishers, Melle, Germany and Aquarium Systems, Mentor, Ohio, 271 pp.

Anderson, D.M., et al. 1994. Biogeography of toxic dinoflagellates in the genus *Alexandrium* from the northeastern United States and Canada. Marine Biology 120: 467.

Antonius, A. 1985. Coral diseases in the Indo-Pacific: a first record. P.S.Z.N.I.: Marine Ecology 6(3): 197.

Ates, R.M.L. 1991. Predation on cnidaria by vertebrates other than fishes. Hydrobiologia 216/217: 305.

Bailey-Brock, J.H. 1987. The polychaetes of Fanga'uta Lagoon and coral reefs of Tongatapu, Tonga, with discussion of the Serpulidae and Spirorbidae. Biological Society of Washington 7: 280.

Baker, B.J. et al. 1985. Punaglandins: halogenated antitumor eicosanoids from the octocoral *Telesto riisei*. Journal of the American Chemical Society 107: 2976.

Balser, E.J. 1998. Cloning by ophiuroid echinoderm larvae. Biological Bulletin 194:187.

Barger, M.A. and G.W. Esch. 2000. Plagioporus sinitsini: one host life cycle. Journal of Parasitology 86(1):150.

Bauchot, M.L., and A. Pras. 1980. *Guide des Poissons Marins d'Europe*. Delachaux & Niestle, Neuchatel, Switzerland, 427 pp.

Bellwood, D.R. 1981. Cyanide—an investigation into the long-term histological effects of sodium cyanide doses upon the gastrointestinal tract of *Dascyllus trimaculatus*. Freshwater and Marine Aquarium 4: 31.

Blanchot, J., and R. Pourriot. 1982. Influence de trois facteurs de l'environment, lumiere, temperature et salinite, sur l'eclosion des oeufs de duree d'un clone de *Brachionus plicatilis* (O.F. Muller) Rotifere. C.R. Academie des Sciences Paris 295 (3): 243.

Bodin, P., 1997. Catalogue of the new marine Harpacticoid Copepods (1997 Edition). Documents de travail de l'Institut des Sciences naturelles de Belgique, 304 pp.

Bouchard, E.C. et al. 1992. Nitrate contamination of groundwater: sources and potential health effects. Journal American Water Works Association 84(9): 85.

Carcasson, R.H. 1977. *A Field Guide to the Coral Reef Fishes of the Indian and West Pacific Oceans*. Collins Publishers, London, 320 pp.

Carney, J.R. et al. 1992. Napalilactone, a new halogenated norsesquiterpenoid from the soft coral *Lemnalia africana*. Tetrahedron Letters 33(47): 7115.

Cervino, J.M., et al. 2004. Relationship of *Vibrio* species infection and elevated temperatures to Yellow Blotch/Band Disease in Caribbean corals. Applied Environmental Microbiology 70(11): 6855.

Chang, C.W.J., et al. 1987. Kalihinols, multifunctional diterpenoid antibiotics from marine sponges *Acanthella* spp. Journal of the American Chemical Society 109: 6119.

Chen, A.C., K.K. Lam, Y. Nakano, and W-S Tsai. 2003. A stable association of the stress-tolerant zooxanthellae, *Symbiodinium* clade D, with the low-temperature-tolerant coral, *Oulastrea crispata* (Scleractinia: Favidae) in subtropical non-reefal coral communities. Zoological Studies 42(4): 540-550.

Chung, A.P.S. 1996. Survival tactic sustains coral-smothering bubble algae. Makai 18(3): 3.

Chung, K-c., and N.Y.S. Woo. 1999. Age and growth by scale analysis of *Pomacanthus imperator* from Dongsha Islands, southern China. Environmental Biology of Fishes 55(4): 399.

Corley, D.G., et al. 1988. Laulimalides: new potent cytotoxic macrolides from a marine sponge and a nudibranch predator. Journal of Organic Chemistry 53: 3644.

Couch, J.A., and J.W. Fournie, Editors. 1993. *Pathobiology of Marine and Estuarine Organisms*. CRC Press, Boca Raton, 552 pp.

Couturier-Bhaud, Y. 1974. Cycle biologique de *Lysmata seticaudata* Risso (Crustace,

Decapoda). I. Cycle biologique des animaux adultes. Vie Milieu 24(3): 413.

Couturier-Bhaud, Y. 1974. Cycle biologique de *Lysmata seticaudata* Risso (Crustace, Decapoda). II. Sexualite et reproduction. Vie Milieu 24(3): 423.

Couturier-Bhaud, Y. 1974. Cycle biologique de *Lysmata seticaudata* Risso (Crustace, Decapoda). III. Etude du developpement larvaire. Vie Milieu 24(3): 431.

Coval, S.J. et al. 1984. Two new xenicin diterpenoids from the octocoral *Anthelia edmondsi*. Tetrahedron 40(19): 3823.

Creed, J.C. 2006. Two invasive alien azooxanthellate corals, *Tubastraea coccinea* and *Tubastraea tagusensis*, dominate the native zooxanthellate *Mussismilia hispida* in Brazil. Coral Reefs 25:350.

Croquer, A., et al. 2005. Impact of a white plague-II outbreak on a coral reef in the Archipelago Los Roques National Park, Venezuela. Caribbean Journal of Science 41(4): 815.

Croquer, A., et al. 2006. First report of folliculinid ciliates affecting Caribbean scleractinian corals. Coral Reefs 25: 187.

Danilowicz, B.S. 1996. Choice of coral species by naive and field-caught damselfish. Copeia 1996(3): 735.

Danilowicz, B.S., and C.L. Brown. 1992. Rearing methods for two damselfish species: *Dascyllus albisella* (Gill) and *D. aruanus* (L.). Aquaculture 106: 141–149.

Darius, H.T., P.M.V. Martin-Patrick, A.D. Grimont, and C. Dauga. 2000. Small subunit rDNA sequence analysis of symbiotic dinoflagellates from seven scleractinian corals in a Tahitian lagoon. Journal of Phycology 36(5): 951-959.

DeMartini, E.E., and T.J. Donaldson. 1996. Color morph-habitat relations in the arc-eye hawkfish *Paracirrhites arcatus*. Copeia 1996(2): 362.

Denner, E.B.M. et al. 2003. Characterization of the bacterial pathogen, WP1, the causative agent of Plague Type II disease of Caribbean scleractinian corals: description of *Aurantimonas coralicida*. Also reported as *Aurantimonas coralicida* gen. nov., sp. nov., the causative agent of white plague type II on Caribbean scleractinian corals. International Journal of Systematic and Evolutionary Microbiology 53: 1115.

Dixon, B.A., S.O. van Poucke, M. Chair, M. Dehasque, HY.J. Nelis, P. Sorgeloos, and A.P. De Leenheer. 1995. Bioencapsulation of the antibacterial drug sarafloxacin in nauplii of the brine shrimp *Artemia franciscana*. Journal of Aquatic Animal Health 7: 42.

Doi, M., et al. 1997. Preliminary investigation of feeding performance of larvae of early red-spotted grouper, *Epinephelus coioides*, reared with mixed zooplankton. Hydrobiologia 358: 259.

Eaton, A. 1995. Measuring UV-absorbing organics: a standard method. Journal American Water Works Association 87(2): 86.

Edmunds, P.J. 1991. Extent and effect of black band disease on a Caribbean reef. Coral Reefs 10(3): 161.

Feingold, J.S. 1988. Ecological studies of a cyanobacterial infection on the Caribbean sea plume *Pseudopterogorgia acerosa*. J.H. Choat et al., eds. Proc. Sixth International Coral Reef Symposium, Townsville, Australia, vol 3, pp. 157–162.

Feller, M., A. Rudi, N. Berer, I. Goldberg, Z. Stein, Y. Benayahu, M. Schleyer, and Y. Kashman. 2004. Isoprenoids of the soft coral *Sarcophyton glaucum*: nyalolide, a new biscembranoid, and other terpenoids. Journal of Natural Products 67(8): 1303.

Fitt, W.K. et al. 1993. Utilization of dissolved inorganic nutrients in growth and mariculture of the tridacnid clam *Tridacna derasa*. Aquaculture 109: 27.

Fitt, W.K. et al. 1993. Recovery of the coral *Montastrea annularis* in the Florida Keys after the 1987 Caribbean "bleaching event." Coral Reefs 12(2): 57.

Fitzhardinge, R.C., and J.H. Bailey-Brock. 1989. Colonization of artificial reef materials by corals and other sessile organisms. Bulletin of Marine Science 44(2): 567.

Garcia-Cuetos, L., X. Pochon, and J. Pawlowski. 2005. Molecular evidence for host-symbiont specificity in soritid foraminifera. Protist 156(4): 399–412.

George, J.D., and J.J. George. 1979. *Marine Life, an Illustrated Encyclopedia of Invertebrates in the Sea.* John Wiley & Sons, New York, 288 pp.

Gladstone, W. 1996. Unique annual aggregation of longnose parrotfish (*Hipposcarus harid*) at Farasan Island (Saudi Arabia, Red Sea). Copeia 1996(2): 483.

Gleeson, M.W., and A.E. Strong. 1995. Applying MCSST to coral reef bleaching. Advances in Space Research 16(10): 151.

Gosliner, T.M., D.W. Behrens, and G.C. Williams. 1996. Coral Reef Animals of the Indo-Pacific. Sea Challengers, Monterey, CA, 314 pp.

Grace, K.J.S. et al. Inactivation of been venom phospholipase A$_2$ by a sesquiterpene furanoic acid marine natural product. Biochemical Pharmacology 47(8): 1427.

Grigg, R.W. 1988. Recruitment limitation of a deep benthic hard-bottom octocoral population in the Hawaiian Islands. Marine Ecology Progress Series 45: 121.

Guzman, H.M., and J. Cortes. 1984. Mass death of *Gorgonia flabellum* on the Caribbean coast of Costa Rica (in Spanish). Revue Biologia Tropica 32(2): 305.

Hall, K.C., and D.R. Bellwood. 1995. Histological effects of cyanide, stress and starvation on the intestinal mucosa of *Pomacentrus coelestis*, a marine aquarium fish species. Journal of Fish Biology 47: 438.

Headlee, L., L. Read, and M. Barnes. 1996. Super Glue use in live rock culture. Sea Scope 13(Spring): 4.

Hellgren, M. 1996. Giant clams promise to revitalize Pacific island economy. Makai 18(2): 3.

Hernandez-Molejon, O.G, and L. Alvarez-Lajonchere. 2003. Culture experiments with *Oithona oculata* Farran, 1913 (Copepoda: Cyclopoiida), and its advantages as food for marine fish larvae. Aquaculture 219: 471–483.

Hoff, F.H. 1996. Conditioning, spawning and rearing of fish with emphasis on marine clownfish. Aquaculture Consultants, Dade City, FL, 212 pp.

Hourigan, T.F., et al. 1989. The feeding ecology of three species of Caribbean angelfishes (family Pomacanthidae). Environmental Biology of Fishes 24(2):105.

Huys R., et al. 1996. *Marine and Brackish Water Harpacticoid Copepods, Part 1.* Synopses of the British Fauna (New Series), 51, 352 pp.

James, D.M. et al. 1993. Metal binding by the trisoxazole portion of the marine natural product dihydrohalichondramide. Heterocycles 35(2): 675.

Jeong, H.J. 1994. Predation by the heterotrophic dinoflagellate *Protoperidinium* cf. *divergens* on copepod eggs and early naupliar stages. Marine Ecology Progress Series 114: 203.

Johannes, R.E., and M. Riepen. 1995. Environmental, economic, and social implications of the live reef fish trade in Asia and the western Pacific. The Nature Conservancy.

Johnson, C. 2002. The rise and fall of Rudist reefs. American Scientist 90(2): 148.

Jurek, J. and P.J. Scheuer. 1993. Sesquiterpenoids and norsesquipterpenoids from the soft coral *Lemnalia africana*. Journal of Natural Products 56(4): 508.

Kalidindi, R.S., et al. 1994. Pokepola ester: a phosphate diester from a Maui sponge. Tetrahedron Letters 35(31): 5579.

Kaplan, E.H. 1982. *Coral Reefs.* Peterson Field Guide 27. Houghton Mifflin Company, New York, 289 pp.

Kittakoop, P., R. Suttisri, C. Chaichantipyuth, S. Vethchagarun, and K. Suwanborirux. 1998. Norpregnane glycosides from a Thai soft coral, *Scleronephthya pallida*. Journal of Natural Products 62(2): 318.

Kleppel, G.S. et al. 1989. Changes in pigmentation associated with the bleaching of stony corals. Limnology and Oceanography 34(7): 1331.

Kraul, S. 1989. Part 56. Production of live prey for marine fish larvae. In, *Advances in Tropical Aquaculture,* Tahiti, Aquacop. Infremer, Actes de Colloque 9: 567.

LaJeunesse, T.C. and R.K. Trench. 2000. Biogeography of two species of *Symbiodinium* (Freudenthal) inhabiting the intertidal sea anemone *Anthopleura elegantissima* (Brandt). Biological Bulletin 199: 126–134.

Lansdell, W. B. Dixon, N. Smith, and L. Benjamin. 1993. Isolation of several *Mycobacterium* species from fish. Journal of Aquatic Animal Health 5: 73.

Lee, K.J. et al. 1995. Molecular cloning of a cDNA encoding putative molt-inhibiting hormone from the blue crab, *Callinectes sapidus*. Biochemical and Biophysical Research Communications 209(3): 1126.

Leis, J.M., and T. Trnski. 1989. *The larvae of Indo-Pacific shore fishes*. University of Hawaii Press, Honolulu, HI, 371 pp.

Li, M,K.W., and P.J. Scheuer. 1984. Halogenated blue pigments of a deep sea gorgonian. Tetrahedron Letters 25(6): 587.

Li, M,K.W., and P.J. Scheuer. 1984. A guaianolide pigment from a deep sea gorgonian. Tetrahedron Letters 25(20): 2109.

Li, M.K.W., and P.J. Scheuer. 1984. N,N-dimethylamino-3-guaiazulenylmethane from a deep sea gorgonian. Tetrahedron Letters 25(42): 4707.

Littler, D.S., M.M. Littler, K.E. Bucher, and J.N. Norris. 1989. *Marine Plants of the Caribbean, A Field Guide from Florida to Brazil*. Smithsonian Institution Press, Washington, 263 pp.

Littler, M.M., and D.S. Littler. 1995. Impact of CLOD pathogen on Pacific coral reefs. Science 267: 1356.

Lutnesky, M.M.F. 1994. Density-dependent protogynous sex change in territorial-haremic fishes: models and evidence. Behavioral Ecology 5: 375.

Lutnesky, M.M.F. 1996. Size-dependent rate of protogynous sex change in the pomacanthid angelfish, *Centropyge potteri*. Copeia 1996(1): 209.

Maida, M., P.W. Sammarco, and J.C. Coll. 2001. Effects of soft corals on scleractinian coral recruitment. II. Allelopathy, spat survivorship and reef community structure. Marine Ecology 22(4): 397.

Manem, J.A., and B.E. Rittmann. 1992. The effects of fluctuations in biodegradable organic matter on nitrification filters. Journal American Water Works Association 84(4): 147.

Mather, P., and I. Bennett. 1994. *A coral reef handbook*. Surrey Beatty & Sons Pty Limited, Chipping Norton, Australia, 262 pp.

McAllister, D.E. 1988. Environmental, economic and social costs of coral reef destruction in the Philippines. Galaxea 7: 161.

Michalek-Wagner, K., D. J. Bourne, and B. F. Bowden. 2001. The effects of different strains of zooxanthellae on the secondary-metabolite chemistry and development of the soft-coral host *Lobophytum compactum*. Marine Biology 138(4): 753.

Michalek-Wagner, K., and B. F. Bowden. Effects of bleaching on secondary metabolite chemistry of Alcyonacean soft corals. Journal of Chemical Ecology 26(7): 1543.

Moe, M.A., Jr. 1989. *The Marine Aquarium Reference, Systems and Invertebrates*. Green Turtle Publications, Plantation, FL, 510 pp.

Moe, M.A., Jr. 1992. *The Marine Aquarium Handbook, Beginner to Breeder*. Green Turtle Publications, Plantation, FL, 318 pp.

Morse, D.E., and A.N.C. Morse. 1993. Marine biotechnology: control of larval metamorphosis, p. 206. In, W. Tien et al. eds., *Biotechnology. Development Center for Biotechnology, Taipai*.

Mosher, C. 1954. Observations on the spawning behavior and the early larval development of the sargassum fish, *Histrio histrio*. Zoologica 39: 141–152.

Nagl, G. 1996. Eliminating H_2S from H_2O. Econ 11(6): 44.

Noga, E.J. 1995. *Fish Disease—Diagnosis and Treatment*. Mosby, St. Louis, 367 pp.

Nursall, J.R. 1974. Some territorial behavioral attributes of the surgeonfish *Acanthurus lineatus* at Heron Island, Queensland. Copeia 1974(4): 950.

Okuda, R.K., et al. 1982. Marine natural products: the past twenty years and beyond. Pure and Applied Chemistry 54(10): 1907.

Patterson, K.L., et al. 2002. The etiology of White Pox, a lethal disease of the Caribbean elkhorn coral, *Acropora palmata*. Proceedings of the National Academy of Sciences 13:8725.

Pearl, H.W. 1995. Coastal eutrophication in relation to atmospheric nitrogen deposition: current perspectives. Ophelia 41: 237.

Perez-Espana, H., and L.A. Abitia-Cardenas. 1996. Description of the digestive tract and feeding habits of the king angelfish and the Cortes angelfish. Journal of Fish Biology 48(5): 807.

Peters, E.C. et al. 1986. Calicoblastic neoplasms in *Acropora palmata*, with a review of reports on anomalies of growth and form in corals. Journal of the National Cancer Institute 76(5): 895.

Peters, E.C. 1993. Chapter 15. Diseases of other invertebrate phyla: Porifera, Cnidaria, Ctenophora, Annelida, Echinodermata, pp. 393–449. In, J.A. Couch and J.W. Fournie, eds., *Pathobiology of marine and estuarine organisms*. Advances in Fisheries Science. CRC Press, Boca Raton, FL. 552 pp.

Pietsch, T.W. 1984. The genera of frogfishes (family Antennariidae). Copeia 1984(1): 27–44.

Pietsch, T.W. 1984. A review of the frogfish genus *Rhycherus* with the description of a new species from western and south Australia. Copeia 1984(1): 6872.

Pietsch, T.W. and D.B. Grobecker. 1980. Parental care as an alternative reproductive mode in an antennariid anglerfish. Copeia 1980(3): 551–553.

Pochon, X., J.I. Montoya-Burgos, B. Stadelmann, and J. Pawlowski. 2006. Molecular phylogeny, evolutionary rates, and divergence timing of the symbiotic dinoflagellate genus *Symbiodinium*. Molecular and Phylogenetic Evolution 38(1) 20–30.

Pontius, F.W. 1996. Regulatory compliance using membrane processes. Journal American Water Works Association 88(5): 12.

Raju, B. L., G. V. Subbaraju, C. B. Rao, and G. Trimurtulu. 1993. Two new oxygenated lobanes from a soft coral of *Lobophyton* species of the Andaman and Nicobar coasts. Journal of Natural Products 56(6): 961.

Rakness, K.L., L.D. DeMers, and B.D. Blank. 1996. Ozone fundamentals for drinking water treatment. Opflow 22(7): 1.

Rasquin, P. 1958. Ovarian morphology and early embryology of the pediculate fishes *Antennarius* and *Histrio*. Bulletin of the American Museum of Natural History 114(4): 327–372.

Reed, J.K. 1992. Submersible studies of deepwater *Oculina* and *Lophelia* coral banks off southeastern U.S.A. Proceedings of the American Academy of Underwater Sciences Twelfth Annual Scientific Diving Symposium, UNC-Wilmington, Wilmington, NC, p.143.

Riddle, D. 1995. *The Captive Reef. Energy Savers Unlimited*, Harbor City, CA, 297 pp.

Ritchie, K.B., and G.W. Smith. 1994. Carbon source utilization patterns of coral associated marine heterotrophs. Third International Marine Biotechnology Conference, Tromsoe Norway: Program and Abstracts: 18.

Robertson, D.R. 1983. On the spawning behavior and spawning cycles of eight surgeonfishes (Acanthuridae) from the Indo-Pacific. Environmental Biology of Fishes 9(3/4): 193.

Roesener, J.A., and P.J. Scheuer. 1986. Ulapualide A and B, extraordinary antitumor macrolides from nudibranch egg masses. Journal of the American Chemical Society 108: 846.

Ruppert, E.E., and R.D. Barnes. 1994. *Invertebrate Zoology,* Sixth Edition. Saunders College Publishing, Harcourt Brace Publishers, New York, 1,056 pp.

Sale, P.F. 1991. *The Ecology of Fishes on Coral Reefs*. Academic Press, New York, 754 pp.

Sammarco, P.W., and J.C. Coll. 1990. Lack of predictability in terpenoid function: multiple roles and integration with related adaptations in soft corals. Journal of Chemical Ecology 16(1): 273.

Santos, S.R., and M.A. Coffroth. 2003. Molecular genetic evidence that dinoflagellates belonging to the genus *Symbiodinium* Freudenthal are haploid. The Biological Bulletin 204: 10–20.

Schultz, L.P. 1964. Three new species of frogfishes from the Indian and Pacific Oceans with notes on other species (Family Antennariidae). Proceedings of the United States National Museum (Smithsonian Institution) 116(3500): 171–182.

Scott, T.D., et al. 1974. *The Marine and Freshwater Fishes of South Australia*. Government Printing Department, Adelaide, Australia, 392 pp.

Shields, R.J., and C.W. Laidley. 2004. Aquaculture of marine ornamental species, year 3. 2004. Marine Ornamentals, December, 9 p.

Siddiqui, M.S. and G.L. Amy. 1993. Factors affecting DBP formation during ozone-bromide reactions. Journal American Water Works Association 85(1): 63.

Siddiqui, M.S., et al. 1995. Bromate ion formation: a critical review. Journal American Water Works Association 87(10): 58.

Smith, J.L.B. 1977. *Smith's Sea Fishes.* Valiant Publishers, P.O. Box 78236, Sandton 2146, South Africa, 579 pp.

Strathmann, M.F. 1987. *Reproduction and Development of Marine Invertebrates of the Northern Pacific Coast.* University of Washington Press, Seattle, 670 pp.

Stubbart, J.M., et al. *AWWA Wastewater Operator Field Guide.* American Water Works Assocaition, Denver, 443 pp.

Symons, J.M., et al. 1994. Precursor control in waters containing bromide. Journal American Water Works Association 86(6): 48.

Tchernov, D., M.Y. Gorbunov, C. de Vargas, S.N. Yadav, A.J. Milligan, M. Haggblom, and P.G. Falkowski. 2004. Membrane lipids of symbiotic algae are diagnostic of sensitivity to thermal bleaching in corals. Proceedings of the National Academy of Sciences 101(37): 13531–13535.

Tucker, J.W., Jr. 1992. Marine fish nutrition. In: G.L. Allan and W. Dall (Editors), Proceedings of Aquaculture Nutrition Workshop, Salamander Bay, 15–17 April 1991. NSW Fisheries, Brackish Water Fish Culture Research Station, Salamander Bay, Australia, pp. 25–40.

Tucker, J.W., Jr. 1992. Feeding intensively-cultured marine fish larvae. In: G.L. Allan and W. Dall (Editors), Proceedings of Aquaculture Nutrition Workshop, Salamander Bay, 15–17 April 1991. NSW Fisheries, Brackish Water Fish Culture Research Station, Salamander Bay, Australia, pp. 129–146.

UNEP/IUCN. 1988. *Coral Reefs of the World. Volume 1: Atlantic and Eastern Pacific.* United Nations Environment Programme, Regional Seas Directories and Bibiographies. IUCN, Gland, Switzerland and Cambridge, U.K./Nairobi, Kenya. 373 pp.

UNEP/IUCN. 1988. *Coral Reefs of the World. Volume 2: Indian Ocean, Red Sea, and Gulf.* United Nations Environment Programme, Regional Seas Directories and Bibiographies. IUCN, Gland, Switzerland and Cambridge, U.K./Nairobi, Kenya. 389 pp.

UNEP/IUCN. 1988. *Coral Reefs of the World. Volume 3: Central and Western Pacific.* United Nations Environment Programme, Regional Seas Directories and Bibiographies. IUCN, Gland, Switzerland and Cambridge, U.K./Nairobi, Kenya. 329 pp.

US EPA. 1988. Short-term methods for estimating the chronic toxicity of effluents and receiving waters to marine and estuarine organisms. EPA 600 4-87 028.

Vallejo, B.M., Jr. 1996. Aquarium culture of giant clams. Journal of Maquaculture 4(3): 7.

Veron, J.E.N. 1993. Cor*als of Australia and the Indo-Pacific.* University of Hawaii Press, 644 pp.

Veron, J.E.N. 1995. *Corals in space and time.* Comstock/Cornell, Ithaca and London, 321 pp.

Voss, G.L. 1976. *Seashore Life of Florida and the Caribbean.* E.A. Seeman Publishing, Miami, 168 pp.

Walker, K.F. 1981. A synopsis of ecological information on the saline lake rotifer *Brachionus plicatilis* Muller 1786. Hydrobiologia 81: 159.

Warner, M., and W.K. Fitt. 1991. Mechanisms of bleaching of zooxanthellate symbioses. American Zoologist 31(5): 28A.

Wiley, R.W. 1984. A review of sodium cyanide for use in sampling stream fishes. North American Journal of Fisheries Management 4: 249.

Williams, E.H., Jr., and L. Bunkley-Williams. 1990. The world-wide coral reef bleaching cycle and related sources of coral mortality. Atoll Research Bulletin 335, National Museum of Natural History, Smithsonian Institution, Washington, D.C., 71 p.

Ya-qing, C., et al. 2005. Food consumption, absorption, assimilation and growth of the sea urchin *Strongylocentrotus intermedius* fed a prepared feed and the alga *Laminaria japonica.* Journal of the World Aquaculture Society 36(1): 68.

Zeiller, W. 1974. *Tropical Marine Invertebrates of Southern Florida and the Bahama Islands.* John Wiley & Sons, New York, 132 pp.

Glossary

Å Ångstrom, 10^{-10} meter

acid-fast staining characteristic of some bacteria

acontia fighting tentacles, extended digestive tract filaments

acrorhagi stinging sweeper tentacles

activated carbon carbon treated with high temperatures

aerobic living in an oxygen-rich atmosphere

ahermatypic coral without symbiotic algae in its tissues

alanine an amino acid

allelopathic toxic to related animals

anaerobic, anoxic devoid of oxygen

anion a negatively charged ion

anthropogenic of human origin

aragonite form of calcium carbonate containing strontium, found in hard corals

archaeocyte amoeboid feeding cell of a sponge

benthic living on the bottom

benthos life on the bottom

bifurcate branched

blue-green algae cyanobacteria

calcite form of calcium carbonate in many shellfish

carbonate carbonic acid

cation a positively charged ion

cavitation when a water pump accidentally draws in air, and the propellers spin uselessly

chitin repeating, cross-linked mucopolysaccharide shell of crustaceans

choanocyte internal flagellated cell of a sponge

cnidarian coelenterate, phylum of corals

cnidocyte firing cell of a coral

coprophagous feeding on faeces

corallite aragonite cup holding a coral polyp

corallum stony skeleton of a colonial coral, connected corallites

cyanobacteria algaelike life with characteristics of bacteria

denitrification anaerobic or microaerophilic conversion of nitrate to nitrogen gas

deposit feeder feeding on detritus, mud, or silt

detritus decomposing plant fragments

DHA dodecohexaenoic acid, an important HUFA

DHW degrees heating weeks (for predicting bleaching)

dolomite ancient form of calcium carbonate

EDTA ethylenediaminetetraacetic acid, a binder of cations

elasmobranchs the cartilagenous sharks, rays, and skates

enzyme a protein that catalyzes a specific reaction

EPA eicosapentaenoic acid, an important HUFA

epibenthic growing on the surface of the bottom

epiphytic growing on the surface of plants

errant actively roaming

eutrophic water body with high levels of nitrates and phosphates

foam fractionater protein skimmer

GAC granular activated carbon

gametes eggs and sperm

gph gallons per hour

Gram-negative, Gram-positive staining characteristics of bacteria

H^+ hydrogen ion or proton, the essence of acidity

head pressure pump output in pounds per square inch; for water pumps, an indicator of how high water can be pushed; for air pumps, an indicator of how deeply air can be pushed below water level

hermaphrodite having both male and female sex organs

hermatypic reef-building coral

HUFA omega 3 highly unsaturated fatty acids

infauna minute animal community living within sand or gravel

isoprene 2-methyl butadiene, a natural fat soluble hydrocarbon

isoyake edible coralline red algae

Kalkwasser German for limewater, or calcium hydroxide solution

limewater solution of calcium hydroxide, also Kalkwasser

LPS corals large polyp stony corals

live sand submerse reef sand containing living meiofauna

lysine an amino acid

macroalgae plant-like attached algae

malacologist mollusc scientist

meandrine, meandroid with ridges meandering like a river

meiofauna infauna capable of passing through a 0.1 mm screen

mesohyl central mostly acellular layer in a sponge

mg/L milligrams (thousandths of a gram by weight) per liter of volume

microalgae microscopic algae in water or as surface scum

microaerophilic living in a very low oxygen atmosphere

minor element occurring in micrograms per liter (μg/L)

monocentric with a single center

monotypic genus containing only one species

mucopolysaccharide a complex carbohydrate combined with a peptide

nanometer (nm) 10^{-9} meter

nanoreef a small reef tank of about 10 gallons

nematocyst stinging cnidocyte

neurotransmitter chemical triggering impulses between nerve cells

nitrification aerobic conversion of ammonia to nitrite or nitrite to nitrate

$^-$**OH** hydroxyl ion, the principal form of alkalinity

oolite type of calcium carbonate secreted by corals and algae

ophiopluteus larva of a basket star

organic containing carbon and hydrogen atoms

organophosphate class of agricultural pocticides

O-ring cylindrical rubberlike seal often shaped as a circle

orthophosphate inorganic phosphate, a plant nutrient

osculum discharge port of a sponge colony

PAC powdered activated carbon

PAR photosynthetically active radiation (part of spectrum) used by plants

parapodium side appendage of a polychaete worm

pelagic drifting or swimming in the water column of the ocean

peptide short chain of amino acids

percent parts per hundred (o/o)

photic zone depth range within which algae can photosynthesize

phycology study of algae

phytoplankton minute drifting aquatic algae

planktivorous plankton eater

planula swimming larval stage of a coral

polycentric with several centers

polysaccharide large carbohydrate molecule composed of sugars

polyvalent ionized with more than one charge, e.g., Ca^{++}

porocyte sponge cell with a hole to allow intake of water

powerhead small submersible water pump

ppm parts per million

ppt parts per thousand (o/oo)

protandrous hermaphrodite male first, changing to a female

protein a specific assemblage of peptides

protein skimmer foam fractionater

protogynous hermaphrodite female first, changing to a male

radula rasping band of teeth in gastropods

reef building coral corals that secrete a stony exoskeleton

reef sand pulverized aragonite

sessile immobile or attached on the bottom

setae bristles, as on polychaete worms

spirocyst sticky cnidocyte

SRP soluble reactive phosphate = dissolved orthophosphate

substrate, substrates the substance(s) acted upon by an enzyme

substratum, substrata bottom(s), such as sand, gravel, or rock

sugar alcohol a nutrient derived from sugar

teleosts bony typical fishes

terpene polymer of isoprene, e.g., diterpine, sesquiterpine, etc.

terpenoid terpene-derived, e.g, camphor, lemon oil, carotene, phytol (of chlorophyll), lanosterol, many marine toxins, etc.

titration dropwise addition of a reagent, where the number of drops to the color change times a factor give the value sought

trace element less than 1 microgram per liter $\mu g/L$)

trochophore early stage mollusc larva

UV ultraviolet light

UV-A 4000–3200 Å, low energy

UV-B 3200–2800 Å, moderate energy

UV-C 2800–1900 Å, high energy

Veliger late-stage mollusc larva

zooplankton minute drifting aquatic animals

zooxanthellae symbiotic dinoflagellates, often genus Symbiodinium

zygote fertilized egg

Index

Acanthocauli, 100
Acanthuridae, 158–159
Acetabularia, 66–67
Acid-fast bacteria, 180
Acropora, 5, 26, 98–99
Acroporidae, 97–99
Actinaria, 90–94
Actinodiscus, 94
Activated carbon, 19–20, 40, 52
Agaracia, 28, 99
Agariciiade, 99
Aiptasia, 92–93
Alcyonaceans, 85–86
Alcyonaria, 84
Alcyoniidae, 86–87
Algae
  brown, 69–71
  control methods for, 75
  description of, 64–65
  fish consumption of, 5
  golden-brown, 72–73
  green. *See* Green algae
  in-tank growth of, 45
  red, 71–72
  symbiotic, 63
Algal mat filtration, 44–45
Algal nodules, 121
Algal turf compartment, 45
Alkalinity of water, 22–24
Alveopora, 102–103
Ammonia
  description of, 14, 20, 33
  stripping of, 43
  toxicity levels, 34
Anadyomene, 68
Anaerobic bacterial decomposition, 34–35

Anemones, 82–83, 90–93
Angelfishes, 162–163
Anglerfishes, 167–168
Annelids, 147–149
Anotrichum, 72
Antennariidae, 167–168
Anthelia, 88
Anthozoa, 82
Antimicrobial drugs, 180–181
Antipatharia, 84
Antithamnionella, 72
Apogonidae, 166–167
Aquarium tank, 6
Aragonite, 30–32, 37
Archaeogastropods, 126
Archohelia, 106
Ascidians, 150
Aspergillosis, 120
Asteroidea, 145–146
Atoll, 3–4
Aurantimonas coralicida, 118
Australomussa rowleyensis,
  110
Avrainvillea, 67

Back reef, 4
Back-up power, 8
Bacteria, 120
Bacterial diseases, 179–180
Ball nitrate reducer, 35
Bank reefs, 4
Barabattoia, 105
Barnacles, 132–133
Barrier reef, 3–4
Bartholomea, 92
Basket stars, 144–145
Beer's Law, 17

Berlin system, 40, 42
Bioballs, 42–43
Biological oxygen demand,
  21
Bivalvia, 128–129
Black corals, 84
Black-band disease, 118–119
Blastomussa, 109–110
Bleaching, 116–118
Blenniidae, 165–166
Blue-green algae, 74–75
Bostrychia, 72
Botryocladia, 72
Bottom media, 29–30
Breeding of shrimp, 136–137
Brine shrimp, 153–154
Brittle stars, 144
Brown algae, 69–71
Brown-band disease, 119
Bryopsis, 69
Bubble contact time, 47

Calcarea, 124
Calcium, 16, 21–22
Calcium carbonate, 22, 37
Calcium reactors, 49
Callidonymidae, 166
Callithamnion, 72
Canister filters, 40–41
Carbon, 19–20
Carbon dioxide, 21, 37
Carbonic acid, 37
Cardinalfishes, 166–167
Caryophyllidae, 110–113
Catalaphyllia jardinei, 111–112
Caulastrea, 104
Caulerpa, 15, 45, 65–66

Cellulose triacetate membranes, 12
Cephalochordata, 150
Ceramium, 72
Ceriantharia, 82–84
Cerithium, 126–127
Chaetomorpha, 69
Chemical oxygen demand, 21
Chillers, 54–55
Chlorine, 14
Chloromycetin, 120
Chordata, 150–152
Christmas tree worms, 149
Chroococcales, 74
Ciliates, 177–178
Cirrhitidae, 170–171
Cladophora, 69
Cladophoropsis, 69
Clams, 129–131
Clavelina, 152
Clavulariidae, 84–85
Clinidae, 165–166
Cnidarians, 77–81
Cnidocytes, 77, 80
Cobalt, 25
Cocurrent skimmers, 46–47
Codium, 68
Coil denitrators, 35
Color rendering index, 57
Color temperature, 57
Colors, 56
Colpomenia, 70
Commercial fishing, 116
Compact fluorescent lamps, 62
Coney, 170
Copepods, 133–134, 173, 176–177
Copper, 25
Coral(s). *See also specific coral*
  description of, 76–77
  ecological types of, 1
  evolution of, 114–115
  Hydrocorals, 81–82
  metabolites of, 77

mixing and matching of, 77
stony, 95–96
Coral reefs
  age of, 2–3
  builders of, 2
  classification of, 3–4
  description of, 1
  evolution of, 2–3
  habitats, 4–5
Corallimorpharia, 94–95
Coralline algae lethal orange disease, 72
Corallite, 80
Cornulariidae, 84–85
Coscinaria, 99
Crabs, 134–135
Cretaceous extinction, 2–3
Crinoids, 140–141
Crustaceans
  barnacles, 132–133
  copepods, 133–134
  crabs, 134–135
  description of, 132
  feeding by, 132
  lobsters, 138
  molting of, 136–137
  parasitic, 182
  shrimp, 135–138
Cuttings
  from hard corals, 98
  from soft corals, 91
Cyanide, 183
Cyanoacrylate, 100
Cyanobacteria, 74
Cyathelia, 106
Cyclopoids, 133
Cycloseris, 100

Damselfish, 160–162
Daphnia, 154
Dascyllus, 160
Deionized water, 10–12
Demospongia, 123–124
Dendronephthya, 87–88
Dendrophyllidae, 113–114

Denitrification, 29, 31, 34–35
Deposit feeders, 148–149
Derbesia, 69
Desulfovibrio, 120
Detritus, 32, 64
Diaseris, 100
Diatoms, 72–73
Dictyospheria, 68
Dictyota, 70
Diethylphenylenediamine test, 14
Dihydroxyphenylalanine, 28
Dinoflagellates, 73–74
Dirona albolineata, 128
Diseases
  aspergillosis, 120
  bacterial, 179–180
  black-band, 118–119
  bleaching, 116–118
  brown-band, 119
  description of, 116
  fish, 179–183
  fungal, 181
  non-infectious, 182–183
  protozoal, 181
  rapid wasting, 120–121
  red-band, 119
  skeletal-eroding band disease, 119
  stress-related necrosis, 118
  white plague, 118
  white pox, 118
  white-band, 118
  yellow band, 119–120
  yellow botch, 119–120
Dissolved organic carbon, 52
Dissolved organic chemicals, 75
Dissolved oxygen, 17–18
Distilled water, 10
Dottybacks, 165
Downdraft skimmers, 47
Drug resistance, 181

Echinoderms
  asteroidea, 145–146

coldwater, 143
description of, 139–140
echinoids, 142–144
feather stars, 140–141
holothuroids, 141–142
ophiurioids, 144–145
Echinoids, 142–144
Echinophyllia, 108
Echinopora, 105
EDTA, 23
Eggs, 115, 171–172
Electromagnetic radiation, 56
Eleotridae, 163–164
Encapsulated dry foods, 156
Entacmaea, 92
Enteromorpha, 69
Environmental stressors, 179
Epitokes, 148
Epoxies, 100
Erythromycin, 120, 180
Euphyllia, 111
Eusmilia fastigiata, 113

Fanworms, 149
Favia, 105
Faviidae, 103–106
Feather stars, 140–141
Feeding. *See* Foods and
   feeding
Filefishes, 172
Filter feeders, 148–149
Filters/filtration
   algal mat, 44–45
   Berlin system, 40
   canister, 40–41
   description of, 40
   fluidized bed, 43–44
   hang-on power, 40
   trickling, 40–43, 49
Fire corals, 81–82
Fireworms, 148
Fishes
   breeding of, 171–173
   care of, 157–171
   diseases of, 179–183

foods and feeding of,
   153–156
larval, 178
types of, 157–171
Flahaultia, 72
Fluidized bed filtration, 43–44
Fluorescent lamps, 58, 61–62
Foam fractionaters. *See*
   Skimmers
Foods and feeding
   brine shrimp, 153–154
   Daphnia, 154
   encapsulated, 156
   live fish, 155
   macroalgae, 156
   meat, 85
   prepared, 155–156
   types to avoid, 179
   vegetables, 156
Fringing reefs, 4
Frogfish, 168
Fry, 178
Fungal diseases, 181
Fungiidae, 100

Galaxea, 106–107
Gastropoda, 125–128
Gobies, 163–164
Gobiidae, 163–164
Golden-brown algae, 72–73
Goniastrea, 105
Goniopora, 102
Gorgonacea, 88–90
Gracilaria, 72, 120
Grammas, 164–165
Grammatidae, 164–165
Granular activated carbon, 19,
   52
Gravel, 29–30
Green algae
   bubbles, 68
   cups and brushes, 66–67
   description of, 59, 65
   fans and fingers, 67–68
   feathers and grapes, 65–66

nuisance, 68–69
segmented, 65
Griffithsia, 72
Groupers, 168–170

Halimeda, 65
Halymenia, 72
Hang-on power filters, 40
Hang-on skimmers, 48
Hardness of water, 22–24
Hawkfishes, 170–171
Heaters, 54
Helioporidae, 85
Herbivores, 75
Hermatypic corals, 1–2
Hermit crabs, 134–135
Herpolitha, 100–101
Heteractis, 92
Heterodonta, 129
Hexacetinellida, 124
Highly unsaturated fatty acids,
   173–175
Himerometra robustipinna, 140
Holaxonia, 88
Holothurin, 141
Holothuroids, 141–142
Hybridization, 115
Hydnophora, 108
Hydrocarbons, 52
Hydrocorals, 81–82
Hydrogen sulfide, 31

Indian Ocean, 114–115
Infectious bleaching, 117–118
Infusoria, 177–178
Iodine, 25
Iron, 25

Jellyfish, 80, 82

Kalkwasser, 22
Kelvin degrees, 57

Labridae, 170
Lace corals, 82

Lamps
  fluorescent, 58, 61–62
  metal halide, 53, 59–61
  power for, 8
  timers for, 62–63
Lancelets, 150
Large polyp stony corals, 103
Larvacea, 150
Larvae, 28
Larval fishes, 178
Leather corals, 85–86
Lecithin, 174–175
Light
  combination fixtures for,
    62–63
  intensity of, 58
  lumens, 58–59
  lux, 58–59
  photosynthesis, 59
  ultraviolet, 57–58
  wavelengths, 57
Limestone, 31
Limewater, 15
Liquefied supplements, 155
Live food, 175
Live rock
  with cycling of tank, 36–37
  description of, 26–29, 35
Livebearing, 172
Lobophora, 70
Lobophyllia, 106, 110
Lobophyton, 87
Lobsters, 138
Lumens, 58–59
Lux, 58–59
Lysmata spp., 138

Macroalgae, 13, 33, 64, 156
Makeup water, 10, 13
Manganese, 25
Marine salts, 13–14
Meandrinidae, 107
Measurements, 184–185
Meat, 85
Merulinidae, 107–108

Mesogastropods, 126–127
Metal halide lamps, 53, 59–61
Microalgae, 173
Millepora, 82
Milligrams per liter, 15
Molluscs
  bivalvia, 128–129
  Gastropoda, 125–128
  Tridacnid clams, 129–131
Molting, 136–137
Molybdenum, 25
Monogeneans, 182
Montipora, 99
Moorish idol, 159
Moseleya latistellata, 105–106
Mouthbrooding, 172
Mulm, 41–42
Municipal water, 9–10
Mushrooms, 94–95, 100
Mussidae, 109–110
Mycedium, 108

Nanometer, 57
Necrosis, stress-related, 118
Needle-wheel skimmers, 48
Nematocyst, 80
Nematostella vectensis, 90
Nemenzophyllia turbida, 113
Neocuproine method, 25
Neogastropods, 127
Neomeris, 68
Neomycin, 120
Neopetrolisthes, 135
Nephtheidae, 87–88
Nessler's reagent, 14
Nitrate/nitrite
  causes of, 36
  decomposition of, 34
  description of, 14, 32–33
  trickling filter production of, 41
Nitrobacter, 29, 36
Nitrofurazone, 120
Nitrogen cycle, 29, 33–37
Nitrosomas, 29, 33, 36
Nodules, 121

Nori, 156
Nostocales, 74
Nudibranchs, 127–128
Nutrients, 5, 13, 75

Oceanic reefs, 3
Octocorals, 84
Oculinidae, 106–107
Oligochaetes, 147
Omega-3 and -6 oils, 174
Ophiurioids, 144–145
Opisthobranchs, 127–128
Overheating, 53–54
Oxidation-reduction potential,
  18
Oxygen, dissolved, 17–18
Oxypora, 108–109
Ozone, 18–19
Ozonization, 18–19
Ozonizers, 51–52

Pachyclavularia, 84–85
Pachyseris, 99
Padina, 70
Paraclavarina triangularis, 108
Parasitic crustaceans, 182
Parasitic worms, 181–182
Parrotfish, 5
Parts per million, 15
Patch reefs, 4
Pavona, 99
Pectinidae, 108–109
Pelycepoda, 128–129
Penicillus, 67
Pennatulacea, 88–90
Periclimenes, 91, 136
pH, 17, 21, 23, 37
Philinopsis gardineri, 128
Phlebobranchia, 152
Pholidichthyidae, 165–166
Phormidium corallyticum, 106
Phosphate, 14–15, 74
Photosynthesis
  description of, 1–2
  light needed for, 59

Photosynthetically active radiation, 58
Phymanthidae, 91
Physogyra, 112
Phytoplankton, 1, 64
Pink grub, 121
Pink spot, 121
Plagioporus, 121
Platygyra, 105
Plenum, 32
Plerogyra, 112
Plesiopidae, 167
Pocilloporidae, 96–97
Polychaetes, 147–149
Polyp, 80
Polyphyllia, 101
Polyphysa polyphysoides, 67
Pomacanthidae, 162–163
Pomacentridae, 160–162
Porites, 102, 104
Poritidae, 101–103
Porolithon, 71–72
Porphyra, 72
Powdered activated carbon, 19–20
Power, 8
Powerheads, 12–13, 38–39
Prepared foods, 155–156
Protein skimmers. *See* Skimmers
Protozoal diseases, 181
Pseudochromidae, 164–165
Pteriomorphia, 129
Pumpless chillers, 55

Rapid wasting, 120–121
Red algae, 2, 71–72
Red tide, 74
Red-band disease, 119
Reef crest, 4
Reef front, 4
Reef mud, 37
Reef tank
  bottom media for, 29–30
  cycling of, 35–37

equipment for, 6–8
nutrients in, 13
Refugium, 45
Reverse osmosis water, 10–12, 75
Rhipocephalus, 67
Rock, 26–29, 35
Rotifers, 173, 175–176
Roundworms, 181
Rudists, 2

Sagartiidae, 93–94
Salinity, 9, 16
Salt mixes, 16, 52
Salt water, 8
Sand, 29–31
Sand dollars, 144
Sandalolitha, 100
Sarcophyton, 85–86
Sargassum, 70–71
Scleractinia, 95–96
Scleraxonia, 89
Scleronephthya, 88
Sclerospongea, 124
Scolymia, 109
Sea cucumbers, 141–142
Sea mat rock, 95
Sea squirts, 150–152
Sea stars, 145–146
Sea urchins, 142–144
Seawater
  calcium in, 21
  description of, 9
  oxidation-reduction potential of, 18
  pH, 17
  salinity of, 16
  strontium levels in, 23–24
Serranidae, 168–170
Shelf reefs, 3
Shrimp
  brine, 153–154
  description of, 135–138
Siderastreidae, 99
Siganidae, 159

Sinularia, 87
Siphonogorgiidae, 87–88
Skeletal-eroding band disease, 119
Skimmers
  algae control using, 75
  cocurrent, 46–47
  downdraft, 47
  hang-on, 48
  needle-wheel, 48
  operating principles of, 46–47
  ozone effects on, 19
  spray injection, 48–49
  types of, 47
  venturi, 47–48
Sleepers, 163–164
Small polyp stony corals, 96
Soft corals, 82, 91
Soluble reactive phosphate, 14
Spawning, 171–173
Sperm, 115
Spirocyst, 80
Sponges, 122–124
Spray injection skimmers, 48–49
Stand, 6–7
Stand-alone chillers, 54–55
Starfish, 145–146
Stenopus spp., 136–137
Stenorhynchus seticornis, 135
Sterilizers, 50–51
Stichodactyla, 92
Stigonematales, 74
Stomphia, 90–91
Stony corals, 76, 95–96
Stress-related necrosis, 118
Strontium, 16, 23–24, 30
Stylophora, 96–97
Stypopodium, 70
Supplements, 155
Symbiodinium, 1–2, 54, 73, 83, 117
Symbionts, 117
Symbiotic algae, 63
Symphyllia, 110

Tangs, 158–159
Tap water, 9–10, 13–14
Temperature
  chilling, 54–55
  monitoring of, 55
  overheating, 53–54
Tethys Sea, 115
Thaliacea, 150
Thin film composite
  membranes, 12
Timers for lamps, 62–63
Total organic carbon,
  20–21
Trace elements, 25
Trachyphyllia, 106
Trematode, 121
Trickling filters, 40–43, 49
Tridacnid clams, 129–131
Triggerfishes, 172
Triplefins, 166
Tripterygiidae, 166
Trochaceans, 126
Trochophores, 176
Tubastrea, 113–114
Tubiporidae, 85
Tumors, 121
Tunicates, 151–152
Turbinaria, 70, 114

Udotea, 67
Ultraviolet light, 57–58
Ultraviolet sterilizers, 50–51
Ulva, 69
Urchins, 142–144
Urochordata, 150–151

Valonia, 68
Vegetables, 156
Ventricaria, 68
Venturi skimmers, 47–48
Vibrio, 117–118, 181

Water
  alkalinity of, 22–24
  calcium in, 21–22
  carbon dioxide in, 21
  hardness of, 22–24
  makeup, 10, 13
  nitrates/nitrites in. *See*
    Nitrate/nitrite
  pH, 17, 21, 23, 37
  quality of, 9–25
  salinity of, 9, 16
  tap, 9–10, 13–14
  temperature of, 16–17
Water motion, 12–13
Water pumps, 38–39

Wavelengths, 57
Wavemakers, 12–13
Weather, 116
Wellsophyllia, 106
White plague, 118
White pox, 118
White-band disease, 118
Wild rock, 28
Worms, 181–182
Wrangelia, 72
Wrasses, 170

Xeniidae, 88

Yellow band disease,
  119–120
Yellow botch, 119–120

Zanclidae, 159
Zinc, 25
Zoantharia, 90
Zoanthinaria, 95
Zooplankton, 1
Zooxanthellae
  bleaching caused by loss of,
  117
  description of, 1, 5, 53, 64,
  73, 83